PRAISE F

Snowflakes
A Flurry of Adoption Stories
by, for and about children and teens

"As hard as adoption is for everyone involved, it is just as rewarding. It takes courage and understanding for the parents to try their best to help the child. As the child grows and learns, the parents grow and learn as well. It is scary for the child to try and fit into a new environment with brand new people. And yet, if it were not for the loving people who took the time to help children in great need, they may hardly even have a chance at life. I am adopted and know these things to be true. There has been much time, care, and love put into this book. It will help others understand the journey of adoption."

~ Ashley, age 18 (adopted in Arizona at age 12)

"Adoption is reaching into the unknown to help a child find a place in your heart. My husband and I adopted five children, and though it has been difficult at times, the rewards far outweigh the problems. I applaud Teresa Kelleher for gathering stories and putting this book together. It will help prospective adoptive parents and will honor those who have contributed. Self-esteem is often an issue for children who have been taken from their parents for whatever reason; they often feel broken and alone. This book will help them to see their experiences are unique, but that there are common threads."

~ Yevet Tenney, adoptive mom and teacher

"The old saying that 'Joys shared are multiplied and sorrows shared are cut in half,' rings true for this precious book. It is a fine collection of individual stories and the many emotions of adoptees and adoptive parents. The willingness of contributors to share a piece of their lives with others helps all of us involved in the circle of adoption feel interconnected and not so alone on our journeys."

~ Lori Morse, adoptive mom and Occupational Therapist

"There is something about asking children to write their own feelings and memories that really gets to the heart of it all: no two adoptions are the same. These stories will be interesting and therapeutic for adopted kids who are still working through their feelings. Good stuff!"

~ Scott Flake, School Psychologist

"There are many ways to build a family, and giving birth to a child is not what makes you a mother. It's the love you nurture each and every day of that child's life. When the youngster comes from an orphanage, it takes a special kind of love to overcome years of emptiness in that little boy or girl's heart. This book is a collection of hundreds of journeys, taken by families and children who trusted that love would be enough to erase bad memories, loneliness, and fear. *Snowflakes* will inspire parents to examine their own hearts. It proves the timeless truth that hope is never lost. And never again will you take for granted that special 'family bond' that shapes us for the rest of our lives."

~ Lin Sue Cooney, adoptive mom and Television News Anchor

"I am a high school guidance counselor who has also worked as a social-emotional counselor in a school setting. In both positions I have worked with adoptive children of various ages. When I was ten years old, a younger brother and sister were adopted into our family. My father-in-law was adopted from an orphanage at age five; he refers to his adoptive mother as his "angel mother." And just recently, my daughter adopted a baby.

I love the sincere, innermost emotions that kids and adoptive parents have been able to share. Their accounts will benefit adoptive children by validating their feelings with regard to adoption. The book will support parents who have adopted children, and it will allow them to understand some of the feelings and attitudes of their adoptive child. They can benefit from the experiences of other adoptive parents, too.

I believe those in the education system can use these narratives as resources to understand the emotional reactions of adoptive children. Thanks for taking the time to put together *Snowflakes, a Flurry of Adoption Stories*. It is a supportive, sincere, and unique resource."

~ Jackie Blair, Guidance Counselor

"This collection is truly valuable, and will be useful to a wide range of people. I am so excited about *Snowflakes, a Flurry of Adoption Stories*. The last section about difficult times is very important so that families can understand that there may be bumps along the road. It's a pleasure to read stories written by adopted children and teens and to be able to visualize the wonderful families who have made a positive difference in their lives. The book is excellent reading for adoption staff and is very insightful for families and prospective adoptive parents!"

~ MaryLee Lane, Founder of Hand in Hand Adoptions

"It is amazing what some children and adoptive families have gone through. The lessons learned from these experiences may be helpful to all parents and families, not just adoptive families."

~ Gaylan I. Jones, M.A., NCSP, School Psychologist

Snowflakes
A Flurry of Adoption Stories

BY, FOR AND ABOUT
children and teens

Teresa Kelleher

with Katie Flake and Paul Kelleher-Smith
Illustrated by Mora Kelleher-Smith

tlc
tender loving
communications

Snowflakes
A Flurry of Adoption Stories
by, for and about children and teens

Teresa Kelleher with Katie Flake and Paul Kelleher-Smith
Illustrated by Mora Kelleher-Smith

This book is a compilation of stories from many people. In order to preserve privacy, some names and states have been changed. Occasionally, a few details have been changed or omitted in order to protect privacy or when they did not relate to the experience of adoption.

ISBN: 978-1-936214-05-1
Library of Congress Control Number: 2009938259

Other publications by Teresa Kelleher:
Adopting From Russia, a Language and Parenting Guide
RUSH into English, Russian to English for Children
Adopting From China – Mandarin
Adopting From Latin America
Easing the Transition, a Parenting Guide

Photographs have all been used by permission.
"The Universe Spins And So Do We" by Maureen Kelleher, www.mkelleherart.com (Back Cover)
All other artwork and illustrations by Mora Kelleher-Smith, http://mkellehersmith.wordpress.com

tender loving
communications

Published by Tender Loving Communications, An Imprint of Wyatt-MacKenzie
Teresa Kelleher
tk.pacifica@gmail.com
Tender Loving Communications / Translation, Language, Communication
P.O. Box 90, Taylor, Arizona 85939

The author/editor donates 10% or more of profits from her books to orphanages around the world and to other causes that benefit children.

For Muriel, guardian angel to more than one hundred "snowflakes."
~ Teresa

For my birth parents, wherever they are.
~ Paul

For my family.
~ Katie

Acknowledgments

Here it is: a book *by*, *for* and *about* adopted children! It's the work of over one hundred people who have been touched by adoption. Thank you to all who shared their experiences. Special thanks to all the children and teens who generously contributed their stories.

Thank you to my team of supporters: Mora Kelleher-Smith, Claire Kelleher-Smith, Maureen Kelleher, Sheila Neck, Debbie Smith, Pam Smith, Lori Morse, Sandra Hostetter, and Pam Flake. Thanks to Denice Westover and Gonzalo Pacheco for technical assistance.

Heartfelt thanks to Dee Oster and Julie Ferdon, editors extraordinaire. You probably did not know what you were getting into when you agreed to "read over a few stories," but you followed through with fervor.

Paul and Katie, you two were the inspiration behind this project. You made it happen. You have enriched the lives of your families in ways you will not be able to understand until you become parents. You also kept me on task with this book. Thank you.

To my family – Roger, Claire, Mora, and Paul – who have lived with this project for three years: I love you and appreciate your willingness to co-exist with "Mom's book." You shared your stories, insights, feedback, honesty, artwork, and willingness to listen. Roger, my love, your patience is astounding. Thank you.

Table of Contents

PART ONE
For Readers of All Ages

PART TWO
For Teen and Adult Readers

Note about the Title

Snowflakes provide a great metaphor for adopted children. They are unique and multi-faceted, and like children, they are affected by their surroundings. Snowflakes are lovely and delicate. At the same time, they must be strong and resilient in order to weather the environments in which they form. Snowflakes in a storm, like all of us in the first stages of adoption, swirl in a flurry before settling down!

My family and I live in the adjoining communities of Snowflake and Taylor, Arizona. Many of the stories herein come from adoptees and their families in Snowflake and Taylor and the surrounding communities. A large number of families here, as in many towns and cities, have been touched by adoption.

Katie Flake, one of the two student editors of this book, lives in Snowflake, Arizona with her parents and ten siblings. She is part of a large family whose pioneer ancestors settled our town in 1878. The name of the town is a combination of their last name and the last name of Erastus Snow, the President of the LDS church at that time. You'll see Katie's adventurous spirit and great sense of humor in her stories.

Paul Kelleher-Smith, my son, is also a student editor for our book. What a guy! Take two parts independence, three parts opinion, and a whole lot of intelligence, mix them together with good looks and talent, and what have you got? Yup, Paul. Though he wasn't always crazy about being involved in "Mom's book project," he hung in there with me for two years by writing, giving feedback on submissions, and reading the entire final draft. I learn from him every day.

Preface

As I was in the middle of editing this book, lo and behold, I came across forgotten references to it from years ago. One of my seven sisters sent me this message more than ten years ago:

> I do *not* tire of hearing about your trip to Russia, Paul Sergei, his assimilation into the family, the girls' reactions, how you and Roger are handling things, etc. I can't think of anything better for you to do than write an article...except perhaps an expanded version in a book! Love, Nancy

Then I found notes in my journal about my decision to follow through. This sentence from years ago still rings true today: "I just hope I can put the thoughts and feelings into words adequately."

The more that is available on the topic of adoption, the better the chances are that children will find homes and families. I hope that adoptive families, and especially children who have been adopted, will continue to share their stories.

This project has been a fascinating endeavor. Stories were rounded up in a variety of ways and arrived to me in various formats. Several families who have used my previous publications contributed their accounts. Vignettes came from families near and far. Family members and friends who have adopted and/or have close connections with others who have adopted shared their views. Some of the anecdotes have come from people I have bumped into in unlikely places.

My goals for this book fall into four categories:

I. To Benefit Adoptees

First, I wanted to give voice to adopted children, by allowing them the opportunity to tell their stories in their own words and to read and know the stories of others in similar circumstances. Adoption is a life-changing passage; if children and teens know that others have navigated the same course, it may help them as they continue on their life journeys. I also want children and teens to see that even if their adjustment to their new home and family has been tough, they are valued, accepted, and loved. Many stories express this theme over and over again.

II. To Benefit Adoptive Families and People Who Know Them

Parents, siblings, grandparents, extended family members, and adoptees all gain by better understanding adoption – whether it's by "walking a mile in an adoptee's shoes" or understanding some of the complex emotions related to adoption. Adoption, like family formation by birth, requires work, adjustments, adaptations, and new roles for all involved. It's an advantage for families to learn from the experiences and insights of others. Much of this book was written by people just like you. Their accounts provide adoptees and their families a jumping off point for adoption discussions in many relevant environments: schools, health care settings, adoption agencies, adoption forums, and foster care settings. The stories reflect the challenges and joys of adoption. They also provide examples of ways in which families have been "built" successfully.

III. To Inform Prospective Adoptive Parents

This book offers prospective adoptive parents a pre-adoption preview of the various stages of the process as well as children's views along the way. The editors have made every effort to include the difficult as well as the delightful to give as realistic a picture as possible of what adoptive families have faced. The good news is that most adoptions are successful with very favorable outcomes for all concerned.

IV. To Give Examples of Successful Adoptions of Older Children and Children with Differences and Challenges

If prospective adoptive parents are contemplating adoption of an older child or a child with challenges, several of the pieces herein will provide valuable information to help you in making your decision.

The book is divided into two main sections. The first is appropriate for people of all ages, including children, and the second, the Teen Section, like "PG" movies, requires parental guidance for pre-teens.

The spectrum of emotions and experiences included offers a peek into the world of the adopted child, both in his or her previous world and in his or her whole new world. I chose not to correct every language error. If you notice the dates following the titles and the references in many cases to how long a child has been home, these will afford you the chance to study the children's development. With careful attention, you will be able to discern the progression of adoptees' language skills at different ages.

I am a language teacher and a parent of biological kids and an adopted son. My comments and opinions have been formed over twenty-five years of parenting and teaching school. I have authored four adoption-specific language sets over the past ten years. As a result, I have also had the remarkable opportunity to carry on e-mail and phone conversations with hundreds of adoptive parents and children all over the world. The present compilation of stories has been gathered with the hope that the final product will enlighten in some small way those who have an interest in adoption. I am particularly proud and pleased to be able to present the words, comments, views, and narratives of children. I am not a psychologist and I do not pretend to be, but it is simple for me to observe a thread of themes that runs through the children's stories: the need for safety, security, affection, attention, love, understanding, and compassion. In essence, it's no more or no less than every human being craves: belonging.

My hope is that families benefit by the labors of the very generous contributors and the student editors. Thanks for reading *Snowflakes: a Flurry of Adoption Stories*. It has been an absolute pleasure to work on this project and it has been and hopefully will continue to be a win-*win*-**win** situation – for adopted children and their families, for prospective adoptive parents, and for children waiting for forever families and loving homes.

Names and dates: You'll see several names repeated. Since we chose not to include last names of adoptees in almost every case, the reader will need to look at the age and home state of the author to differentiate. Also, when soliciting stories, I suggested that for difficult or very personal stories, the authors might wish to change their names. Several contributors did so. The coming home date is provided at the beginning of some entries; this is done to give the reader information on how long the adoptee had been in his or her new surroundings when writing the story.

TERESA KELLEHER

❋ x ❋

PART ONE

For Readers of all Ages

C H A P T E R   O N E

Children's Stories:
In Their Voices

"I am like a falling star who has finally found her place
next to another in a lovely constellation,
where we will sparkle in the heavens forever."

~ Amy Tan

The Rainbow
By Daniel, age 8, 2006
Pennsylvania

After a long day my new family and I finally got home from Russia. I was two years old. God blessed us with a rainbow in the back yard. That was the first time I ever saw a rainbow. The rainbow reminds me that I will always have a family.

Amazing Adoption
By Debbie, age 12, November 2008
Arizona

Adoption is an amazing thing because you can find out how other people have different ways. It makes you understand about different places and how different people live. I got to come here and learn how Americans talk in a different language and how they live. In the future, when I'm older, I want to go back and visit my birth country. I want to see what's there and how the people there live.

How I got adopted is remarkable. It turns out that I am related to other kids who have just recently moved to my town. So now I have cousins here from the Marshall Islands. I have visited with them twice. Two of them are older than I am and the other one, the girl, is two or three years younger. It's exciting to have that connection with my birth country and my biological cousins. I'm glad they are here.

Everyone says that it's cool to be adopted. I agree. I say, "Yeah, it is cool!" I will adopt when I'm older. If kids are poor, they can get taken care of. It helps kids. I feel proud to be adopted.

My Born Family and My New Family
By Alejandro, age 8, December 2008
Home to New Hampshire 2005

I'm Alejandro. I'm eight and I'm in second grade. I was born in Guatemala. I turned five years old in Guatemala and a couple of weeks later, my family came and adopted me and now I live in New Hampshire. When the adoption lady showed them my picture, they didn't want to see any other pictures of children. They wanted me to be in their family.

I remember when I was four and my born mother and father brought me to be adopted and they didn't tell me until we got there. My little mother in Guatemala told me she loves me and she was giving me a new family. I was scared and sad. I didn't like my foster family. I didn't know what was going to happen to me.

I want to tell you something if you are going to get adopted by a new family. They think you're cute and they want to love you and take care of you. Let your new family love you. Love your new family. Have fun with them. I have a sister and she plays with me and tells me things. She's in fifth grade. She is glad I'm her brother.

If you get adopted, it doesn't mean your born mother doesn't love you. It just means she wants good things for you and good things to happen to you. So she puts you on adoption so you can have a better life than she could make for you. She put you on adoption because she loves you and a happy life is what she dreams for you. I'm not mad at my born mother anymore.

It will be sad because you'll have to miss your born family, but you will be happy with your new family. You can still love your born family and you can remember them. I remember my born family. My born mother was nice and she made me rice and beans in a pot on the fire. I had two brothers and two sisters. My baby sister got adopted before me and I thought she was in heaven. One year after I got adopted, my parents took me to see my baby sister. I was six and she was three and we looked just alike and we hugged each other and had fun together. My mother sent a picture of us to my little mother in Guatemala so she could see us together and she would feel good. My brothers and my other sister are still with my little mother in Guatemala. I still love them and someday I hope I can see them again. My mother helps me send money for children in Guatemala for food and toys and clothes.

It doesn't matter if you have brown skin. I like being a brown person. Nobody where I live cares what color I am. When I was in kindergarten, I had a girlfriend. I asked my parents if I married my friend when I grow up, would she turn brown or would I turn white. Mom told me that I would still be brown because that is the skin color God chose for me, so it is the right color. And God chose white for my friend, so that is her right color. That is what God thought we would look our best in.

It's all in a Name
By Angelika, age 9, August 2007
New Hampshire

Hello, my name is Angelika. My name has not changed since I came home from Russia. Angelika has always been my name. Most of the people I know don't make fun of my name or say it wrong. If someone says my name wrong on accident, I don't mind. If they say it wrong on purpose, I won't be happy! In Russian, my name means "little angel." Sometimes I am not a little angel to my brothers. I do things like change the music station to something they dislike.

I was born on February 1, 1998 in Revda, a small town north of Ekaterinburg, Russia. My parents visited me in May and adopted me on August 9, 2001, when I was three and a half years old. My dad blew bubbles with me and the other kids when he visited at the orphanage, and we played with balloons too. I got a necklace with my name on it from my parents, and I got lots and lots of pictures taken of me. I had such a wonderful time when my parents came to visit. Now on Gotcha Day, I look at those pictures from when I was in Russia.

I did not like the ride home on the airplane. I yelled and screamed. I do not remember a lot, but I know I scared people on the plane. I was so loud that almost everyone moved away from us on the first part of the trip home. I guess I finally settled down when I could listen to music on my headset. My mom says I was so excited that I never did sleep at all on the whole way home.

When I finally got to my new home in Boston, I got lots of toys. My new brothers' names were Dan, Jared, and Jason. My three brothers were great! Dan played with me a lot. We still spend time together. When my brothers watch me, we make dinner together and watch a movie.

After I lived in Boston for about a year, my family moved to New Hampshire. We got a new house and it's on a farm. We have three chickens, three sheep, one llama, two horses, two dogs, four cats, and a tortoise. Every summer we let cows from one of our friends stay in our fields to eat grass. Our farm is fun. The animals are lots of work, but they are fun to play with, too.

Here are some facts about me. My favorite color is turquoise because it stands out from other colors. I have tons of turquoise jewelry. My favorite sport is basketball, and I play on a team. I also play lacrosse in our city youth program with a friend of mine. I love to read, especially books from the *Magic* series, because the writer describes everything well. My favorite food is quiche, but I will try anything. I like some Russian foods, like pickled beets. My family doesn't really have a way of celebrating Russian culture, but I'm interested in learning about it. I still know a few Russian words, like "cat," "dog," "underwear," and "grandma." I'll probably study Russian again in the future, and my parents and I have talked about going back to visit when I'm older.

I think being adopted is kind of cool because it makes me special in my family. I am from halfway around the world! Every once in a while the subject of adoption comes up. One of my best friends was adopted, so we talk about it some. Another girl at my school was adopted from Ethiopia. I have thought about the possibility of adopting, but I'm still too young to give it much thought.

Buttons
By Elise, age 10, 2006
Pennsylvania

I remember when we first got on the airplane to come home from Russia. I was four years old. There were buttons on the airplane chair. I was pushing the buttons all the way home because I was so curious. That was fun. My mom and dad told me that every button had different music in the headphones, but I don't even remember that. I just remember that I liked pushing the buttons.

Note by Elise's mom, 2006:

* It is worth noting that these buttons were only an example of all the things that Elise was curious about in her new world outside of her orphanage. She wanted to see and experience and get her little hands on everything! She took big sniffs of anything that had a scent, and she ate anything and everything we put in front of her. (Of course we were careful not to deviate too quickly from the foods she was used to eating, but one of the first English phrases she learned to say was "Excuse me," because she was constantly burping from her new eating patterns.) She felt so free and couldn't wait to take in this whole new world!

The Girl That Came From Russia
By Galya, age 12, December 2008
Home to New York 2002

There was a girl that came from Russia and her name is Galina but they call her Galya. She lived in an orphanage because her parents did not want her. She was four when she went to the orphanage. It was very sad to see her go to an orphanage instead of to a home with a family. When she was six years old, she came for a visit to Buffalo. She stayed for a month. She learned to speak English very, very quickly. She lived with people named Tom and Leslie. They really wanted her. A few months later they came to Russia to visit her in the orphanage for a few days. It was very sad when they left, but they promised that the next time they would take Galya home. That winter, they came back and this time they adopted her.

Have you guessed that I am Galya?! Now I live in a nice home and I'm happy to be in a family with my mom, my dad, and my big sister, Jordan, who was twenty-four years old when I came home. Jordan rides horses. At first I was very afraid of horses, but now I love them too.

My mom and dad are great! Nothing was really too hard for me when I came here. It felt like the right place to be. My sister lived near us for about three years before she moved to Kentucky to go to college. It was very sad for me when she moved. I didn't like it when she left but I still see her about four or five times a year. When she visits we go horseback riding together. I always cry when she leaves!

I go to the Elmwood School. I have a lot of friends there: Alex, Justin, Anthony, Nico, Taylor, Spencer, Samantha and Robin. Grace, Lily and Emily live on my street. I met James in summer camp and Caroline and Wesley in soccer. Sarah is my very, very best friend. She used to go to my school, but she moved to the suburbs. I love to do sports because they are the best thing ever. My mom is a dance teacher and I am in her class.

It's kind of like I have had two lives. My life in Russia was miserable. I try to forget it. There is no memory of Russia that I want to keep. I probably won't ever go back to Russia (my mom says maybe I'll change my mind one day and want to visit). I've even forgotten Russian.

Here it is better because I have a family, friends and fun. There are even things like carnivals and theme parks. I will go to college some day. I have a good home and now I am so happy!

My Adoption from Kazakhstan
By Abe, age 10, July 2008
Home to Snowflake, Arizona 2005

My birth family was very poor, and my birth mother could not keep me. She took me to the orphanage. They took care of me very well. I grew there. I had lots of mothers there, six or seven. There was one mother who was really good. When I did something bad, she would put me in time-out. She took care of me and fed me. She let me watch TV. We didn't ride in any cars. We just walked everywhere. There was a doctor who helped my back when it was hurt. She helped me get better.

In the orphanage I would play outside when there was snow. Sometimes we would go outside and play with snowballs. When there were lots of storms, though, we wouldn't go outside.

There was a time when my adoptive parents came into a room at my orphanage with lots of kids in there, and I was there too. I remember talking to them and talking to Marina. She helped them with the adoption. I was very sad because they were there talking to me and then they left. I didn't think they were going to come back for me.

Soon they came back and adopted me. We drove in a car together and went to an apartment. I had never been to an apartment before. It was awesome! I was very nervous of my parents because I was afraid they would be mean to me. I kept thinking, "I have a new family now. I'm not in the orphanage anymore."

My parents fed me. I really liked the new food and it tasted good. I had never had an apple in the orphanage and I liked it a lot. I loved the yogurt, and I kept asking my mom if we could buy yogurt. I ate tomatoes, cucumbers, carrots and corn. I didn't like meat; the meat in the orphanage was yucky, so I didn't want to eat it. My favorite new food was yogurt. Oh, I love yogurt!

I remember the plane ride to go meet my family in America. I was riding with my dad and Katie, my new sister. I remember eating a lot on the plane, going to the bathroom, watching TV, and sleeping. My dad was so big and scary at first. I'm not scared of him anymore. I saw that he was bald. I liked that part. It was funny. I was glad to get off the plane.

When we got to Arizona, it was night time and I was asleep. When we got off the plane, there was my family with lots of signs. I was scared because there were lots of people and they were all hugging me. Nobody had hugged me before in Kazakhstan. It was very different.

I remember my first day in America. I woke up in my house and I wanted to go see the chickens. I called them "bac, bac, bac" because I couldn't say *chicken*. The chickens scared me because they would bite my fingers. I saw dogs and cats and they all scared me too, but I wanted to chase after them.

I was afraid of my big family for a while because I couldn't speak English. When I went to school, I kept thinking, "Where am I?" I didn't know my teacher, and the other kids were mean to me.

I started liking my family because I had a nice sister. I liked my brother McKay, too. We played in our coats and boots. I wore the boots a lot. I feel good about my family now. I like Mom and Dad the best because when I do bad things, they can fix it. When I do good things, they are happy. That is all I'm going to say today.

My Christmas Present to You
By Ally, age 10, December 2007
Texas
(Note: Ally wrote this story for her parents as a Christmas gift her fourth Christmas home.)

Once upon a time there was a Mom who was going to have a baby girl. The girl was named Elena. She loved Elena very much. She thought Elena was a beautiful girl and she was glad that she got a girl. Elena had a brother. When Elena was born the brother was five years old.

The Mom took good care of Elena. And the Dad loved her as much as the Mom did. As Elena was growing up, no one taught her that the true meaning of Christmas is loving one another and that it was a time to show our love for Heavenly Father. She didn't know it was such a wonderful time of the year.

One time when Elena was five years old she and her mother went to the market in Russia. Elena went to the bakery and her mother went to get butter for the bread. Elena got lost in the store. It was very sad. The mom yelled, "Elena, Elena!" Everybody said, "Who is Elena?"

Then these men came and said, "Do not be afraid because we are going to help you." They took Elena to this place where a lot of kids were. She made friends there and the kids became nice to her. They even took her blueberry picking.

It had been a whole year since Elena had seen her family. She still missed them a lot. One day this new mom and dad came in and said, "We will take her." Then they left. Elena thought they were going to be her new mom and dad, but they left. She was confused; it was very sad.

In a couple of months they came back. Elena saw them and she was glad. They played with her on the playground at the kids' home, and it was fun being with them. This time they took her with them. When it was time to leave the kids' place, she had to say good-bye to everyone. The other kids were sad and so was Elena.

Elena and the new mom and dad had so much fun together, but Elena was still sad. The first night she slept with them she was sad and crying. Her new mom spoke to her in Russian and told her, "It is going to be OK; nothing is going to hurt you." Then she hugged Elena, gave her a kiss, and said "Good night." Then Elena went to sleep.

When it was time to go to her real home in America, Elena got to see her new brothers, Ethan and Hayden. She even met a new Grandma and Grandpa. That was the best day ever because now she had a family again and she felt safe and loved.

My Name
By Sergei, age 11, July 2008
Home to Chandler, Arizona 2004

My name is Sergei. Sergei means trust. My parents thought it meant "warrior." When I first came here to visit, my name was Seriozha. When I started living here, my family began calling me Sergei. Now my name is Sergei Allen. It makes me proud because it's a cool name.

Picturing the Past
By Kayla, age 10, November 2008
Home to Florida April 2008

I never knew what I looked like when I was a baby. But I really wanted to know. I didn't know if I was cute, or what I liked to eat or do. Then my mommy got a picture of what I would have looked like. I was a cute baby Kayla. I had little hands and big eyes. In my picture, I am lying on a pink blanket. I had a little hair. I had no teeth. Bye. Thank you from cute baby Kayla.

(Note: Kayla was adopted from Kostroma, Russia. In this story, she is talking about an age-regressed baby picture that her mom ordered to give her an idea of what she looked like as an infant.)

Changes
By Elina, age 9, June 2009
Home to California October 2007

My name is Elina. When I was seven years old and I was being adopted I saw my mom sitting on the couch. I ran up to her and hugged her. Then I saw two other people and one of them was named Charlotte and the other was named Ryan. They were my aunt and cousin. He looked strange to me because I had never seen him before. He took a picture of my shoe, and I was laughing because I thought it was hilarious. Then I saw a weird gadget. It had words and things in it. I had no idea what it was, but I found out later that it was a translator.

Then my mother left and when she came back she brought me a fuzzy, fuzzy teddy bear and I loved it. After that I came in a strange car and I kept taking my seatbelt off because I didn't know the rules. We went to a store and Mom and Anya shopped for food that I wanted. Then we came to the hotel. I played hide-and-seek with my mom. She found me under the table. I didn't sleep under the table and I never fell asleep on that bed in the hotel. I just couldn't sleep at all.

My aunt had a strange clock gadget. We saw a talking cucumber in a movie called *Veggie Tales* and the cucumber was jumping and jumping. When the tomato came, well, it was funny. It was in English and I couldn't understand anything they were saying, but the cucumber was dancing funny. But this is not the whole story, you know, because I finally fell asleep then. My mom was dressing me when I was asleep. She was changing me out of my little slippers that I got.

My mom woke me up early because, of course, it was time for the plane. On that plane my ears were hurting like crazy. In the plane a lady gave me some water. I liked that lady. She was pretty and nice. After the plane, we came to an airport again and I then I flew on another plane. Then I saw these other people in another airport and I figured out they were my grandma and grandpa. They had a puppy. I loved that puppy and I figured out it was for me. We drove and then stopped at a food place to get a milkshake. My mom had to change, but I didn't know that until she told me later. The puppy had peed all over my mom, all the way from her tighty-whiteys up to the top of her shirt!

We came to a house and I figured out that this is where I was going to live. I saw this nice room and it was for me. I thought it was beautiful and it had anything an orphan kid could dream of. It had a nice bed, books, and stuffed toys (just what I needed). The house had a lot of food. It was a good house. I saw a rocking chair in this room that was called the living room. I kept rocking and rocking on it the first night I was here. I still rock by myself sometimes, but sometimes I rock with my mom now, too.

That day I met a neighbor named Charlyn. She was a friend and she loved me, too. She was a silly, silly one because she laughed a little like a pig!

The next day my mom, my grandma, and I went to a shoe store. My mom got me nice shiny shoes. They were kind of like high-heels. I wore them every day because I loved them. We went to Costco, too, and my mom got me a nice glass doll called Aurora. They got food and other things before we went back to my house. I played on my mom's organ and I tried to play on it but I was just fooling around with it, you know.

My mom made some soup and I hated the soup she made. It was a sweet potato soup and I hated that soup! I don't know why, but I just didn't like it. Then I fell asleep.

Then the next day was Halloween. I saw these weird monsters and I thought they were real. I was terrified. Someone came to the door like a skeleton on roller skates. I thought it was real. Then my mom had me dress up like a kitten on my head and I felt like a fool. I felt embarrassed. I decided I wanted to dress up like a scary thing, not a little kitten. Who would want to dress up like that on Halloween? I got a marker and marked some tiger stripes and whiskers on my face. I wanted to look scary, not like a kitten, and I went trick-or-treating. Then I fell asleep. Maybe I was going to sleep because there were a lot of new things happening at once.

The hard times lasted a long, long time. Sometimes I felt scared, mad a little, happy, or terrified! The hardest thing was getting to know the people. Getting to be friendly with other kids still is hard, but when things are hard for me, I talk with my mom about it. You know, some people have hard times too, not only me. Well, bye-bye. That's the end of the story. Hope you liked it.

Learning a Language and Leaving a Language Behind
By Victoria, age 11, December 2008
Home to Arizona 2005

Being a Gemini, as my mom would say, I like to talk. It has always been important to express myself. Being adopted meant losing this aspect for who knows how long. Being adopted was very scary, sad and frustrating when it came to a new language.

Friends are important to me. Having friends means having someone to talk to or tell your feelings to. Imagine suddenly losing your best friends and all those you know and depended on in the orphanage. Leaving them behind was very sad and scary.

I was scared because I did not know if I would make new friends in America. I thought, "How can I, when I don't speak the same language?" I felt like I was a mute. I couldn't talk. I couldn't communicate my needs. All day I heard gibberish. I missed the Russian language so much that every night for months, I would speak to myself in Russian. My parents only knew a few words. I so desperately wanted to keep my language.

Not being able to communicate, I was frequently frustrated while learning a second language. There were days I wanted to speak to my new mom about what happened at school, but couldn't make my feelings and thoughts clear. Some of my schoolmates would make fun of me because I didn't understand what was being said or what was going on. I couldn't make myself understood. I pretty much felt stupid. I made up my mind to learn the new language, which was English. I made it a priority.

By and by I steadily learned a second language. After three years, I was deemed proficient and released from the English Language Learner program. I was even chosen to receive recognition for achievement as an English Language Learner. I am very proud of myself. I learned that learning a second language can be fun – with time, effort and teachers who made it fun.

My advice to anyone learning a second language is to not give up. Figure out what method and techniques work best for you. Having a Russian/English tutor meant a lot to me when I first arrived here in America. I would think of all the things I wanted to ask my parents and have the interpreter ask them. It was a wonderful feeling to be able to finally tell my adopted parents how much I appreciated them.

On a final sad note, no matter how hard I tried to retain the Russian language, I eventually gave it up in favor of becoming as American as I could. As of now, I do not know if I will ever learn to speak Russian again.

C H A P T E R   T W O

Adoptees on Adoption

"We, you and I, are bound together in an inescapable web of destiny.
I can never be all that I was intended to be
until you become all that you were intended to be."
~ Martin Luther King, Jr.

Adoption is Destiny
By Jessica, age 15, February 2009
Arizona

Sometimes I hear people make comments about adoption. They never say anything to me directly, but I do hear them talking about it. I'd like people who are not adopted to know that it's not a bad thing. I was adopted when I was a baby, so it hasn't been an adjustment for me. I feel this family is where I belong, and I'm sure I'm loved. It has definitely been a great way for me to grow up. Adoption gives you an opportunity to have a better life. It was always meant to be for me to be a part of this family. Adoption is destiny.

I have a friend who was adopted when he was quite a bit older, already a teen, actually. He says it took some getting used to. I want to say to him and to others that have been adopted that they shouldn't feel weird or bad about it. I think it is cool. Parents who allow their kids to be adopted want something better for their children. If it is challenging because of someone being adopted when they are older, I say to try to make the best of it. Everything will work out over time.

I've always wanted to adopt and I definitely plan to when I'm older. I will probably adopt a couple of children, maybe one from here in the U.S. and also one from another country. My cousins have adopted from other places, and I think that is great. Adoption is for the best.

Message to a New Sibling
By Sergei, age 11, July 2008
Chandler, Arizona

I'm from Russia. We're going to adopt a new child from Ukraine. I think it will probably be a sister. I think it will be Lily because we have seen a picture of her. She will need to know some stuff about our family.

Our house is safe. My mom and dad took a picture of it to send to me when I was in Russia so I would know it was safe. Now you won't have to be scared.

We have a lot of pets: two dogs, two cats, two birds, and an aquarium full of fish. Our dogs are nice. They don't bite and they like to play. My mom and I take care of the dogs. I don't spend much time with our cats, but sometimes they rub against me when I watch TV. The cats like my sister Elizabeth very much, so they come to her when she calls them. Maybe you could feed the fish and have the job of playing with the pets.

Being in our family means building trust. When our parents call you, you come the first time every time. You do what your parents say because they want you to build trust. They tell me what time they will pick me up from school, and they make sure to pick me up on time. My dad plays soccer with me, my mom plays *Uno* with me, and we all swim together. They spend time with me because they love me.

Mom and Dad are going to love you, too. We'll all help you learn about our whole family and we'll all teach you English. This family is very nice, so they will love you, and you will love them, too!

Lilya with Aunt Teresa shortly after
coming home from Ukraine

Lilya's Words
By Lilya, age 7, February 2009
Home from Ukraine to Arizona November 2008

It is fun and happy here. We have dogs to catch. And we have two cats. I was catching the birds, but they are too fast.

The difficult thing, I was scared. I saw clouds there in the movie video. I said I don't want to go there. I didn't want clouds. I don't like clouds. I like sun better. I don't like rain. In a big boat in a big storm you might fall off the boat in the rain.

I feel funny now. My dad makes me laugh. He was counting funny. He says the wrong numbers. It's not right. I say, "Nice try, Dad!" He's so funny.

One time I was taking out toys from my brother's room. Mom teaches me a better way. One time I was sad and she hugged me and told me things would be better. Then we laughed.

Sergei, my brother, makes me mad. He says, "You are robots," and he plays with food.

I like school because I have one hundred and nine friends. My teacher helps me with my English.

(Note: Lilya didn't want to be anywhere where there were lots of clouds and rain. She has been home three months with her mom, dad, sisters, and brother in *sunny* Chandler, Arizona.)

One Very Happy Girl
By Nikayla, age 10, August 2008
Snowflake, Arizona

I feel that I was very lucky to come to this country because I mean I was absolutely starving when I was a baby in Russia. When I look at pictures of myself when I was first adopted, I was covered with sores because all the orphanage had to feed me was sour milk and I am allergic to milk. When I watch videos of me in Russia, I feel weird because it amazes me how I was so small and how now I am in fifth grade.

Someday I want to go back to Russia because it looks so beautiful, and of course I want to learn the language.

I am thankful to live in the United States because I live in a home in the nice town of Snowflake and I have loving parents.

I think being adopted is awesome and I just love it when people notice because it makes me feel special and great. I think most people are surprised to find out that I am Russian-American.

The Fun of Being Adopted
By Anna, age 12, March 2009
Home to Arizona 2005

The fun of being adopted is that I stay in one place. I don't move every day. Before I was adopted, I moved a lot. I lived in ten or eleven different foster families. The first time I was three or four years old.

While I was in the foster homes, I had a lot of different feelings. Some feelings were scary because you don't know where you will go after you leave. It was also hard because of sets of rules. You had different rules at each foster home. When they came to get me to go to a new home, I would always get scared. I was thinking, "Where am I going to go now?" I hoped I would be going somewhere comfortable and safe. I hoped that the parents would like me and treat me well. Usually I was scared for a while, but then when I got used to it, I wasn't afraid.

But if the house was bad, I did not grow happy and safe. The scariest ever was a house that had no rules. I was about five years old when I was there. It was scary because everyone could do whatever they wanted and the kids of that family, I called them "the troublemakers," did bad things. When they behaved badly, I got blamed for it, and they acted like sweet, adorable children that did nothing wrong. They acted like I was a mean, rotten, bad, person, and I got in trouble because the parents didn't believe me when I said I didn't do it because I was the foster child.

But there were good feelings too. A couple of times were when I got settled in, I sometimes got rid of my scary feeling. I then would feel happy and would like that house. One of the foster families was about to adopt me but something happened so they didn't. They were a good family, so I felt sad. After a while, though, my family came (the family I have now) and they adopted me. It was nice and I felt good inside. I still feel glad and joyful about being in this family.

Have Hope
By Daniel, age 9, September 2008
Pennsylvania

Adoption means something very special for me. It changed my life forever. I feel very special to have a family. For kids who have not yet been adopted, I would say, "Good luck. I'll pray for you. Never give up hope."

I Was Scared, But Now I'm Not
By Ally, age 12, July 2008
Texas

Sometimes I get up in the middle of the night and cry. My mom comes and asks me, "What's the matter?"

I tell her, "I'm scared about bad guys hurting me."

I have come to realize that every night in Russia in the Children's Home I was guarded by police, because they wanted to keep the bad guys away from us. They thought they would come in the night and take us away. One night we children heard noises outside that sounded like someone trying to get in. I was really scared, and that is why I'm scared about bad guys getting me.

But I know my mom and dad will do everything to keep me safe and I trust them. I'm glad that I have them to take care of me.

I Changed My Name
By Anna, age 12, December 2008
Home to Arizona 2005

My name is Anna. I got to pick my name after I got adopted. I do not like my old name. My parents agreed that I could have a better name. My first and my middle name were both storm names before, and I didn't want those names anymore. People used to make fun of my names when I lived in Florida. Here no one knows those names so they don't tease me about that. I talked with my mom and dad about it, and we decided to change my name. We looked at names on the Internet. When I looked at all the names, I liked the name Anna. I chose Anna, and they started calling me by my new name. I also got a new last name. I'm very happy that I got new names.

High Hopes
By Elise, age 11, September 2008
Pennsylvania

Adoption was great for me because I got a family. I think others at the orphanage think I'm so lucky to be adopted. I would say to them, "Keep your hopes up. Keep hoping." It's great to let people know that I'm adopted because it might help them adopt and inspire them to adopt too. Do I think about adopting someday? Yes! It's a definite yes because I want to do that.

Fitting In
By Anna, age 10
Ohio

I was born Vinnitza, Ukraine. My birth family was from a little village near the city. My birth parents couldn't take care of me when I was young so they put me in an orphanage called the Baby House. I was born with one arm and PFFD (one leg is much shorter than the other because I'm missing part of my thigh bone). At that time in the U.S.A. a young couple with two boys were wanting to adopt from Ukraine, and they had to do a lot of paperwork and a lot of scheduled appointments with social workers. Then they went through files of pictures of boys and girls who were up for adoption and they saw me. The people there kept on talking to them about a little boy named Andrushka, but they wanted to meet me. Then they went to meet me, and they met me and knew that I was theirs. The few weeks they had to wait to go to court, I told everyone in my orphanage, "That's my mama and my papa!"

When we went to the U.S.A., I was three years old. I learned English really quickly and went to a church called LifeSpring. I went to Sunday school and learned how to navigate the Bible. I gave my life to Jesus and decided I wanted to be baptized.

My parents were friends with a family that had a girl named Bethany. She was really shy around other people, but not with me. We became best friends. People always ask us if we are sisters.

When I was about eight years old, I got a service dog from Circle Tail. His name is Hydro. He picks things up for me and opens doors for me. I also train him with 4H and placed 1st for obedience in my county at last year's fair. I'm still working with him and we'll compete in this year's fair too. I also raise ducks and chickens for 4H – even though I don't live on a farm!

I am on the Clippard YMCA Barracudas Swim Team. I like swimming freestyle, and my second favorite stoke is backstroke. I also like butterfly and breast stroke. My mom and dad say that I am a fish. I started taking swim lessons when I was six or seven. I started because I wanted to learn how to swim, and because knowing how to swim is a safety issue.

I have two older brothers and two younger sisters. My younger sisters are adopted, too. Sometimes, when I go someplace new, I feel like I don't fit in, but I just keep trying anyway. That's the only part about being adopted that makes me sad. But lots of kids feel like they don't fit in – even kids who are not adopted or don't have disabilities. But being adopted usually makes me happy because I always feel like I fit in with my family and friends.

My Family Cares
By April, age 12, February 2009
Home to Florida 2004

The way my family cares is that they treat me nice sometimes. When I'm agreeable, they treat me nicely. They help me with problems if I let them help me. Sometimes I argue. When I argue, they tell me that there is another way rather than arguing. They talk it out with me. Sometimes I let them; other times I don't. Sometimes I still argue and get mad. We're all learning together how to be a cooperative and happy family.

Sometimes you might not want to try what your parents say but you have to trust that they know what they are doing and saying. One time my parents told me to fix the homework that they corrected and I didn't want to because I thought it would take a long time. They said that if I did it then and tried hard, I would get it done faster. I didn't want to admit it, but they were right. It just took twenty minutes doing it their way, but my way would have taken an hour! So think about it. Your parents are probably right all the time. You should listen to them. I learned that if you do it their way it's quicker, but if you insist on doing it your way, it takes *forever*.

I was adopted on April 26, 2004. What makes it special is that it was also my eighth birthday. The coolest thing is that my family took me in. They care so much for me they wanted to make my life better. My mom buys me nice and pretty clothes. She buys me things I don't even need like extra shirts. I got a ton of Christmas shirts so I don't even wear my old ones! When there are rough days, she takes her time to help me and to work things out. She has me sit and think about it until I make the right decision. I get angry at first, but then I calm down. If I don't understand something, she explains it to me and tells me why it will happen a certain way. The reason she does this is because she loves me. My dad is patient about that too. He has the time to work it out with me.

The advice I want to give to adopted kids is that if you have a problem during the day (during school), stop and think about it and calm yourself down. Think about if your choice is right or wrong or if it would get you in trouble. When I was younger that was hard to do, but now I'm getting way better at it. If you stop and think, you get better and better all the time. That's what has happened to me.

My Thoughts about Adoption
By Elizabeth, age 9, September 2008
Missouri

I'm Elizabeth and I'm nine. I'm glad to be adopted, and you should be too! Usually I keep my feelings about adoption to myself, but being adopted makes me feel that I am special inside. Nobody can take that away from me. Sometimes I like to talk about adoption, but when I'm around strangers I don't liked being asked questions about it.

I know two girls and one boy from church that are adopted from Russia. There is a family that adopted a new baby. Also, there is a girl named Hally. She is adopted from Vietnam and she is my friend. I also have three cousins that are adopted from China, but I don't get to see them very often because they live in another state. I do like to talk about Russia, but just with people I know. My classmates ask about adoption when we have to share about our culture and when the teacher asks for baby pictures. People think that I'm a twin to my brother, but I'm really from another country.

I would like to tell other adopted children to just be you and be proud that you have a family that loves you and that can take care of you. Anything can happen if you just be yourself and be proud that you are from Russia or any of the other beautiful countries in the world.

I have not thought yet about whether or not I might adopt a child when I'm grown up. I'm still only nine years old, so I'm not sure yet if I want to have kids or not. But I'm proud of who I am and I'm glad to have a special place in my family.

Sergei's Adoption Thoughts
By Sergei, age 12, February 2009
Chandler, Arizona

I know that lots of kids get adopted and many don't. I am sure glad I got adopted. I will never forget getting a new family. It was weird when I first came for summer camp because I didn't know who I'd be staying with for the three weeks. But I fell in love with the family, my family, and I didn't want to leave.

The most amazing thing about adoption for me has been being in a safe place. It took a while for me to feel safe because I didn't know what my parents and new sisters were like. They helped me by coming in my room to hold me at night if I had bad dreams.

My new sister, Lilya, just came home three months ago. She was surprised because we have a pretty house and she had fun exploring it. She annoyed me a lot by copying things I did and calling me a baby. It annoyed me, but I felt that that it was good that she was here because every boy and girl should get adopted and have a family. Now, three months later, it's still crazy with a new sister in the house, but I'm getting used to it. It is fun that I have someone to play with. Sometimes she'll play what I want, but I'm not too interested in playing princesses.

She's getting better about not taking things out of my room. I tell my mom and we tell her not to do that. My parents have to talk with her about leaving my stuff alone. It's getting better, but she still doesn't listen all the time.

I haven't thought about whether or not I'll adopt a child in the future. It's a lot of paperwork and a lot of traveling. I do think that more kids should get adopted, though. I think people should check on kids and see who needs families. People can work through churches to tell others about adoption. They can show pictures of kids and orphanages. Then more children will get homes and families.

Stories and a Wish
By Natalya, age 9, August 2008
Snowflake, Arizona

I love to hear stories about when I was adopted. I love to hear the story about when I was afraid of my dad because I had never seen a man before. I like to look at the pictures of me when I was little. I wish I had some pictures of me when I was a baby, but I don't. I used to say Russian words, but my mom taught me how to speak English because speaking or hearing Russian would make me throw up. I would say, "I not Russian! I American!" I don't want to learn Russian again, because I think I wouldn't understand

English then. I feel scared when people ask me if I am adopted because it makes me feel creepy. I just wish I had been born from my mom's tummy instead of being adopted.

Moving and My Two Moms
By Ally, age 11, January 2008
Texas

We just moved to Texas from Arizona and though we now live a bit closer to Russia, it feels like we are further away from Russia. I really love it here in Texas; it is very beautiful. I feel like my Russian mom is glad this happened. I know she would be happy to know I am safe and well loved and taken care of. I think she was always worried about being able to feed me and take care of me. I think she also worried about "bad guys" hurting me. I know it is really hard to lose a child. I really miss her and I will never forget her. But I am glad this happened; I love my new family and I will always. I will be with my family forever and not a thing will change that.

Thoughts on Adoption
By Galya, age 12, December 2008
Home to New York from Russia 2002

Sometimes I want to talk about adoption – with friends and my family. When kids at school ask me in a surprised way, "You're adopted?" I just say, "Yeah, I am," but sometimes I get annoyed. I don't always want to talk about it.

When I see the video that my dad made, I realize how many kids need homes and families. If other kids get adopted, I think that is great. I would say to them, "Good for you!" I will probably also adopt when I am older because a lot of kids need a home.

(Note: Please see the story "Second Chance Children," in section XVII. Deciding to Adopt and Making a Match.)

Why Do You Ask?
By Arona, age 18, April 2008
Snowflake, Arizona

My family isn't your everyday family. There's just something a little different. Usually people find this out when they see us all together; they are surprised that we're all one family. Over half of us ten kids are adopted. And we all have different ethnicities, which is pretty sweet. My spot in the family is the middle child.

I became a part of this family when I was six years old. My parents had four kids already, two of them biological and two adopted. My bro and I made it six. We were adopted in a Utah courthouse. I'm an African-American and so is my bro. That's what makes us just a little bit different from the rest of our family. My mom and dad and oldest sister are Caucasian, my second oldest sister is Hispanic, my oldest brother is Hawaiian, my second brother is Caucasian. My bro and I are black Afro-American and Cree Indian, and the three youngest kids are Caucasian.

Sometimes people don't believe that my mom is really my mom. When people look at me and ask her the question, "Is she adopted?" my mom just answers, "Why do you ask?" It makes me feel happy that she thinks that it doesn't matter; I'm just one of her kids. It doesn't bother me that people ask because I know that they are interested and curious. It only bugs me when people are rude about it.

My Two Moms
By Rachel, age 12, May 2009
Arizona

My two moms are my birth mom and my mom. I'm glad my birth mom had me, but she didn't take very good care of me. She was good because she took me to the doctor and took me to all my check-ups and everything. She wanted the best for me, so she let me go to a family with a mom that could care for me.

I was eight when I came to my forever family. My mom now is really good. She takes care of me and cares about me. She takes me places, gives me what I need and she helps me. She loves me and wants the best for me.

On Mother's Day I think about my two moms. On Saturday I went shopping with my mom. It was just me and my mom. Out of the blue I said,

"I always wonder where I would be without you...without my family. Where would I be without you guys?"

I want to say to my mom now that I am thankful to her. I want her to know that she does have an impact on me. I do love her and I know that she loves me.

Adoption Made It All Good
By Jashon, age 18, February 2009
Snowflake, Arizona

When I came to my family I was on the plane and I was crying. I was too young to know I was being helped. I know that my birth family didn't treat me right because I used to have cigarette burns on my stomach, but I didn't understand what it meant to be adopted.

I'm not the only one in my family who is adopted. It's probably easier for me because most of my other brothers and sisters were adopted too. I am a bit curious about my biological family, but probably wouldn't look them up. I don't feel any need or desire to learn about them.

I can't think of any big challenges I've had. Life has been really good. One funny thing is that people expect a lot out of me because of my sister. She is a star athlete, so people expect that I might be too. But I'm just a computer nerd.

Next year I'll graduate, in 2010. My plan is to go to college and focus on computer technology. I haven't thought about the future beyond that yet.

Adoption programs are good; they help people have a fresh new start. It's a great experience. I haven't had difficulties or challenges because of adoption. I have lots of friends and a good life because I was adopted.

The Mother Who Gave Me Life and the Mother Who Loves and Takes Care of Me
By Ira, age 17, May 2009
Home to Florida 2006

I have two mothers in my life. One is my biological mother and the other one is my adoptive mother. I love them both very much, but I guess it's two different kinds of love. I love my biological mother for giving me birth and *trying* to take care of me. I love my adoptive mother for loving me, caring for me, and being always there for me when I need her. It's a very interesting experience to have two mothers. I am thankful for my biological mother because if she didn't give birth to me, then I wouldn't live a happy life with a mother that loves me and teaches me everything I need to know about life. Being adopted is such a great feeling because everyone loves you unconditionally. I am very proud to say that I was adopted and have two moms. God doesn't put people that you *want* in your life. He puts people that you *need* in your life.

Not Your Typical Adoption Story
By Nash, age 19, July 2008
Montana

Let me first start by saying that my story is probably not nearly as exotic, trans-oceanic, or cross-cultural as half of the stories in this book, but with that being said, my mother and the editor of said book feel that I have something to contribute. I'm the talkative type, meaning I rarely (if ever) turn down the chance to throw my two bits in. So think of this writing as a quarter thrown from my hand into the coin-slot of your imagination.

I am American. I have been my whole life. So when I say that my adoption story is not exotic, I mean to say that I didn't have to cross an ocean, learn a new language, or adapt to the perils of modern American society to integrate with my new family (and to all the people out there who do – man, are you in for a wild ride! I mean that in the rollercoaster sense, though – it has its ups, its downs, it's scary as can be, but in the end, you get off and all you can think is "That was great! Let's do it again!"). I was born in Fayetteville, North Carolina. English is my first (and as far as fluency goes, only) language, though there have been times where the sound of my voice has been altered by the twang of a Southern drawl. (I don't do that anymore.) I'm as American as apple pie, major league baseball, Interstate highways, fireworks on the 4th of July, and capitalism. Even with all these home-court advantages, though, it was still a challenge being the adopted kid.

This is the point where I have to digress from my story and tell a few others for the sake of understanding. My biological parents were roughly a quarter of a century apart in age. When I was born, my mom was 37, and my dad was 63. No matter how you look at it, 63 is a pretty ripe old age to be fathering kids (not that I'm complaining!), so it's not altogether shocking that when I was seven, my biological father passed away. Shocking – no, shocking isn't the word for it. It was earth shattering. I was seven. As far as I was concerned, "death" was the place people go after nursing homes – a magical place where Rice Krispie treats flowed like water and all you did was sit around and watch all the old cartoons that got cancelled. What I had never realized until after it affected me directly was that *people just do not come back from being dead.* So there I was, the only child of a single mom.

Due to my powerful unwillingness to relive any part of the following five to six years, I'm going to fast forward to June of 2001.

June 2001 was a magical time. I had just finished sixth grade. I was learning to play the trumpet (and was dueling for first chair in band with a guy I had known since I could walk). I had a bunch of friends that I had known for what felt like a really long time. And for summer vacation, my mom was taking us to Montana to go on a horseback pack trip. But little did I know that sinister workings were afoot, as a family friend had phoned my mother about two months before we were set to leave.

The call, I am told, went something like this:

"Trish! How are you? What have you been up to?"

"Oh, we're great, we're going to Montana for a pack trip!"

"Really? Where are you flying in to?"

"Some town I've never heard of – it's called Bozeman!"

"Trish, I know the greatest guy in Bozeman. You really should meet him."

"Al, I can't call a guy I've never met! That would be crazy!"

In the end, though, she called him. And that was how we met Mike. (He was "Mike" then, and he's "Dad" now, but there's more story to tell as to how that particular transition took place.) Mike met Trish, and sparks flew. Six months after we flew to Bozeman to pack into the woods on horses, we pulled into Bozeman in a car with the earthly possessions we didn't sell in a U-Haul behind us. Trish and Mike were married the following May, and I officially became the child of an integrated marriage. You may be thinking this is a little off topic for the subject of adoption, but read on. It gets more pertinent with every passing word.

I don't know exactly when my mom started floating the concept of being adopted by my stepdad, but I want to say it started sometime between when they got married and when my dad gave me my first hunting rifle. I was a little weirded out by the concept – not to sound insensitive – but at the time I thought adoption was something that you did to kids from orphanages in foreign countries. Turns out I wasn't correct. I think part of it had to do with the fact that I was convinced by society's stereotypes of integrated families that they just didn't work. The kids hated and resented the other parent, and tension inevitably ensued. That, to me, was just how integrated families worked. I didn't think they could actually, legally, *officially* be considered a family.

But I gave up on that concept about the same time that I realized that this guy my mom married was straight up *cool*. For a start, he had television (Mom killed ours shortly after the biological dad passed on). But on top of that, he hunted. No matter your stance on gun rights, it's fairly undeniable that the average city slicker kid (or any thirteen-year-old male, for that matter) thinks guns are pretty cool. They're the stuff made immortal by countless Rambo spinoffs and Western movies, and this guy my mom married not only had a safe full of them, but let me (in a controlled environment, of course) shoot them! How cool is *that*? And as if he didn't have enough of a John Wayne air about him, he had horses, and he rode them too! Not only that, he played guitar, and he listened to classic rock. Heck, if it hadn't been for this guy, I *still* wouldn't know who The Who, Jimi Hendrix, or the Eagles were. Slowly but surely, I began to realize – this dude is *the man!* And it was about then that I stopped calling him "Mike" and transitioned to "Pop," which slowly morphed into "Dad." Strange how these things happen, huh? On April 17, 2002 (Which was also the eighth anniversary of my biological father's death, strangely – sometimes you just can't plan this stuff. The workings of the universe just make it turn out like that.), my stepdad legally became my dad in the inner chamber of Judge Mike Salvagni at the Law and Justice Center in Bozeman, Montana.

I'm out of the house now, attending college in a far-off place, but I'm never going to forget April 17, 2002. That was the day I gained a second father, who gained a third son. And he's been "Dad" ever since.

CHAPTER THREE

At the Orphanage/ Life before Coming Home

"Where we're coming from is only
half as important as where we are going!"
~ unknown

The Baby Home in Tomsk
By Susie, April 2008
Florida

Every time we went to see Katie at the baby home, it was spotless, cheery, and always smelled good. You would think that if one hundred babies and little kids lived in a place together that it might smell bad, like urine or dirty diapers, but it didn't. There was always something good cooking, and the meals smelled great. The dining area for the kids was really cool, complete with little kid-sized tables and chairs. We wished we could stay and eat!

We got to spend two hours two times each day for the three days of our first trip in a playroom where other parents were playing with their kids, too. There were three other families visiting with their children, and it was nice to have a chance to speak with them. I think the playroom was strictly for this purpose. It was a very large and open room that could easily accommodate five or six families meeting their children. It reminded us of a dance studio or gymnastics room. There were mirrors on the wall at one end and the room was filled mainly with large toys: a ball pit, tubes to crawl through, and a wooden rocking horse. A bin of smaller toys was located to one side.

We did have an interpreter with us at all times during every visit on both trips. That was nice, as it allowed us to be able to ask questions and to say things to our new daughter. Katie was shy around strangers, including our interpreter. She didn't speak much at all and didn't want to be hugged or held by either one of us, so we did have a concern at first. We wondered if our daughter might have encountered abuse earlier in her young life. That concern was immediately eased, however, when we saw her playing with and cuddling a baby doll. She also interacted well with her caregivers and she liked playing with her friends from her group of about fifteen two-year-olds. She would make brief eye contact with us after the second day of the first visit. Our initial fears were unfounded.

The baby home was well run and the director was totally awesome; it was evident that she loved her kids immensely. The caregivers were also very caring. We saw them carry different children to an examination room or to a room for speech therapy, and they cuddled and hugged the kids often. All the horror stories about neglect in the baby homes didn't apply to this one.

No School until Age Nine
By Paul Z., age 16, April 2008
Home to Arizona 1999

When I lived in Bulgaria, I did not go to school because there was no school to go to. There was no money to build schools with. So I had to stay in the orphanage all day. In the morning, I would go to the orphanage cafeteria and eat breakfast. The cafeteria was small, with about ten windows looking out toward the highway out of town. There were five small tables that each could seat three to four people. The breakfasts were usually hot cereal and bread. For drink there was always water. There were not very many special breakfasts.

After breakfast I went outside and I watched cars drive by. The orphanage was located in the middle of a big town. The place where the orphanage was located was poor. The houses there looked like the paint was all chipping off and people had no money for beds so they had to make them. Our beds were made out of wood and they did not have any mattresses on them. It was a very poor country, so we didn't have much of anything. We had one blanket and one pillow to sleep with. The bedrooms were very small and there were four people in a bedroom. They used bars for windows.

After watching the cars go by, I ate lunch. For lunch we usually had boiled eggs. We were not allowed to get seconds, so I did not always get plenty of food. I did not have a favorite meal. There weren't choices.

There were not any fun activities, there was no entertainment, and there was no TV. There were no board games or videogames. After lunch I stayed in the orphanage and talked to people: the caretakers and some girls my age. After that, we had dinner. For the dinner meal we had one raw potato. Then after that we had to go right to bed. We were too young to stay up late.

Life in the orphanage was very tough. Now when I think about it, I am glad that I am out of there.

The Pink Backpack
By Janna, June 2008
California

The orphanage director was talking to our new daughter when we walked in to meet her for the first time. She looked at us, came over to us right away, hugged both of us, and went back to sit with the director. The director was telling her in Chinese that we were her mommy and daddy. She came over to us and hugged us again and went back to the chair where her pink backpack was. I can't tell you exactly what was in it. She was very protective of her things and that little bag was all she had.

She opened her backpack and pulled out a bag of marshmallows. I helped her open them, and she immediately shared them with Sean and me, which I thought was a very good sign. She also had a baggie in it, with gifts for us that the foster mom must have sent. Sean received a necklace, which he was allowed to wear. I received a bracelet, which I wore for a few minutes, and then she decided to pack it away again. *Maybe I have to earn it back?* I thought.

The first evening in our hotel room, Lili cleaned up her playthings and went to her backpack. Sean was watching her and said to me, "She's got tears in her eyes." I went over to her, helped her zip her bag, and picked her up and held her. She started wailing, calling out for "Mama Wang," her foster mom. She cried and cried and cried. I was so sad for her. She got down off my lap, put on her backpack and shoes and grabbed my hand. She led me to the door, wanting to leave. I told her no, we weren't leaving, and took her back to the couch. She screamed and cried, pushing me away. It was so hard to see her grieving so badly; her heart was broken. She wanted to go home. She didn't understand yet that she was going home with us. I took the backpack off and put it on the couch next to us. I just held her as she cried. Every now and then she'd start pushing and hitting, but she finally just gave out. She lay on my shoulder and cried herself to sleep.

As hard as it was to see her in so much pain, it isn't a bad thing. She needed to grieve the loss of all she'd known in order to be able to move forward with us. It's comforting to know she loves her foster mother so much. It means she's able to love us, also.

The Day I Met My Mom and Dad
By Zenna, age 8, 2008
Home to New York 2006

The day that my mom and dad were coming to meet me started out different from other days. There was someone who worked in the *dyetsky dom* who was in charge of really pretty dresses and shoes for special occasions. She came and brought me to her room and put a beautiful pink dress on me and some shoes that I loved. Then, I went into the office where I met my mom and dad. They had brought me a teddy bear that said, "*YAH tib-YAH loo-BLOO, Zenfira.*" I was very shy and didn't say anything but when my mom showed me that the bear had underwear with a hole for the tail, I laughed. Then, she made me a little bear with play dough. Valentina, the head of the *dyetsky dom*, thought that I was not acting like I usually acted – I was being too quiet, so she brought us all into another room where my friends came and we all played with the bear. I also showed my mom and dad that I could do a headstand. My mom and dad had brought stick-on earrings for me and my friends so we all stuck on the earrings and I even stuck some on my dad! That day was a very exciting day because it was International Women's Day so we were putting on a show in our theater. I sang a song with my friends Liana and Vika and then I was in a sweeping contest. After lunch, it was time for my mom and dad to leave. I did not know that they were going to adopt me. I just thought they were visiting because of the show, because there were other people visiting that day too. But I was glad that they left the bear because I took it everywhere with me from that day on. And when they came back to get me, I brought the bear to New York where it now sleeps on my bed.

My School in Russia
By Nastia, age 17, April 2007
Home to Florida April 2006

I was in five different schools when I was in Russia. I liked my high school there. It was good because the school was bigger than this one. It had four stories and there were a lot more people.

The teachers were really strict. You couldn't talk during the class hours. You couldn't even get up and throw away trash without asking the teacher. We didn't get to pick our classes either. They just made you a schedule for a whole year. We had ten classes for the whole year and we went to six different classes every day. Classes were only forty-five minutes long, but sometimes we went to double classes, which means we stayed in the same class two times in a row.

We didn't have lunch time; we just went home around two o'clock and then we had lunch. We didn't have cheerleaders or other things like that, but I really liked to go to Russian high school because I had a lot of friends there.

Visiting Our Daughter at the Orphanage
By Kathy, April 2007
In Kazakhstan before Almira came home to Louisiana

Today we went to the orphanage; this was day seven of visitation. I let Almira pick an activity I had for us to do. She chose the bracelet making kit, so I brought that and the video camera. Maria checked with the orphanage director and made sure that we could film inside the orphanage. He said we could; he is a wonderful and understanding man. I started off filming, and Almira wanted to see how the camera worked. She took off from there; she was running down halls going in all the rooms and talking to people. You can hear her on the video jabbering away in Russian.

We got to meet her family, Family #5. Almira showed us her bed; she sleeps in a room with ten other girls. Next door was a room with about ten beds for the boys. There are a lot of older boys in her group. She video-taped them today and said all of their names; she doesn't want to forget anything. We met her teacher, a very nice Kazakh man that seems to be in charge of her family. The social worker, Tatiana, was with us a lot today. She comes and goes and sits in on our visits. You can tell she wants Almira to be happy. She asked Almira today if she had any doubts about going home with us, and Almira said an emphatic, "No!" By the end of our orphanage tour we had an entourage of kids following us.

We saw the sewing room with the most incredible embroidery I've ever seen. The lady there gave me a beautiful embroidered handkerchief. We also went in the music room, where four of the girls performed for us. Next, we went to a computer lab and the chemistry classroom. We ran into Almira's geography teacher who told us that Almira does very well in geography. We also went and visited the youngest family there, Family #9, the seven- and eight-year-olds. Finally, we went back and finished making the bead bracelets we had started. As always, it was hard to leave.

Zyka
By Pat, MaMaw of Caitlyn, December 2008
Louisiana

It was a cold, gray November in St. Petersburg, but on the day before Thanksgiving, the sun came out as if smiling at us. This was "Gotcha Day," one of the dearest days in the life of an adoptive family. I was proud to be accompanying my daughter Christine as we went to Baby Home #1 to pick up little Caitlyn, eighteen months old.

The prior visits had been short, but oh so precious. My daughter and new granddaughter had bonded on that very first visit in September when they spent their moments hugging, rocking and laughing together. I watched in amazement as they became mommy and daughter. How could one become so attached in such a short amount of time? We left a stuffed bunny with Caitlyn that day.

We learned while we were back in the U.S. that the caretakers had let Caitlyn have her bunny, named Zyka, while we were away. They had even let her sleep with it. On this next visit, in November, I was sure Caitlyn wouldn't remember Christine or me – after all, she was just a baby! But she came into the room clutching Zyka ever so closely, and those big brown eyes looked around expectantly and latched onto her mommy's. We felt sure then that she was aware of the connection. And although Caitlyn was a bit shy, in minutes the two of them were mommy and child once again, hugging and laughing, my daughter playing her hair over the baby's face as she had previously done. Watching the giggling was priceless.

Memories of Guatemala
By Alejandro, age 8, November 2008
Home to New Hampshire 2005

I remember my home and my family in Guatemala and some of the things we did. I remember playing with my sister and brothers. I was the youngest except my baby sister. She was adopted, and then I was adopted a long time after her.

I remember our little house and the road. It was on a hill, and our cousins lived near us. A lot of people lived in little houses. Some didn't have a door on them and some were sort of like tents. Ours had a door on it, and once we got locked out. My family lifted me up into the window, and I landed on the bed and unlocked the door. My sister and I had one bed, my brothers had one bed, and my born mother and the baby had a bed. We didn't have other furniture, but we did have a little table and the beds. We didn't have sheets and pillows and pajamas.

I sold bread with my mother and my job was knocking on the doors. My sister and I went out in the day to get all the sticks for the fire to cook on. We had a fire on a little metal shelf and a pot to cook the beans and

rice. My born mother made rice and beans and *arroz con leche,* but sometimes we had no food. We picked mushrooms to eat.

I liked cats because I was of afraid of the mice in our house, and the cats
would chase them away. I remember the little river where we washed our
clothes and our plates and we played in the water. We went to the cemetery
sometimes on the holiday and had a picnic there.

Sometimes if my father came and he drank wine, my sister, my
brothers, and I would hide in the woods until he went to sleep. Sometimes
he was nice, and sometimes we were scared. Sometimes he lived with us
but not some other times.

I was only four when my born mother in Guatemala brought me to be
adopted. Sometimes I miss my born mother and my sister and brother that
are still at Guatemala and I cry. My mom hugs me and I tell her about my
family in Guatemala.

I remember what everything looked like and some things we did, but
I don't remember anything we said in Spanish. When my mom was trying
to adopt me she learned some Spanish because I only spoke Spanish. I
learned English really fast after I got adopted. Mom kept learning more
Spanish so I would have two languages. But I stopped speaking Spanish and
I wouldn't listen to it anymore because I was getting good at English and no
kids in my town spoke Spanish. I don't know Spanish anymore. My mom
takes lessons sometimes and she practices so we can speak Spanish together
if I decide to learn Spanish again when I want to.

To Love Him Is To Love Her
By Michelle, 2009
New Hampshire

Before adopting Alejandro, I didn't know I would have such intense
compassion and respect for his birth mother. It has been three and a half
complex and amazing years since our adoption and I am filled with gratitude
to her and to God for the privilege of becoming Alejandro's mother just after
his fifth birthday. At times, as with my biological daughter, I find parenting
to be a fulfilling but very challenging occupation. But loving them is always
easy! Alejandro is an optimistic, energetic, loving person full of enthusiasm
for life. It has been obvious all along that Alejandro was loved and treated
with affection by his birth mother in his baby and toddler years. He joined
our family knowing how to give and receive love. I am awed that Alejandro's

birth mother had the selfless courage to provide all she wanted for him through adoption. To love him is to love her.

At Night
By Rick and Donna, 2006
Pennsylvania

We had learned enough Russian to communicate with our newly adopted four-year-old daughter, Elise, who spoke fluent Russian. (She, by the way, was not interested in speaking Russian from the moment she was ours. She wanted to learn English.)

For the first several nights after we adopted her, Elise wanted to sleep wearing just her underwear. After we prayed, sang, and tucked her into bed, we didn't hear a sound from her until the next morning when we came to greet her. We were surprised (and impressed!) that everything was so still and silent that entire time, especially considering the fact that she was sharing her bedroom with her two-year-old brother whom we had adopted at the same time. We awoke in the mornings expecting to hear them talking, playing, or giggling, but rigid orphanage routines at bedtime had obviously been established for them, and they did not deviate from the rules. From what we could tell, bedtime meant

- No wearing pajamas. Sleep in underwear only.
- No moving from your bed from the moment you lie down until the moment someone comes for you in the morning.
- Be silent. If you are not tired, just lie there without making a sound.

We must admit that we actually liked this routine at first because it gave us all a chance to get a good night's sleep, which was very encouraging to us after returning from our exhausting adoption trip. However, after a few nights, it became evident that there was more to the bedtime routine:

- If you need to use the bathroom during the night, sit up in bed and "cry" until someone escorts you.

Ah. So much for the good night's sleep. Certainly we wanted Elise to just get up and go to the bathroom if she needed to, but we quickly learned that changing any part of her orphanage routine was not so easy. Even with our Russian phrases, our English words, our gestures, our expressions, and our role playing, we were unable to get it across to her that she could just go on her own. She continued to sit up in bed and "cry" until one of us would come and escort her to the bathroom.

There she sat on the toilet, night after night, with us smiling by her side and saying as many encouraging phrases of praise in Russian and English as we knew. She seemed to understand what we were saying, but we were convinced that she was too afraid to test it. We can only imagine what the consequences may have been for not following the rules in the orphanage. (She had alluded earlier to consequences of "no eat" and "more sleep.")

Finally, it happened. I heard a rustling in the kids' bathroom during the night. When I entered the hallway and could see the bathroom, there she sat on the toilet! As excited as I was for her to finally break through, I could tell she was nearly scared to death. She looked at me with huge eyes, and she had an intensely nervous expression on her little face. Before she could continue on any longer in fear, I dashed to her and hugged her little bare chest.

"*Mahl- ah- DYETS! Mahl- ah- DYETS!* (Good job!)

She melted into my arms in relief as she sat there on the toilet. She knew that she had understood what we had been trying to get across to her, she was relieved that everything was OK, and she was proud of herself.

Tears All Around
By Charlyn, 2008
Georgia

They say that some moments in time become burned into your memory because you are completely immersed in the emotions of that moment. The memory of picking up our two little boys from Baby Home #1 in Yaroslavl, Russia is such a moment. I remember the sounds of quiet in the room while we waited and the sudden cries of my older son, Pasha (now Nick), and the look of questioning and hesitant smile of my younger son, Andrey (now Drew), when they saw us.

And I remember the hurried steps of the caregiver and her obvious state of concern as she came running over to me. Although my Russian was limited and her English was even more so, I knew that she was concerned that she had almost missed us and that she had something to give us that she considered to be very precious. I couldn't imagine what it was. She kept pointing to the two envelopes and then to the boys and then to me, and through her tears, she had a big smile on her face. When I opened the envelope, I began crying, too. As the tears of joy streaked down my face, I opened two little envelopes that are now my most treasured possessions. Inside each little envelope was a christening necklace and a small card that recorded the date of my sons' christenings. At that moment, I knew in my heart what I had already begun to sense – that my sons had been well loved and cared for by these caregivers. I knew it even more when, as we made preparations to leave, in addition to my husband and me, the orphanage workers were all crying. Tears of sadness because my boys were leaving their orphanage home, mixed with tears of joy because our boys were going to their new home and we were going to be a family. Tears all around – for we all knew that Pasha and Andrey had been and would be loved.

A Birthday Party at the Orphanage
By Kathy, April 2007
In Kazakhstan before Almira came home to Louisiana

We have just returned from the orphanage and Almira's fourteenth birthday party, and I can honestly say it was not like any birthday I've ever been to. Almira was waiting outside for us when we arrived at the orphanage. There were also several other children there from her family (her group at the orphanage) to help us carry everything inside. We first went upstairs to where her family suite was, and the ladies there were getting everything ready for the birthday party. We had ice cream cakes, baklava, and an apple cake made at the orphanage. We also brought candy and fruit.

Right after arriving, we were taken downstairs to a small theater. Chairs were all set up for us, and the director (or leader) of Almira's family came and explained to Maria that the kids were going to put on a special show for us. They sang and danced, and then some of the children from Family #9 came in and did a little dance as well. They are the seven- and eight-year-olds. Almira's family director, who takes care of Family #5, did all the announcing. He talked about the family and how talented all the children were. One young man played the accordion with an older man; they were really good. The family director introduced us to several of the students after the performance and said many of them would be competing in a competition in Astana. They are athletes, singers, dancers, and artists. After the performance, I actually had to stand up and give a speech. This request was quite unexpected! Several of Almira's friends came and gave her homemade cards, and one friend gave her fresh flowers and kissed her cheek. The family director talked about how loved Almira was and that she was the shyest in the family of almost thirty.

After the performance, we went back upstairs to the family suite and all the children gathered in the foyer area. The kids' places were all set at the table with bowls full of rolls, baklava, fruit, and candy. Then the ice cream cakes were put on the table. The family director spoke some more and they presented Almira with a large picture of birch trees with a big bow on it.

The children sat at a long table in the hallway and the adults went into the kitchen with a table set for them. After the family director shut the door, he went to a small closet and pulled out a bottle of vodka. Little shot glasses were put all around the table. I know my eyes had to be as big as saucers. I tried to tell them I don't drink, but he poured me one anyway. They explained that you took a sip of vodka and then ate some of the sausage or cheese that was on the table. I'll admit I did swallow a little bit on that first toast; it singed my throat. I then switched to juice. No one drinks water here; that just kills me. My throat and mouth were so dry that I could hardly talk. We ate a little bit and mostly visited. After a few more rounds of vodka shots, hot tea with milk was served. We were there until after 6:00 and did very little visiting with Almira. The teachers and people at the orphanage made several comments today that they hope we will love Almira and take good care of her. I promised them we would and that we already loved her. I also promised that we would keep in touch with them and let them know how Almira is doing.

We did enjoy the visiting with the other folks from the orphanage and found out a lot about Almira and some of the other kids in her family. It was fun overall, but still nothing like any child's birthday I've ever been to. By the time we opened the door to leave that small kitchen, Almira was standing at the door waiting for us. She walked us out and we told her we would see her tomorrow. I couldn't tell if she was overwhelmed today with all the attention or if she was embarrassed, but she was really quiet. The festivities of the day and the comments made by all made it clear that they really do love her. However, when Maria reminded Almira that Boris was coming to pick her up tomorrow, she responded "Good!" I think she is so ready to be gone from the orphanage and into a family of her own.

Orphanages – No Match for Home and Family
By Teresa, February 2009
Snowflake, Arizona

Many orphanages do an admirable job of giving children as positive an environment as possible, despite many hurdles. We were told by our agency and adoption contacts in Russia that each orphanage is supplied with a building, heat and electricity, food, and meager staff salaries – nothing more. No clothing, no toys, no books, no crayons or drawing paper, and no medicines are routinely provided. Much of the money paid by adoptive parents in adoption fees goes directly to the orphanages to purchase these basic necessities. Only if there is money left over, can "extras," such as educational toys, warm clothing, and holiday treats be bought. Adoption fees fund the purchase of equipment and supplies to improve the lives of the children who stay behind.

Orphanages, out of necessity, maintain very structured environments with strict schedules. Knowing that affection and attention are important to every child's normal growth and his/her ability to have a healthy emotional life, many orphanage workers try very hard to offer children as much nurturing as possible. Nevertheless, it's next to impossible for caretakers to provide the kind of attention that children receive in a family environment. Many orphanage workers dedicate themselves to being surrogate family members, reaching out to offer more than what is expected of them. We have heard stories of orphanage workers who wanted to adopt children, but they could not afford to feed, clothe and provide medical care for a child.

In many cases, orphanage workers encourage children to call them by their names or call them "Aunt _____," saving the names "Mama" and "Papa" for the adoptive parents who come to take them to their forever homes. Many adoptive parents report that their new children greeted them as "Mama and Papa."

At our son's orphanage, the one hundred or so children who lived there were divided into family groups of twelve or thirteen children. Surely this grouping added more of a family feeling and allowed children to bond more easily with adult workers and other children. It seems common for children to have one special "Mama" to take care of them in particular, giving them love and attention and tucking them in at night, probably an arrangement made specifically to help children learn to bond and love as normally as possible. All the caretakers we met seemed genuinely interested in the children and their well-being. Orphanage directors in Russia, we were told, are all pediatricians. Our son received very good medical care, even seeing specialists when he was recovering from a serious illness as an infant.

As we left our son's apartment after visiting with him one day, the rest of the children of his group were in the potty room, each sitting on a little plastic "pot." We assumed that this was the daily routine: after mealtime everyone proceeds to the potty room. It was quite a sight: ten or eleven two-, three-, and four-year-olds chatting and laughing and smiling, "doing their time" on their little pots.

I know their routine included group story time and group music time each day. The arrangement of the furniture made it evident that there were also "circle" activities for smaller groups of five or six children. Teaching supplies (paper, crayons, paints, puzzles, etc.) were stored up high and we were told they were available only for "therapy," as they are quite expensive. The lawn (snow-covered when we were there in December), had some playground equipment and trees. The children played outside each day whether it was warm or cold.

We were impressed with our son's environment and were relieved to see that he had toys, plenty of food, and enough warm clothing. He got along well with his little friends and orphanage staff. He even had religious instruction. In short, life was pretty good for him overall during his first three years. It's evident that he was in a very good orphanage, and we are very appreciative. Nevertheless, it was no match for a home and family. As hard as it was for the staff at the baby home to say good-bye, they were elated to know that our son would now have the commitment, stability, and love of a family. We are indebted to them for giving our son a very good start.

C H A P T E R   F O U R

New Siblings and Families Speak about Adoption

"It is the sweet, simple things of life which are the real ones after all."
~ Laura Ingalls Wilder

Reactions of Siblings to Adoption
By Teresa, 1997
Snowflake, Arizona

When our adoption process dragged on and on (almost three years), our bio kids' attitude about adoption seemed to change from excitement to nonchalance. When we expressed interest in learning about a few boys that our agency said might be possible matches, our kids' responses were, "We want a sister," and "Whatever. I don't want to think about it anymore." Their waning interest was certainly understandable; two and a half years is an eternity to a child.

Then the director of our agency showed my husband and me a video of a little boy who seemed to us to be a good match for our family. We were watching the video when our daughters unexpectedly entered the room. They were instantly attracted to the little guy on the TV. "That boy is so cute and so sweet. Let's get *him* for our brother." When we questioned their immediate positive reactions (because of the not-so-happy comments we had heard from them earlier), they responded with, "Yeah, but he's so *sweet*. And besides, he would be so happy with us!" Well, it turned out that we did adopt the little boy on the video and he was sweet – and feisty! – and he *is* happy with us, just as we are happy with him.

A – D – O – P – T – I – O – N
By Tanya, June 2008
Alabama

A is for Always and forever. Oh yeah, and for adjustments.
D is for Devotion to children and family, lots of devotion to children.
O is for Overwhelming. It has been overwhelming at times, and now we experience overwhelming love.
P is for Patience. A big dose is good; an infinite quantity is better.
T is for Trust. It continues to grow.
I is for Incredible. Adoption is an incredible experience and a wonderful way to build a family.
O is for Opportunity. Adoption brings opportunities for growth, flexibility, learning, and love.
N is for Never. Never can I imagine life without adoption or life without our adopted children.

The Two Sergeis
By Colin, age 8, December 2008
Arizona

My name is Colin. I have two Russian cousins. Wow! They are both named Sergei. Well, one is named Paul, but his Russian name is Sergei.

I have a lot of fun with them. Sometimes we go to movies, or goof around, or jump on my trampoline. We love to mess around on the trampoline. Sometimes Paul launches me, which means that when I start bouncing, he jumps on the trampoline too. When we both land on the trampoline at the same time, I get a double bounce and go up really high. Sometimes Sergei, Paul, and I wrestle, either on the trampoline or on the floor. But what we really like to do is play *Halo*, *Fusion Frenzy*, or *Star Wars Battlefront*. When we play Spies, I always want to be on teams, but Sergei always wants it to be a free-for-all. I hate doing free-for-alls! Now, back to business. I am eight, Paul is thirteen, and Sergei is eleven. I like to play a lot of stuff with them, my cousins, the two Sergeis. That's my story.

Colin typing his story about his two Russian cousins while Paul looks on

McKay's Story of his Siblings' Adoption
By McKay, age 9, September 2008
Snowflake, Arizona

My name is McKay and I am nine years old. I am the youngest in my family. I live in Snowflake, Arizona and I have ten brothers and sisters. I have a brother and a sister, Abe and Katie, who were adopted from Kazakhstan three years ago.

I'm glad that I have Abe and Katie for a brother and sister. I was six years old when they came to live with us. I remember my mom was video-taping Abe the first time he saw our chickens. He kept on saying some words from Kazakhstan and I couldn't understand him. It was pretty funny. All Katie wanted to do was to swing on our swings.

I liked having them as my brother and sister. Now it feels like they weren't even adopted. It feels like they were born from my mom because they have been here for so long and I can barely remember them not being here.

At first we had three boys in our bedroom. Abe slept in a single bed, and Levi (my brother who was eleven) and I slept on the bunk beds. Now Levi moved into the room with the big boys and Abe and I sleep in the bunk beds, and we got rid of the other bed. Abe and I play with light sabers and wrestle a lot, and we like to kickbox with each other.

My mom asked me what it would be like to not have Abe here, and I said I wouldn't have a brother that is my age to play with. Sometimes we fight, but I am still glad that Abe is my brother.

Katie is a fun sister. She does headstands with me, and flips, and I ride with her on the bus. She talks with me and I like that.

We have a fun and happy family and I am glad to be a part of our family. I feel like Katie and Abe have made our family better. I love Katie and Abe and everybody else.

A Little Brother
By Kristen, age 14, 1998
Arizona

The biggest event in my life this year was the addition of a little brother to my family. Getting new siblings happens all of the time, but the way my brother came to our family was different. The adoption process took three years altogether. Since he was three when he came to our family that means that we started within three months of the day he was born, and we didn't even know about him until last July. But it gets even better than that; he came from Russia speaking fluent Russian and not a word of English!

It has been a huge challenge adjusting to him and having him adjust to us. It all started in December 1997 when my parents got off the plane from Russia carrying him. He seemed like such a sweet, innocent little boy, but we soon found out the truth. After about one day of being an angel, he settled into his regular routine. I didn't think that a child coming from a Russian orphanage would be spoiled, but he proved me wrong! He was so used to getting his way that when he didn't, he would SCREAM! It also complicated matters that we couldn't explain what we were doing because of the language barrier.

One of the greatest moments with my brother was when he first came home. Ever since leaving the orphanage, he had used his coat as a security blanket; he wouldn't take it off. But as soon as he walked into our house, which he recognized from pictures, he immediately took off his coat.

Now, even though my brother has only been with us for three months, he has adjusted really well and already speaks fluent English. I think that he is the best thing that ever happened to my family. We laugh more now than we ever have before and we are enjoying *almost* every minute of having him around!

Grandkids – Grand Kids!
By Debbie, February 2009
Taylor, Arizona

Every grandparent experiences the excitement of waiting to see his or her grandchild for the first time. Will he look like our family? What color will her hair and eyes be? I have had the opportunity to experience grand-parenthood eight times. My husband and I were given the gift of two beautiful granddaughters through adoption. The anticipation of seeing them for the first time was like receiving a surprise package and unwrapping it, not knowing what beautiful gift is hidden inside. We waited nine months for five of our grandchildren and the anticipation was equally exciting. All of the questions I had about them were the same as for our two adoptive children.

Our first granddaughter was in Kansas when our daughter and son-in-law went to pick her up. They came home after four days, and I went to my daughter's home to meet Jessica for the first time. I was so excited to see our new granddaughter and to finally see a child in my daughter's arms. She – and we – had waited so long. I walked inside and my daughter came down the hall toward me from her bedroom. Right behind her was the most perfect, brown-eyed, black-haired baby girl. She crawled down the hall and then pulled up on her mother's legs and peeked out to say hello. This sweet ten-month-old had rosebud lips, little full cheeks, and flashing eyes. She was the first of our grandbabies to have dark hair and brown eyes like me. As the months passed, it was amazing to see how much like our family she was in many ways.

As Jessica grew, she helped to complete out family. Her cousin Alexis was her best friend. They were two peas in a pod. They were born only a few months apart and loved to play with one another, sharing giggles and lots of smiles. All of our friends called them "Salt and Pepper," one being blond and the other having dark black hair. They are still close now, fifteen years later.

Three years later, we were blessed with another beautiful girl who came to us from the Marshall Islands. Again, our daughter and son-in-law went on a journey of a lifetime. We kept Jessica, then four years old, and anxiously awaited the new baby to be added to our family. Seven days later we had a grand homecoming. Our whole family met at the airport, looking like the teddy bear brigade, each of us waiting anxiously to give her that special gift that would welcome her home. We watched as people disembarked one by one, and finally we saw them: our daughter and son-in-law, and in their arms, a petite, fifteen-month-old baby girl. She had hardly any hair, but what she did have was dark brown just like mine, and she had the biggest brown eyes I have ever seen. Clinging to her new mother, she also held in her arms a little plastic container of Fruit Loops, which she guarded with her life. I can't even begin to imagine what this tiny little girl was thinking. You leave your tropical island home in a jet plane and fly through the clouds and stars with two people whom you have just met. Then when you get to your new home, there is a crowd of strangers speaking in a strange language. She did not understand anything we said to her, and though we did not speak the same language, love conquers all, and we each waited our turn to hug and hold her and let he know how long we had waited for her. I do remember that when each of us held her she lowered her head and cuddled into us as if to say, "Please don't hurt me." She had a gentle spirit and it reflected in her actions. My daughter and son-in-law named this sweet girl after me; we share the same first name. I was very honored then, and as she grows, I am even more proud that we share our name.

Like Jessica, Debbie had a cousin who was born only a few months before she was. His name was Derek, and from the beginning, these two understood each other perfectly. They loved to play and giggle, and they spent many hours outside chasing sun rays and rainbows. Debbie could soothe Derek with her gentle spirit and tiny tender hands. She would stroke his forehead and instantly calm him when no one else could. One particular day, Derek had not had a good morning and seemed to be mad at the whole family. He had thrown himself on the floor and would not look at anyone. Debbie-Tai came in and just started patting the top of his head gently. He stopped crying and looked up and they instantly smiled. Our family all believes that these two must have been little angels in heaven together hopping happily from cloud to cloud before coming to us. Maybe they were waiting to see each other again when they came to our family.

Each of our grandchildren is a unique piece of our family puzzle and without any one of them our family picture would not be complete. I am so thankful for them all and know that from the moment they were all born, they were meant to be in our family. I am proud of all of my grandchildren and want them to know what gifts they have all been in my life. Thanks, kids!

Calm, Cool, and Caring in the Phoenix Heat
By Melissa, February 2009
Arizona

When my brother Sergei had been home a while, he asked our parents a couple of times, "Aren't you going to help any other little kids like you helped me?" I was amazed that a seven-year-old thought of other kids around the world who needed a home just like he once did. So later, when we hosted Galya from Ukraine through a summer program, it was wonderful to see Sergei's response to her.

One day I had to drive the kids to a doctor's appointment. It was 100+ degrees outside and the car was hot, probably over 125° F (52° C). I watched my little brother get in the car, and then use a towel to buckle Galya's seatbelt. He told her not to grab the seatbelt because it was hot, and then he carefully tucked the towel between the buckle and Galya so it would not burn her. I was so impressed by his care and concern for her. I was then and still am so proud of him!

A "Flake-y" Family
By Noah, age 15, January 2008
Snowflake, Arizona

I am the sixth child of Shon and Pam Flake. I have a total of ten brothers and sisters, two of whom were, in fact, adopted. Their names are Ekaterina Dee and Abraham Vitaliy. I remember several years ago when Katie

(Ekaterina) came to stay with us for a couple of weeks. She was Katya then and she was very shy and scared. She didn't know very much English, so we all tried our best to learn some Russian so we would be able to communicate a little. The conversation I remember the most with Katya took place near the time when she came home to live with us. We were joking around calling all the girls *boys*, and the boys *girls* in Russian. The first memory of Abe was of him getting off the plane at the Phoenix airport. He was so tired. He had had a thirty-hour trip, and he, Dad, and Katie were just dead tired.

When I tell people that I have ten siblings, most have a feeling of awe. Then I tell them that two were adopted, and they usually think that my family must have a hard time getting along and that there must be much fighting and anger. I must be honest, there is some yelling and anger, but that would be the same in any family no matter how many kids there are.

Nowadays, when I think of Katie and Abe, I hardly remember their Kazakhstani names. To be totally honest, I am not even sure that I spelled their Kazakhstani names right. They fit in with our "Flake-y" family so well that sometimes I forget that they were even adopted. They bring a feeling of completeness into our family. Adoption is a wonderful thing, and I know that it was right for my family. Some of the experiences with Abe and Katie have made me realize that it is not for everyone, but I am happy and privileged that I can call them my brother and sister.

Kayla and Zenny: Two Little Pearls
By Sherry, November 2008
The sisters were reunited in Florida April 2008

From the day we adopted Zenna, she always wanted to be reunited with her older sister, Kayla, who was still in Russia. We started the paperwork, but the process was taking a long time. Fingerprints, clearances — everything seemed to be moving in slow motion.

We went on our first visit in the fall and envisioned having Kayla home by Zenna's birthday in the beginning of December, then by Chanukah. But we heard nothing and were getting very discouraged.

Then, for winter break, we went to Disney World with my family. One night, we were waiting to eat dinner at the Japanese restaurant in World Showcase in Epcot. To pass the time, we went walking through the department store there. They have a water tank from which you can pick an oyster and claim the pearl. We decided that would be an interesting souvenir, and each of the granddaughters picked one. We also picked a few for friends at home. In all, I guess we got about a dozen. As each one was opened, we "oohed and aahed." They were truly lovely. But when Zenny's oyster was opened, it contained twin pearls.

"Very rare," the seller stated.

I don't know about that, but I do know that Zenny's was the only oyster that night that contained more than one pearl. We felt that it was a sign that the girls would be brought together again. In fact before too long, Zenny and Kayla were together, wearing matching pearl necklaces.

Family Experiences and Family Additions
By Paul Z., age 13, 2004
Home from Bulgaria to Arizona 1999

I have lived with my forever family for six years. The first year I went to school, I learned how to spell words and every spelling test we had I got almost all of the words correct. I visited the Phoenix Zoo when we had a field trip. When I was growing up, my favorite toys were wagons. Funny books like *Amelia Bedelia* were always my favorites. After I had been with my family a few years, we adopted four other kids. Their names are Ashley, Stephanie, Craig, and Angel. They used to live in Oregon, but now they have lived with us here in Arizona for four years.

We have had some fun activities as a family. We have visited Yellowstone National Park and Meteor Crater. We went camping and have gone to family reunions. We went to Idaho and visited our brother Doug. Sometimes we go out to eat, go bowling, and go to movies. I have participated in wrestling and track, and my family traveled to my tournaments. We have a good time together as a family.

My favorite foods are fajitas and Chinese food. Christmas is my favorite holiday, and the story of the "Work and the Glory" is my favorite story. My favorite hobbies are to play basketball and to hang out with my friends. Now I like MP3 players.

I participate in church activities and in scouting. I have a lot of friends at my church. We complete service projects and have activities (for example, going to Clear Creek, being in an Easter Pageant, going on a fifty-mile hike, and doing the Klondike, a snow campout). When I got to high school, I started playing in the band. We competed at State and got a rating of Excellent. As you can see, I stay busy.

My life has been both good and bad. I have had some sad experiences, but most of the time my life has been happy.

Galya's Adoption: Mom's Point of View
By Leslie, 2008
New York

My husband Tom and I dated for quite a few years before we got married. Although we were very compatible and very much in love, we weren't quite sure our age difference could stand the test of time. He was a nineteen and I was thirty-one when we met, and when we married, he was thirty and I was forty-two. I had a fourteen-year-old daughter from a previous marriage who Tom and I were now raising together. I had decided, for numerous reasons, not the least of which was the possibility of birth defects in women over the age of forty, not to have any more children. However, as time went on, for Tom, the lack of his own child became an increasingly heavy sorrow.

Tom was a news photographer for our local TV station. Being one of the most talented at the station, and possessing an adventurous spirit, he was often sent overseas to cover stories. Over a period of time, he shot footage in orphanages in Tanzania, Italy, Honduras, and finally, Ukraine. Upon arriving home from this last trip, he shocked me with the news that in the orphanage he had met his young "soul mate," in the form of a ten-year-old girl named Masha, and that he wanted to adopt her.

We had never discussed adoption before. Tom was a risk taker (sometimes to the point of doing what I considered foolish things). I, having led a very sheltered childhood, was completely the opposite. Yet, when I had watched stories of foreign adoptions on TV, shows such as *60 Minutes, 20/20,* and *Oprah,* I thought, *How wonderful those people are!* Since adoption was something I had always wanted to do, I agreed to go ahead with the process. Taking the plunge was certainly an act of faith. One "friend" warned me about all the horror stories she had heard about adopted children. (The stories scared me, but luckily for our future daughter, not enough to keep me from undertaking the adoption!)

In not too long a time, we learned that Masha could not be adopted. Her mother would not relinquish rights to her even though the she had been taken away from her family. This is a sad twist of the adoption laws in Ukraine, and it pains us even today to think about what happened to Masha.

In Ukraine, even when a child is removed from the home and the family can no longer have custody, the parents still have some rights and can determine if their child will be placed for adoption.

We slowly made our peace with the idea of losing Masha and began to move on to the idea of adopting another child. We signed up for a program in which a child from Russia would stay with us for the month of July and then go back to the orphanage while we completed paperwork to adopt her. The big day of her arrival was July 2, 2002. Only one parent was allowed through airport security to meet the child. Unfortunately, Tom went. Galya appeared to be terrified. Probably his beard and mustache, plus the fact that she had been around so few men, scared her. She came through the gate holding Tom's hand looking absolutely stiff with fear. Silent tears streamed down her face, and her body was frozen even when I lifted her to hug and try to comfort her. The translator couldn't get a word out of her. At a reception for the children, she wouldn't eat anything except a little bit of melon, which she threw up in the car. I must confess that I thought, *Here we go. We've got a kid that will never bond with us.*

She was as sweet looking as her photo, inappropriately dressed on that oppressively hot day in long jeans and a "Summer Miracles" t-shirt (the name of the program that sponsored the children's visit to the U.S.). Of course, none of the children owned their own clothes. Clothing in the orphanages was always communal as we later learned when I sent her back with a fleece jacket and then saw it worn by another child who appeared in a video someone shot.

We arrived home, changed her into some summer clothes, and gave her a balloon. She thought that was the most amazing thing she had ever seen and called it a *"sol-a-key."* Russian-speaking people we asked thought that word meant something like a cylinder. Apparently, Galya didn't know the word for balloon, so we figured that even her Russian vocabulary was not too good. She batted the balloon around the house and backyard for hours, jabbering in Russian and giggling. Unlike most children, adopted or otherwise, there were no tears but only laughter when the balloon became irretrievably stuck in a tree. Well, my initial fears were certainly assuaged within a matter of a few short hours. Galya fit comfortably into our family dynamic that very first afternoon. In fact, when we look at the video of her arrival at the airport, through the drama of her tears, she seems to have one eye on us, checking to see what our reaction is to her discomfort. Certainly today we know her to be quite the little actress and comedienne.

As a coming home gift, we had a little dance outfit for her and a CD of Mickey Mouse music. She spent hours dancing to "Meeekey Mouse" on our back deck, and by the end of a week, knew the words to every song. She was fearless in a swimming pool, though the people from the orphanage swore that there was no way she could have ever gone swimming before as there was no opportunity to do so in the orphanage and most likely the same with her biological family. (In fact, Galya describes her original family life as incredibly empty and neglectful. Once, upon seeing a mother pushing a baby in a stroller, she commented to me that she never had one. I asked her how her mother took her outside and she said, "She didn't.") In short, she embraced every aspect of her new life.

Though I'm by no means a religious person, I do think there is always a reason for every event in our lives. I can't explain or justify why we lost Masha and I sincerely hope her life turned out well. But I do think that all of us in this household, my husband, my older daughter and myself, do feel that Galya is our "soul mate" and was destined for this family. Sometimes I feel as if I am the one who suffers from amnesia and I just can't remember the first six and a half years of her life. If one can imagine the slight sense of revulsion one feels toward say, the bodily functions of a child who isn't one's own, I never felt that, even from day one with Galya. It is so easy to forget that she isn't of my own flesh and blood. My only thoughts on the subject are that I would have given anything to have seen what she looked like as a baby. And I just cannot imagine how in the world anyone could have neglected such an extraordinary and unique child.

Lilya and Sergei, Two Very Different Blessings
By Elizabeth, age 18, February 2009
Arizona

One of my most fortunate experiences in life has been to have two adopted siblings. Both have been a blessing to our household, yet the processes couldn't have differed more.

Sergei has been a member of our family now for five years. At the age of seven, Sergei came from Pskov, Russia to be a Smith. Because of his three-week stay the previous summer, Sergei's adjustment to our family was very easy. He wanted with all his heart to be a Smith and we were ready to dive in and teach him. All of us were overflowing with love for our new family member. However, because I was the youngest prior to Sergei's arrival, the adjustment was a little difficult for me. Suddenly becoming a big sister to a seven-year-old at the age of thirteen is somewhat of a shock, to say the least. Sergei seemed to only enjoy pestering me and whacking me when he could get away with it. It seemed that while he was just dying to marry my older sister, I remained tantamount to dirt. More than that, I had to share the role of being the "funny kid." That was uncalled for in my book! However, we began to find ways to play with each other, and while there was certainly some sibling rivalry, I began to thoroughly enjoy playing with him. I grew used to the idea of being the big sister, and of course, now I can't imagine what life would be like without him.

Lilya was very different. She has now been a member of our family for a little over three months. I believe that I have a very special and perhaps the strongest bond with my little sister because I got the opportunity to travel to Ukraine and bring her home. It is so much easier for me to understand why Lilya can be a stinker because I have seen where she comes from. I regret that I never had that understanding with Sergei. Unlike Sergei, Lilya was not so sure she wanted to be a Smith. She didn't have the three-week visit that he'd had, but rather had spent some time in Italy with a family that decided adoption was not for them. She repeatedly told us that she wanted to be in Italy and that she'd go back as soon as she could. She told us that she would not be learning English, and I suppose she expected us to simply deal with that. However, after three months, Lilya hardly speaks of her Italian family anymore and when she does, she mentions them merely as a matter of conversation, not competition. It should also be noted that she hardly uses her Russian anymore; she only speaks to us in English. So much for her goal, huh? She is still learning the rules of being a Smith, and I love to watch how Sergei handles that. As far as I'm concerned, he's a marvelous big brother. Though I must say for someone who enjoys pestering, he doesn't deal well with being bothered himself.

Both my brother and sister have been incredible blessings to our family. I cannot wait to see how they continue to bond with each other. Through both processes I see mainly immense differences, but also I see the similarities. Both have brought such joy, humor, blessing, and ultimately, completion to our family. The two have inspired me to adopt a child of my own someday, and for that I am so grateful.

Love Comes in Many Colors
By Anna, mom of nine, September 2008
Snowflake, Arizona

After having two children, we were not able to have any more. Both my husband and I wanted more children. The first thing we thought of was adoption. We got our paperwork finished. It was about that time when a news story came out about two young men who were adopted that had killed their adoptive parents. No way did we want to adopt anymore!

A year later we were still yearning for more children. It then occurred to us that our reason not to adopt was not a good one. We realized that not all adopted children have problems. Every person in prison is not adopted! We have seven adopted children and two biological children. Our family theme is "Love comes in many colors." We have eight nationalities in our family. This has been such a blessing in our family and in our community. We are all different on the outside, but on the inside we are all the same.

Love comes in many colors

Adoption across Race Lines
By Christy, mom of 12, 2007
Oregon

I know there are many doubters when it comes to adopting across race lines; believe me, I heard from them when we started down the path. But instead, I listened to my internal voice, the voice that said that it was the right thing to do, the voice that guides me and pushes me to live a life of doing things that are important. I wasn't entirely sure that adopting an African-American baby was right. I wasn't without doubts at the time. But then I asked myself these questions: "If not me, then who? Some white foster home? And besides, who's to say who it's OK to love? Should our ability to love be determined by the color of our skin?"

Before we adopted, we realized that children are considered hard to place simply because they don't match our skin color or have the misfortune of being older than five. Yes, of course it's true that I can't teach my African-American daughter what it is like to be the strong black woman I want her to be. The question is could a white foster family do a better job? At least I can teach her how to be a strong woman and how to love people as people, regardless of race. I can also attempt to provide her with strong black role models in teachers, doctors, and mentors to support her in the ways I can't. She is black, she is beautiful, and I want her to feel, believe, and live that.

Would she be better off in a black home? Possibly. However, that is not the reality of the choice for most black kids who need families through adoption. Does she deserve less because she's black? No way! And what about me? Do I deserve less? Do I deserve not to be able to enjoy her gregarious spirit, her deep loud laugh, her immense creativity, and her unconditional generosity, just because I was born a different color?

To all those doubters on mixed-race adoption, what I want to know is this: what are *you* doing to change the system? It's not for you to judge me and put conditions on me because of the color of my skin or hers. Does she wish for a black mother? Maybe. Will she have issues to overcome as an adult because she was raised in a multi-racial family? Possibly. But what's the bigger issue? Being raised by a family of whatever color, or never having a permanent family at all?

Three-fourteenths and Counting
By Grandma Jean, March 2009
Arizona

Paul Sergei, our first Russian grandson, came here when he was just a little guy — so cute and very quiet at first. He was three years and eight months old.

Three weeks after he had been home with his family, I called to see how things were going. One of his sisters, who was about nine years old at the time, answered the phone. I asked her how much Russian she had learned. Her response was, "We don't need Russian anymore because Paul is already learning lots of English words." After having had such a good beginning with his new family, he has gone on to become an avid reader with an *amazing* vocabulary.

He has also become a very competitive *Scrabble* player (great word game!), and loves to "bingo," which means playing all seven letters at one time – and getting fifty extra points for it. If you don't believe me, just challenge him to a match!

I now have three beautiful grandchildren through international adoptions, and each is a wonderful addition to my "brood" of fourteen grandkids.

CHAPTER FIVE

First Meetings and Early Days Together

"Those who bring sunshine to the lives of others
cannot keep it from themselves."
~ James Barrie

Orphanage, Day One
By Teresa, December 1997
St. Petersburg, Russia

Dear girls,

Today your new little brother was "born" into our family. There is only one way to say it: he is precious! He didn't seem at all afraid of us…just a bit timid, as we had expected he might be. He was willing to walk over near us, and we just smiled and waited. I said in Russian, "I'm your mama," and he understood me. We gave him your gift to unwrap today, and it was an enormous hit. We played on the floor with the little red car for a long time – many big smiles as it wound up and zoomed around. It didn't take long at all for Sergei to catch on to how to make it work.

Seriozha (Seriozha is the nickname that they call Sergei here.) sat on my knee and looked at the Russian picture/word book, sometimes with me saying a word and him repeating, and other times with him answering when I asked in Russian, "What's this?" Then he sat with Dad for a long time (playing with the little puppy that Rachel sent) and with the car. They got along famously, making universally recognizable "boy noises"! Sergei looked at the pictures of both of you girls with interest. We think he has an under-standing of who we all are – as much as possible for a three-year-old who has never lived in a house with a family. The water therapist, Ina, told me (in Russian, of course), "We love Sergei very much." When I thanked her, she said, "Thank *you* very much." We hugged each other and both cried: inter-national tears of joy! Love, Mom

Soccer
By Sergei, age 11, July 2008
Arizona

The first time I came to visit my new family, I was in summer camp. That was in Chandler, Arizona, in the summer, five years ago. I got a new soccer ball when I first met my family. I thought it looked like fun to play soccer. I learned how to kick the ball, and my dad taught me not to touch the ball with my hands. I remember that my shorts were too big, and I had to hold them up when I ran and kicked. It was a good thing because then I didn't touch the ball with my hands.

Even though it was over one hundred degrees outside, I still kept on playing soccer. I kept saying to my dad, "Let's go play more soccer!" He was willing to play with me, and it was fantastic. We played in the back yard even when it was extremely hot. My dad wanted to go inside, but I still kept wanting to play. We were sweaty and so hot that we felt like we were going to die. Finally we went inside and sat down to rest. We drank cold water from the fridge with plenty of ice.

After summer camp was over, about three weeks, I went to the bus that would take me to the airport. It was time to go on the flight back to Russia. I didn't want to let go of my sister's hand because I didn't want to leave my family. It was pouring rain, and everybody had a lot of tears, too. The whole family was crying, and so was I. One of the women who worked with the adoption agency had to pull me away from my sister Kristi because I didn't want to leave my whole family. I cried for a little while on the bus, but I was okay for the plane trip. When I got back to the orphanage, the adoption workers asked all of us kids, "Do you want to live with your families?" and everybody screamed, "Yes!"

My mom and dad came to pick me up in Russia, about four months later, right after Christmas. When I saw them, I was quiet but I felt excited to get to my new house. Inside I felt shocked because I didn't know they were going to be there. I was overjoyed to leave with them. I was not sad to leave the orphanage because I knew I now had a family that could take care of me very well. I still play soccer with my dad whenever I can.

Pajamas – a Pretty Big Deal
By Teresa, 2000
Snowflake, Arizona

I am so thankful that I had learned enough Russian before we traveled in order to be able to talk with our son a bit and also to understand some of the precious comments he made in our first weeks together.

The second night we spent with Paul, I gave him a bath at Roald's apartment in Moscow. He played delightedly with a plastic container, pouring water repeatedly over his head and face while giggling and squealing. He "swam" back and forth in the warm water, reveling in the freedom of the water and the big tub.

After wrapping him up in a towel, carrying him to the bedroom, and setting him down on the bed, I pulled out from the suitcase some "footie" pajamas that we had brought for him. I held them up and said in Russian,

"These are for you." He covered his mouth with both hands, gasped, and his eyes got big and round. As he took his hands away from his face, he said in an excited, hushed voice, "They're *blue*!"

I can only imagine what thoughts were roaming around in his head. We'll probably never really know for sure what those blue pajamas represented to him.

Baby Needs New Shoes!
By Charlyn and Greg, September 2008
Georgia

Everything that my husband and I had read about international adoptees had prepared us for meeting a "very small-for-his-age" little boy. However, we noticed on our first trip to meet our oldest son that he seemed big for his age. So when we were trying to buy clothes that we would bring him home in, I really had no idea what sizes to buy. I guessed as best as I could and tried to find things that would stretch or adjust (smaller or larger) as much as possible. Shoes were a whole different story. I had no idea. I decided to use his age (seventeen months at the time) as a gauge and took several pairs of shoes that were supposedly "about" what a seventeen-month-old would wear. Well, you guessed it. After finalizing the last of the paperwork that was required at the orphanage, we were ready to change him into his new clothes so that we could leave. (The orphanages usually keep the children's orphanage clothes.) Luckily, his outfit fit well. Then, we tried on the first pair of shoes – way too small; then the next pair of shoes, still too small; then another pair – still too small. Oh, no! What were we going to do? About this time, the orphanage director realized what had happened, smiled and left the room. She came back in with a pair of brand new "Scooby Doo" tennis shoes (which I'm sure had been donated by a prior adoptive parent) that fit perfectly. For the next two to three weeks, those Scooby Doo shoes were the only pair that he could wear. He loved them and so did we…and while he has long since outgrown them, we still have those shoes!

Roald's Kitchen
By Teresa, 1998
Snowflake, Arizona

When we arrived in Moscow from St. Petersburg after traveling all night, we were greeted at the train by the older gentleman who would be our host in Moscow. We had the good fortune of being the guests of Roald, a stocky, bearded, seventy-something, retired Math professor. His university salary had been meager and his retirement pension was abysmal; who knows how he made contact with our adoption agency and agreed to become a host for adoptive families in order to supplement his income, but we're glad he did.

Roald's home provided a comfortable "nesting place" for us for the five days we were in Moscow waiting for our paperwork to be finalized. His apartment occupied part of the fourteenth floor of a huge and fairly bleak Soviet-era apartment building. Though the stairwell and elevator were unadorned cement and metal, the apartment had a warm atmosphere with wooden floors and modest but comfortable furnishings. The entry hall had doors leading to the living room, the only bedroom (Roald slept on the living room couch for the duration of our visit), a "split" bathroom (the sink and shower in one small cubicle and the toilet in its own tiny water closet), and the kitchen. The windows of the compact apartment's living room afforded us a view of people skating and ice-fishing on the frozen Neva River far below.

Roald's kitchen was particularly memorable. Small and cozy, it was furnished with a padded and pillowed bench-type sofa against the wall farthest from the stove and sink, a kitchen table directly in front of the bench couch, a few straight-backed wooden chairs on the opposite side of the table, and a television on a stand near the door, which was between the refrigerator and the stove and opposite the window. The counters were cluttered with the domestic odds and ends that were the heart and hearth of Roald's apartment: a tea kettle, pots and pans, utensils, storage bins, dishes, packages of a variety of foods and drinks, a bread plate, and vegetables. We spent hours in the kitchen each day, eating, drinking tea and coffee, chatting with Roald, staying warm, watching news and cartoons, and getting to know our new son.

Roger, Paul Sergei, and I were assigned seating on the bench couch, though as often as not, Paul Sergei ended up on Roald's lap to watch TV when the meal was over. "*DYEH-doosh-ka*" Roald willingly answered Paul Sergei's incessant questions and patiently explained why tomatoes are red and why the snow packed by the side of the road is dirty. Natasha, Roald's friend and neighbor, prepared hearty meals for us, eager to demonstrate for me how to mix cream cheese with jam for breakfast and how to cook borsch for the mid-day meal. We managed to converse at length on a variety of topics, using an odd mesh of Russian, English, a bilingual dictionary, drawings, and gestures. Paul Sergei was soon dubbed *"pah-chee-MOOCH-ka"* by Roald, which means "little child who asks 'Why?' all the time."

Because the temperature in Moscow hovered around -25° F (-32° C) that week, a thick layer of ice remained on the kitchen windowsill for the duration of our stay. Roger and I had never seen two inches of ice on the *inside* of a windowsill before! The steaming tea kettle and the boiling pot of borsch supplied warmth and coziness to the compact room. Roald and Natasha gave our son the gift of providing a caring and supportive "bridge" he could cross to travel between the orphanage that had been his home for over three years and his forever home with us in Arizona. Roald's kitchen was an ideal spot in which our precious *"pah-chee-MOOCH-ka"* could transition safely from the orphanage to his new parents.

A Sister's Patience Pays Off
By Jewel, September 2008
Snowflake, Arizona

When my parents told us they were planning on adopting two children from Kazakhstan, I couldn't believe it at first. Most people might think that we – with nine children already in the family – had plenty. We had always felt, though, that our family wasn't quite complete, and I trusted that my parents knew what they were doing.

We had involved ourselves in a program where the children would have an opportunity to come and stay with us for three weeks and then go back to Kazakhstan, where they would stay in the orphanage and wait for parents to finish the paperwork. When Katya (now Katie) first came to stay with us, the first thought I had was that I had never seen such a sad little girl.

We didn't know this at the time, but Katya had been raised an only child by her mother, and had only been in the orphanage for three months when we met her. She was very sweet, but very quiet (mostly due to jet lag and the fact that she spoke no English, and although we had an English-Russian dictionary, we were far from able to carry on a conversation). The first few days she was with us, I didn't see her smile once. I really enjoyed spending time with her, but I wanted to hear her laugh, or at least see her smile.

One day when I didn't have to work, my mom thought it would be fun for me to take Katya down to my grandparent's barn and show her the horses they kept there, assuming that she hadn't had opportunities to see large animals before. I was impressed by how brave she was. Although it's normal for most children to be afraid of such large animals, she was willing to pet them and she enjoyed picking weeds to feed them. At that point, I began to see her softening and even showing some signs of contentment.

Later, when I showed her the trampoline and helped her to jump on it, I finally saw her smile. After helping her swing on the swings, I got what I had been waiting three days for – she began to laugh out loud! I was thrilled to see her finally showing her true personality – it really was a fun bonding experience for us, and one that I shall never forget.

On Russian TV
By Wendy, August 2008
Snowflake, Arizona

My husband and I had the privilege during the adoption of our second daughter to be followed around the city for a day being filmed by a TV news crew. They wanted to interview a couple who was adopting a Russian child. First we went to the orphanage to get our daughter. It was a good two-hour drive on a horribly bumpy road to get to the orphanage in the town of Artium. During the drive, the TV journalist assigned to us asked us questions regarding how we chose our daughter while the cameraman filmed us.

We explained the story of how we had adopted our first daughter from Vladivostok when she was a year old. When she was three, she insisted that we go back to Russia and get her "white hair sister, the one with blue eyes." We had told her over the course of a few months that she didn't have a sister in Russia, but our daughter didn't give up. She would tell us, "But she doesn't have any shoes! She doesn't have food! We have to go get her!" To make a long story short, after an extensive search, we found the "white-haired, blue-eyed angel" who needed to be in our home.

This was our second trip for this adoption, and we were due to adopt our daughter at the end of the week. The day the crew followed us we were getting our daughter's visa picture taken. Then we went to some government offices to get more paper work completed, and then back to the orphanage. They filmed us with her at the orphanage – playing with her there in the little guest playroom – in the room set aside for visiting prospective parents.

Afterwards, my husband and I followed the camera crew and journalist back to the TV station for the official interview. We were interviewed for about twenty minutes and were asked some very interesting questions: Why would you want to adopt Russian children when you already have children? What do you like about Russia? Will you be proud to have a Russian child? Will you teach your child about Russia? They asked what we did for a living which allowed us the money to be able to adopt. They asked how our other children felt about us adopting, as well as how our family and friends would accept this Russian child. Some questions I can't remember because they were so odd. What they really wanted to know was why we would want these children that Russians didn't want. The economy was so poor at the time and children were being abandoned in large numbers in their area.

My husband and I felt very blessed to have been chosen to be the people to be interviewed for this news special. We really felt God must have had a hand in choosing us to do this little bit of ambassadorship on behalf of the United States and adoption advocacy. In our hotel at the time, we had run into a couple who had mentioned how they couldn't wait to get out of Russia. They hated everything about it. They felt like the people were rude, the food was horrible, and the water was undrinkable. My husband and I looked at each other and said, "What country are they in?" We loved Russia! The people were so kind, the food was interesting and amazing. The architecture was gorgeous.

Of course, we couldn't wait to tell the news people all that we loved about their country. We also told them how well our other Russian daughter was doing in the U.S. and that she was very proud to be a Russian American. We let them know that our daughter's heritage is very important to us and we would surely do all we could to help our daughters see and learn the good about their culture and people. We explained what a privilege it was to be able to come into their country to adopt these beautiful children. We also gave them some information about my not being able to have children, why our family was so large, and what kind of lifestyle we lived.

While we were still at the studio, they showed us what they were going to air that evening: the whole story. The story included footage of other orphanages around the city and hundreds upon hundreds of children. They gave us a video of the interview, in Russian of course, and explained that our copy of the video would not have footage of children.(They were not allowed to let footage of their children leave their country.) They said that along with our interview, they wanted their people to see the thousands of orphans in dire conditions. (During our adoption process, we were only ever allowed to see the child we were adopting. At no time did they allow us to see inside the orphanage proper.) That evening, they aired the interview and story/footage of our day to their city of over a million people.

Afterwards, we had people stop us on the street telling us that they saw us on TV and thanking us for caring for these children. When we went to the airport that weekend to fly home with our new daughter, two Russian women, vendors, ran up to us. They had little toys and thrust them at us, saying in Russian, "We saw you; you are the ones we saw on TV. This is the little Russian girl you adopted! Please take these toys for your two little Russian girls!" My husband and I felt like celebrities.

Adopting my two Russian daughters was an amazing experience. I have no doubt that divine providence led me to my daughters and helped to arrange the details so that these specific children could be in my home. I will be forever thankful to the birth mothers of my daughters for giving them life.

Good morning!
By Teresa, January 2008
Snowflake, Arizona

How can you tell if it's the middle of the night or morning when you wake up in the winter in Russia? You can't! And if you're three years old and your internal clock is confused because you have just traveled halfway around the world, it's impossible to tell what time it is when you wake up in the dark.

Deep into the early morning hours on our fourth day home, I heard a little voice in the dark: "*DOH-brai OO-tra.*" (Good morning.) It was Seriozha testing the waters, so to speak, to see if someone else was awake. I quietly slipped out of bed so I wouldn't disturb Roger and whispered, "*DOH-brai OO-tra*" to Sergei as I picked him up from his bed on the other side of our room and gave him a hug. I tiptoed out of the bedroom and down the stairs with Sergei, moving carefully and quietly so we wouldn't wake the girls. The kitchen clock read 4:30. I snuggled with Sergei for a few minutes in front of the remaining coals in the woodstove. We spent precious time together for the next two hours, playing before the rest of the family woke up.

The next morning, the same routine: again the "*DOH-brai OO-tra*" sounded at 4:30 a.m. Again, we quietly crept down the stairs and played.

The following morning, again, the same greeting sounded in the dark. I was getting worn out, and I realized that I was contributing to a schedule that we couldn't continue; 4:30 was just too early! From our double bed across the room, I whispered back to Seriozha, "*NEE OO-tra. spa-COIN-ah NOH-chee. DAH ZAHF-tra*," (It's not morning. Good night. See you tomorrow.) I lay there listening for a few minutes to see what would happen next. A tiny shuffling noise came from his bed as he settled back under the covers. Soon I could hear his breathing change. Just like that, he had accepted the fact that it was still night, still time to sleep, and he had dozed off again, seemingly very much at peace with the fact that my husband and I were right there in the room with him and would be there in the morning too. "We'll be here every morning, kiddo, forever. Sleep tight."

Paul Patrol
By Paul, age 14, July 2008
Snowflake, Arizona

When I first came home from Russia, I was three and a half years old and I wasn't very tall, not even tall enough to see onto the kitchen counter. I had a fascination for foreign objects and things I'd never seen. My family had to keep a really close eye on me so I wouldn't get in trouble or danger. My dad, mom, and sisters had to take turns watching me every minute. They called it "Paul Patrol." I would take whatever my little hands could find, sweeping along the kitchen counters to grab those objects that had been purposefully stored out of my sight. One day on an exploratory mission, I managed to run into my mom and dad's bathroom and lock the door before anyone could catch up with me. My mom was freaked out because she thought I might get hold of a razor or chemicals. She talked to me through the door to keep me out of mischief until my dad could get upstairs and unlock the door.

Now I wonder why these things happened. Probably I was on overload because of all the new experiences I was having. There were too many new things all coming at me at once. I certainly had more freedom then than I'd had in the orphanage.

Special Shoes for a Special Boy

Special Shoes

By Claire, age 14, January 1999
Snowflake, Arizona

Imagine walking into a room filled with children. A little blond boy with big blue-green eyes sees you. "Mama," he says. He runs to you as fast as he can.

He has seen pictures of you and knows you are his family. You tell the interpreter that you love the little boy. It is translated into Russian, and the little boy smiles. *"YAH tib-YAH loo-BLOO,"* he says, "I love you," in Russian.

When you leave the orphanage with the boy to head back home, you offer to leave his shoes. "No, keep them. Special shoes for a special boy," the matronly caretaker replies. It breaks your heart as you see the three-year-old cutie hug his best friend Misha and say, "Bye-bye." However, you know he will have a better life and more opportunities in the U.S.

Leaving the orphanage with the little boy is quite an experience. He is intrigued by turning on lights. He has never been outside at night before. He flushes the toilet every chance he gets, amazed. Imagine such a change in your life.

One year later the little boy is no different from any other American boy. People never ask, "Is he adopted?" The little boy is excited because he is going to play T-ball next summer. He has new shoes that are bigger and more American. He has almost forgotten his boots, and past, in Russia.

A Tantrum is a Tantrum is a Tantrum
By Janna, 2008
California

I've learned that a temper tantrum from a five-year-old pretty much looks the same no matter where you're from. Now that we're home, Lili is becoming very comfortable – which is a good thing. With that comes testing and seeing what Mom's going to let her get away with. Any time I tell her "No" about something (which I try not to do a lot at this point, but sometimes it's unavoidable), she starts that long, drawn out, whiny cry and runs up to her room, shuts the door, lies down on the floor and rolls around kicking and hitting until she ends up under the bed. It's a sight to behold, let me tell you! I usually let her spend a few minutes getting it out of her system and then I go get her and sit with her until she calms down. That hasn't been happening very quickly, though, I think partly due to our communication barrier right now. In between fits, she has pretty much stuck to me. I understand her need for that, but it is draining. By bedtime we are both physically and emotionally exhausted.

People ask how we're doing; I always say we're doing well, and I believe we are, but I also want to be real about our days and not paint a picture that's inaccurate. It's hard. Lili cries – often. She's not easily consolable. She's five and wants her way all the time. Real life is setting in. The newness is wearing off for the other three kids, and Lili is testing boundaries. It's a hard place to be right now. Sometimes she makes her defiance very clear, but other times, I think she's as frustrated as we are. I know it just takes time. I know we aren't the only family to be going through this. I knew to expect this transitional period for our family, but none of the logic makes the tough days easier.

Several adoptive moms have said that when you adopt an older child, you can't base your days on the chronological age of your child. It can be compared in some ways to having a newborn. I'm told to expect this phase to last four to six months. I've tried to remember those days from when my older kids were newborns. Nothing got done: laundry piled up, dishes stayed in the sink for days, stuff was scattered everywhere. With each of my older kids, my mom came and stayed for two weeks after I'd had a baby. She took care of just about everything, and all I had to do was take care of myself and the new baby. I can't imagine not having had her there to help. Once

Sean's mom even took our laundry to her house and worked on it for me. This time, bringing home a child that was almost five, I didn't expect to be back in that place. And yet, here I am.

Katie and Abe's Adoption
By Levi, age 14, November 2008
Snowflake, Arizona

Both Katie and Abe were accepted into the Flake Family. We had already met Katie when she visited for a summer program, and now she could speak a little bit of English. We were all anxious to meet Abe. He wasn't able to speak a word of English when they first came home.

As I said, I had seen Katie before, but that was just after her mother had died, and she had been in sorrow then. A few days after she had arrived the second time – after being adopted – she was brightening up to our family and remembering our names. Katie was beginning to enjoy having a family again, and she was learning more English. She seemed to know how much we had to go through to adopt her.

When Abe came home, it felt like my love had grown an extension because we had worked hard so that our family could keep on growing. I'll never forget the first time I saw Abe. He was half asleep, and he looked happy to be on the ground again. Then he saw Mom, and the familiarity brightened on his small skinny little features. He ran forward, and Mom went up and gave him a loving hug.

I attached to Abe right away when he first got here. I had a wooden sword that my brother Shiloh had made for me. Abe was staring at it the first time he saw it, so I let him play with it. There was a problem, though, because he didn't know how to use the locks on the bathroom doors. He locked himself in there and couldn't get out, so he hit the door with the wooden sword to get somebody's attention. He got Mom's. She was glad he was all right; we all were. We all laughed at the holes he put in the door with the sword! Of course we taught Abe and Katie how to use the locks so they wouldn't get locked in the bathroom again.

Meeting Abe
By Jayze, age 18, November 2008
Snowflake, Arizona

The morning after our family picked up Katie and Abe was a slow one. We had had to drive the three hours home after staying up late waiting in the airport the night before, and we weren't able to get to sleep as early as we usually did. For some reason, however, I didn't feel the urge to stay in bed longer than usual; I got up earlier than anyone else and was wandering around the house in those early hours of the day when my new little brother, Abe, came running out, eyes wide open, looking at everything with awe. I'd been hearing about this boy for weeks, and as a family, we'd been working to adopt him for a couple of years. That morning, I got to spend an hour or two showing him our chickens, the playhouse, the dishes, and anything else he was curious about. He talked the whole time, pointing and I'm sure asking tons of questions, but I didn't understand a word of it. All I knew in Russian was how to count to ten and how to say, "Brush your teeth," so I didn't know what he was saying, but I had an awesome time meeting my new little brother, Abe.

Seeing Christmas through New Eyes
By Debbie, July 2008
Chandler, Arizona

It was hard to send Sergei off to wait for us in Russia. He had been at summer camp with us for three weeks. My husband could hardly stand the wait and worked nonstop on the paperwork that needed to be done. It was hard to wait, but I had peace that this was the way it was to be. I had been waiting thirty years; a few more months would not be so bad. So for the next four months we prayed and sent our son letters with pictures of us and of things we wanted him to see. We tried to paint for him a picture of what it would be like to be a part of the family.

One morning in December, my cell phone rang and it was the program director saying she had just received word they had a court date for us on December 29th. We asked our daughters if they could postpone Christmas until our return. They were willing to wait because we would be coming home with the best Christmas present ever: their new brother!

We flew to London where we had an overnight layover. Christmas day in London things were shut down to bare bones operations and after an all-night flight and waiting for a train to help us get to a hotel to sleep, tears filled my eyes. I was so tired and I asked God, "Why did we have to travel on this special day of the year?" God answered in his still small voice and with a mighty picture inside my head. I heard him say, "I gave you my son many years ago and this year I give you your son." Then as the tears flowed I saw a young woman, a man, and a donkey trying to find a place for her to have her baby, and suddenly the wait for the train didn't seem so long and I didn't feel quite so tired.

We made it to the hotel and we made all the connections to the city where we were to see our son. I can't express the joy I felt or the joy on our little guy's face when, after four and a half months, our eyes met again. The next day we went to court and the adoption was official. Praise God! He planted the desire in my heart and then he gave this perfect gift to fill that need.

Later that evening in our hotel room, our son was sitting on his daddy's lap and said, "You are my papa, that is my mama, and I am your son." Those words will be remembered forever. Our God who for thirty years prepared me for this day placed them in our son's heart. It has been three years now and things are going so well; we are a family. I still talk with God daily and pray for my children, but now I have a face for all four of the children that I am a mommy to and thank the Lord daily for the children that grew inside my womb and for the one that grew in my heart for all those many years. And yes, we are tired, but we are filled with the joy and love that come from God's presence in our lives.

Sergei and his mom

Katie's First Horse Ride
By Molly, age 12, June 2008
Snowflake, Arizona

On the first day that Katie and Abe came home to Snowflake from Kazakhstan, we went to my grandma and grandpa's house, where they have horses. We saddled up the oldest and gentlest horse, Chester. My friend Lexi was there with us and she rode Chester with Katie and me. Yes, there were three of us on one horse. This was Katie's first horse ride, and Lexi didn't have much experience, so I was the only one there that knew how to ride a horse. Well, Katie figured that if you kick the horse, it will slow down, but really it makes the horse go faster. Katie was sitting there, kicking poor Chester until he was running at full speed. Katie and Lexi were screaming their heads off! Katie was screaming in Russian and Lexi was screaming in English.

"Katie!" I yelled, "Pull!" (That's how you stop a horse.)

So Katie pulled as hard as she could. Chester jerked to a stop. For the rest of that ride, Katie yanked Chester back whenever he started walking too fast, and when she finally wanted to get off, she pulled on the reins so hard that Chester started backing up. Luckily, Chester never reared up, so none of us got hurt, and Katie was proud of herself for riding a horse.

Humorous Moments Relieve Tension
By Elizabeth, age 18, January 2009
Chandler, Arizona

I have really appreciated the humor and frequent laughter in our home since the arrival from Ukraine of our new seven-year-old sister. Both offset the tension of having a new sibling integrating into our family. Lilya has only been here three weeks, but her English abilities are rapidly growing. Today I had the privilege of experiencing two great new English moments!

Expressing Opinions
Though we don't usually watch TV while eating, I had missed the season finale of *America's Next Top Model* and I was allowed to watch it over dinner. As the winner was announced, her pictures from the season flashed across the screen. My mom and I took the liberty of sharing our opinions.

My mom stated that she didn't like a certain picture. Quick to defend my opinion, I told her, "I actually really *like* this picture!" You can bet Lilya was not going to let her opinion go unnoted. In a proud display of her new vocabulary, Lilya boldly shouted, "I *like* spaghetti!" Laughter ensued.

Karma

My brother, Sergei, was adopted five years ago, and as the former youngest, he is not accustomed to being pestered. However, Lilya is a big fan of bothering Sergei; I can't help but laugh. On the way to McDonald's, Lily decided to put her arm around Sergei's shoulder just to bug him. After a couple of minutes of continuous shouts of "Stop it!" my older sister turned around and told Sergei, "You know what? You deserve every bit of this. You did this all the time when you came home!" I could hardly contain my laughter when my brother responded, "What do you mean?" My only answer to him was, "Karma, Sergei. It's karma." Without hesitation, Lilya resumed her pestering, whacked Sergei's shoe, and yelled, "Kama, Sergei!" Needless to say, the car was filled with laughter (except from Sergei, of course).

A Christmas Stocking Story
By Teresa, May 2009
Snowflake, Arizona

When we found out that our travel date to bring our three-year-old son home from Russia would likely be in December, I determined it was best to prepare for Christmas early that year. It was actually quite a good way to put my "nesting" energy to work and keep the pre-travel "what-ifs" from being at the forefront of my mind.

Fast-forward to December 24, 1997. We had been home with our new son for exactly one week. Thank heavens I had done the Christmas shopping and gift wrapping ahead of time; it never would have gotten done in those frenzied, exhausting, and somewhat difficult first days at home! But I had overlooked one detail: I had not made a Christmas stocking for Seriozha.

He probably would have been ecstatic with any stocking, but I wanted him to have one like his sisters' hand-made stockings, from the same holiday-patterned material and in the same design I had used for each of the girls years before. That afternoon, I dug through my sewing bin to find the fabric and pattern. I cut out the pieces, pinned them together, and began stitching. As I worked, I realized that Seriozha had poked his head around the corner and was peeking into the laundry room, where I had set up the sewing machine on the counter.

He came closer and stared at the stocking taking shape on the sewing machine. I put my arm around him and we had a little conversation in Russian. My phrases might have been a bit choppy, but the communication was as crystal clear as an icicle.

"What's that?" he asked.

"A Christmas sock," I responded. (Luckily, I knew the word for *sock* in Russian.) "It's for you."

"For me? Why?" he asked, this time with a quizzical look.

"Grandfather Frost. Tonight," I told him. "Tomorrow morning. Apple. Orange. Candy. From *DYEH-doosh-kah mah-rohss* for you. Here," I attempted to explain, pointing into the stocking.

"*DYEH-doosh-kah mah-rohss* is coming tonight? Here?" He knew and understood Grandfather Frost very well. He had received a chocolate version of the Russian "Santa Claus" as a going away gift from Valentina, the orphanage director. But he was still confused. He raised his eyebrows and his eyes got big. "Here?"

"Yes. Tonight. Grandfather Frost. Candy. Orange. Apple. For you," I explained as best I could with the Russian I knew. "Tomorrow morning, by the tree, this sock, for you."

Seriozha ran off to tell his sisters about the Christmas *sock*. Shortly afterwards, about halfway through dinner, he got down from his chair, headed up the stairs, turned and announced, "It's bedtime." Tomorrow morning couldn't come soon enough.

C H A P T E R   S I X

Travel, Culture, and New Worlds

"Great love and great achievement involve great risk."
~ Tenzin Gyatso,
the Dalai Lama

My Plane Trip from Kazakhstan
By Abe, age 9, March 2007
Home to Snowflake, Arizona 2005

The plane trip was scary because I looked out the window and saw so many city lights. I knew I was joining a new family and I didn't know what it would be like. It was fun, too, because I had a backpack full of food, books, and a submarine game. When the plane landed, it felt like my brain was dropping down!

I liked my room at my new house. There were toys. My brothers' toy guns were my favorite. The floor was neat because there was a carpet on it. I liked my bed too. Everything was a new experience for a while. Then I got used to my new home.

Ants and New Treats
By Debbie, age 12, and her mom, November 2008
Home to Taylor, Arizona 1998

One of my favorite memories is from when my mom and dad came to pick me up when I was adopted. That was in 1998, when I was only one year old. We were getting ready to fly out from the Marshall Islands. My parents were hoping to fly home one day earlier than they planned at first because they wanted to get me home and they wanted to get back to my big sister. So there we were, in the airport on stand-by, anxiously waiting to see if we could get on the plane. I was over by some benches playing with ants. I was trying to grab them. My mom said I was daintily picking them up between my pointer and my thumb. When she saw that I was going to eat them, she swept them away.

I was very tiny for my age. The doctor gave me a physical and I was healthy, but my mom says I was very small – just skin and bones. I guess I was eager to try all kinds of foods. I wanted everything. My mom says that I ate rice and cheese and that I gobbled up every kind of food they had at the hotel. All of it was good and I wanted to eat it all; it was a new experience for me. When we traveled on the plane, they gave me a plastic tub full of Fruit Loops. I was willing to share the Fruit Loops, but I didn't want anyone to take away that plastic tub!

A Post Card Home

Dear girls,   December 10, 1997

The Winter Palace is beautiful. St. Petersburg is an incredible city. It's lighter than we thought it would be this time of year (from 9:30 a.m. to 4:30 p.m.). When we arrived at the orphanage today, the kids in Sergei's group were all bundled up in wool coats, mittens, and hats, with scarves wrapped around their necks, and they all wore felt boots – out playing in the snow. They looked like a little flock of sparrows all puffed up to stay warm. Sergei spotted us, lit up, and came running in our direction. We fed all the "sparrows" M&M's, which, of course, were popular. We can't wait to give you a hug and introduce you to your brother.

Love, Mom and Dad

Zenna the Brave

By Sherry, November 2008
Florida

When we adopted Zenna, she had never been in a hotel before. We brought her to our hotel in the region after court and because there was some paperwork problem, we were stuck in the hotel for hours. All of a sudden at about 8:30 p.m., the problem was solved and we got into a van with another family for the trip to Moscow. Zenna quickly curled up on my lap and went to sleep. When we got to Moscow, it was about 1:00 a.m. Zenna's dad carried her out of the van, into the very fancy hotel, and, after checking us in, up to our room. Zenna opened a sleepy little eye, looked around, and went back to sleep. Later on, the hotel brought us a cot, and we moved her to the cot. The next morning (actually later that morning), the doctor arrived to check Zenna out prior to our visit to the U.S. Embassy. She was so tired that we couldn't wake her up, so the doctor just started doing whatever parts of the examination he could with her still asleep. He was a **big**, TALL guy, and Zenna was a teeny little six-year-old girl. When he started to measure the circumference of her head, Zenna opened her eyes and looked up. Remember: this doctor was a total stranger, my husband and I were virtual strangers, the hotel was certainly different from anywhere she'd been before, and she was not even in the bed she went to sleep in the night before. Did she scream? Yell? Cry? No – Zenna the Brave just looked up at this doctor and advised him that, "I have a small head." This is the essence of Zenna: she is courageous, resourceful, and smart.

Russia

By Mora, age 9, December 1997
Arizona

Russia is the largest country in the world. It is 17,075,400 square kilometers. It is very cold there. Only reindeer and arctic foxes are able to survive the cold. Most of Russia is in the arctic, and it is also in Asia and Eastern Europe.

Russia used to be ruled by czars until 1917. A czar is like an emperor. He controls everything. From 1917 to 1991 Russia was ruled by the Communists. In 1991 the republics demanded freedom.

Moscow is the capital of Russia. Moscow has really tall buildings and huge churches with colorful onion comes. It has fourteen million people.

Another interesting city there is called St. Petersburg. It is called St. Petersburg because in 1703 Czar Peter the Great decided to make a European city on the Neva River, and he named it after St. Peter. Then he changed the capital of Russia from Moscow to St. Petersburg, and he made all of the royalty move and build their palaces there. When the Communists came along, they changed the capital back to Moscow.

Russians eat lots of good food. They eat things like soup, bread, cabbage, cucumbers, potatoes, sausage, and lots of dairy products. Their main meal of the day isn't at night like ours. It is at about 1:00 or 2:00 in the afternoon. At night they have tea or coffee and bread with cheese and sausage.

Russians are very good painters. They paint eggs, pictures, and matryoshka dolls. Matryoshka dolls are wooden dolls that open up and inside of each one is another.

Russia is a very interesting country. Some day I

Russian Church with Onion Domes

want to go there because my brother is from St. Petersburg. We will go exploring the beautiful buildings and cities together!

A Comparison
By Alec, age 11, January 2008
Home to Virginia 2006

Russia is different from the U.S.A. in several ways. A lot of Russia is cold because much of it is by the North Pole. One day the temperature was -30° F (-34° C). It gets even colder, but that's the coldest weather I felt. People in Russia eat soup in the winter to stay warm. They grow and eat lots of vegetables. That's one way people have enough food, and it's also one reason they are healthy. Another difference between Russia and the U.S.A. is language. The alphabet that Russians use is different from the alphabet in English. It can be pretty confusing to read in English after learning to read in Russian. The last difference I'll write about is the onion domes. Those are roofs that you can see on churches in Russia. They are called onion domes because they are shaped kind of like onions. There are even some that are painted with gold, and that makes them really beautiful. The U.S.A. and Russia are different, but each country has some good features.

Fall Travel
By Teresa, December 2000
Snowflake, Arizona

It was three years ago this week that we took our trip to Russia to bring home our son. We were impressed with how beautiful Russia was in the "fall" – snow, icicles, and temperatures of -20° F (-29° C). Our train ride from St. Petersburg reminded me of *The Polar Express* by Chris Van Allsburg: snow, ice, frost, steam, half-light, and half-dark. What a vivid memory I have of looking out the train window as we slowed several times throughout the night to pass by icy train stations in small rural towns. The "smoke steam" rose from the train and from the log buildings and curled around dim, yellow-lighted lamp posts and icicles hanging from the eaves of wooden station houses. The train clattered and clanked over the rails through moon-white meadows and black-treed forests. It was surreal. Here we were in a train compartment, nestled with our three-year-old son of two days, wide awake with emotion, staring out into the Russian landscape, wondering what the future would hold. After four hours, our son finally slept.

Russia, Where I Was Born
By Paul, age 12, 2007
Snowflake, Arizona

Russia is a very special place to me. Russia is where I was born. I was adopted at the age of three. I want to tell you about some of my home country's history and information, starting with the mighty and great czars of Russia.

The Russian culture has a very rich history, some of the figures being great and some more evil. Let's start with the very first Russian czar. First you need to know what a czar is. A czar was a king- or queen-like figure that ruled Russia in the beginning of Russian history. The first czar was crowned in 1547, Ivan the Fourth. Ivan would go on to become know as Ivan the Terrible. He was a very suspicious man who at times would even act insane. With his neurotic way of behavior, he hired a police force and began terrorizing his people. Among some of his terrible deeds are the following: he arrested several aristocrats and had them put to death; in a fit of anger he killed his own son; he burned many towns and cities; and he heavily taxed the Russian peasants.

On a lighter note, Czar Peter the Great, an heir to Ivan the Terrible, was much better. He helped the Russian military and brought western influence into Russia. In short, Peter the Great brought Russia out of the Dark Ages. Even in this time of great advancements, Peter still kept the peasants heavily taxed.

Catherine the Great, a czarina, was also a very good influence to the Russian people. She encouraged the arts and suggested school for those who could afford it. Even though she did many great deeds, she put even more taxes on the Russian peasants. In the year of 1917, the peasants decided that they were tired of being repressed. This led to what is now called the Bolshevik Revolution. To keep it simple, the peasants thought that if they could rid themselves of czars, they could end their oppression. The peasants stormed the palace and held the last czar, Czar Nicholas, and his family captive. They then killed the whole family. Little did they know that this would plunge them into a 73-year-long reign of communism. During this period of time, America had an interesting time with the Russian government.

In the year 1957 Russia and the U.S. began a race to see and explore outer space. The space race commenced in October 1957 when Sputnik 1 was launched. On July 21, 1969, American Neil Armstrong became the first man ever to set foot on the moon. The space race ended in approximately 1975 with Apollo and Soyuz joining together and the passengers conducting joint experiments. Although the space race era was exciting, it is nothing compared to the "nail biting" Cuban Missile Crisis era.

In the year 1962, about fifteen years after the end of World War II, Cuba was allowing the Russians to keep missiles in Cuba. The U.S. didn't want Russia to keep missiles in their "backyard." The U.S. then blockaded Cuba and didn't allow any missiles in. Russia, not wanting war, pulled out. Now that you have a background on Russian history, it's time to tell you about Russia the country.

Russia is the largest country in the world. Even with the land being so big, agriculture is scarce due to the harsh climate and poor soil. Russia has the most diverse climate in the world. The temperatures can range from 100° F (38° C) to 90° F below zero (-68° C). Since it can get so cold, half of Russia has permafrost beneath the surface. Russia is so large that thirteen cities have over a million inhabitants. Moscow, the capital, had ten million, three hundred forty-two thousand people as of 2005. So you're thinking, "What on earth do the people do for a living in such a large country?"

Some important Russian industries are farming, mining, and fishing. As I mentioned earlier, Russian agriculture does not do well, due to poor soil, lack of rain, and short growing seasons. Even with all these hindrances, Russian farmers still manage to grow barley, flax, fruits, oats, potatoes, rye, sugar beets, sunflowers, vegetables, and wheat. Russia is also rich in minerals. They have deposits of coal, petroleum, and natural gases. Among some of their more lucrative deposits are platinum, iridium, and nickel. Fishing is also one of the major industries, one reason being that the Russians love caviar, salted sturgeon eggs. Fishing crews fish inland and in the Atlantic and Pacific Oceans.

With all of the good food that is produced, Russians have a very hearty and rich diet. Not surprisingly, Russians must store a lot of fat for winter. With almost any Russian meal you'll find some sort of meat, whether it's in soup or sausage form. In Russia, it's also common to find soup on the dinner table. One of Russia's most favorite soups is *schi* (pronounced 'shee'). Schi has been served as a main course for over a thousand years. The main ingredients of schi include cabbage, meat, carrots, and dill (which is usually sprinkled on top). Pelmeni, another common Russian dish, is minced meat wrapped in thin pasta-like dough with onions and garlic for spice. The pelmeni are cooked like raviolis (boiled in water) and eaten. One Russian dish that does not include meat is blini. Blini are much like French crepes, thin pancakes. They are often served when there are religious rites or festivals. They are topped with butter and sour cream or caviar, but never both at the same time.

There's more to Russia than just Russians. There are many more ethnic groups. The population is diverse. Although eighty-three percent are native Russian, there is still seventeen percent left, which includes Tatars, Ukrainians, Chechens, Germans, Kazaks, and Jews. Most members of each ethnic group practice a religion.

Religion is an important part of Russian culture. Most Russians are Christian. Russia has over five thousand Russian Orthodox Churches. Islam is the second largest religion, with eight hundred parishes and mosques. Russia also contains almost ten monasteries to support its Buddhist populations. Ten percent of all Russian Jews live in Moscow.

Sports play an important role in Russia. The Russian government promotes sports heavily. Russians, like other people in the world, enjoy sports. The favorite sports of Russians are gymnastics, soccer, and ice-skating. The Russian gymnastic and ice-skating Olympic teams are always very good, due to hard training. Although the Russians may have good Olympic teams, soccer is arguably Russia's favorite sport. Russia also has many sports camps for children and adults alike.

We now know that Russians have gone through many hardships. They have had an interesting time with America. We also know the size of Russia, the industry of Russia, the foods that they eat, the diverse ethnic groups, and what sports they like. Where are the animals? The Siberian tiger originally inhabited forests of eastern Asia and northern China and many other places. They also live in Russia's Far East. Siberian tigers eat about twenty pounds of meat every day. When the Siberian tiger knows that it won't eat for a period of time, it can eat up to a hundred pounds of meat to sustain it over a long time. Siberian tigers prey on various deer, wild boars, fish, and if they have to, they can eat porcupines. Some neat facts about the Siberian tiger are that a Siberian tiger's roar can be heard from up to a mile away and it is the only tiger known to withstand the extreme cold.

Russia is a huge country that has many different foods, cultures, and industries. Russia also has an intriguing history. Now that you know about Russia in general, you can visit Russia and nothing will be a surprise to you. I hope to visit Russia someday myself. I think that I'll go bug my parents for a plane ticket to Russia.

Party Preparations and Missing Home
By Kathy, April 19, 2007
Before bringing Almira home to Louisiana

This was our tenth day of visiting and even Almira was counting down the days. Almira walked us to the door again today and seemed sad that we were leaving her. We did leave a few minutes early because we are going to buy supplies for her birthday party tomorrow with her family group at the orphanage. The caretakers are making Almira a cake and will serve tea. We bought four ice cream cakes and lots of fruit for the kids. There are now twenty-six kids in her family at the orphanage. We wanted to be sure to have enough for everyone.

Today has been a hard day. The time away from Sarah and everything familiar has really caught up with me. We were told again today that we may not get a court date before the holidays (May 1st and any additional days that the Kazakh government chooses to take). This was a crushing blow to say the least. I'm not sure I can emotionally take it if we have to stay an additional week and a half. Everyone here is nice, and we just live for our visits with Almira, but I've never been away from Sarah, our other daughter, this long, and my heart hurts because I miss her so much.

City versus Small Town
By Nastia, age 17, November 2007
Home to Florida April 2007

It was really weird when I had just moved to be with my new family because I thought the name of our town and the other small towns nearby were just names of the streets. But when I found out they were towns, it was strange. I was used to a large city. I thought my new town was really small and there was nothing here to do, but now I'm kind of used to it and I don't really care because everybody says the same thing: "There's nothing here to do." But you still can always find something to do if you try. My town is small, but that's the way it is. I guess I will have to get used to it.

Elizabeth's Initial Reactions
By Carole, September 2007
Missouri

Don and I officially became parents again on December 9, 2002, when we adopted three-year-old Elizabeth Nicole, born August 14, 1999 in Yaroslavl, Russia. She had lived in the orphanage since leaving the hospital at one month old.

Airline Challenges
Everything went quite smoothly during our trip to bring Elizabeth home: our adoption hearing, Elizabeth's physical, and appointments at the adoption center, American Embassy, and Russian Consulate. We flew home on two separate airlines, one of which declared bankruptcy during our trip and the other experienced a big strike and a bomb scare. That added to the excitement of the trip, but presented no difficulties for us, though.

The Circus
The weather was bitterly cold, so we didn't do much sight-seeing. Our facilitator's college-age son was our driver for a sight-seeing trip. Another college student took our little group to the Moscow Circus on our last day, and it was terrific. Elizabeth was barely three, but sat mesmerized by the acrobats and the trained animals. All of the costumes had a wonderful ethnic flair. There were some interesting camels, too. Trained house cats juggled fire batons with their feet, among other more spectacular acts, and Elizabeth was absolutely transfixed by the show.

Seatbelt Stress
We had no significant problems until the flight home, when Elizabeth became absolutely hysterical over the seatbelts. This started before the plane took off, so it wasn't air pressure changes. She screamed bloody murder and cried for hours when we strapped on the seatbelt in the airplane, and nobody, not even a kind Russian woman seated in front of us, could calm her down. We don't know if she had never been restrained or maybe had been for some unpleasant purpose. We were told possibly for toilet-training. Anyhow, by the time we reached Chicago, she had accepted the seat belt and even latched herself in before finally falling asleep during the

last leg of our journey. She has had no problems with her car seat, thank goodness. She's strong willed and wants to do everything for herself, so we let her fasten the seatbelt and she was okay with that.

Mom, the "Security Blanket"

We were told that Elizabeth had very little exposure to men at the orphanage. She attached to me almost immediately, but I would say it took several months before she effectively attached to my husband. I was Elizabeth's security blanket for weeks. She clung to me like plastic wrap and would not even let me go to the bathroom by myself. After a few weeks, she relaxed considerably and let her daddy fix her breakfast, and she would even accompany him to Walmart, that most wondrous of places. She had rarely ridden in a vehicle, and apparently ate mostly porridge, vegetable soup and bread at the orphanage. You can imagine her fascination with an entire store full of food, candy, and toys. Her favorite foods at first were bananas and canned peas; she would down a whole can at one sitting if we let her.

Language Development

Elizabeth's English language came along well in the beginning; she learned several important phrases early on, such as "Stop that, Michael (her new brother)," and "Mommy, I'm done," (yelled *loudly* from the bathroom). She memorized "tvinkle, tvinkle, little zar" in its entirety and most of the alphabet song in her first few weeks home, although we doubt she had a clue what she was saying. Michael was patient with her and with everyone else's focus on her. He thanked us several times in those first weeks for bringing him a little sister. It still brings tears to our eyes now when we think back to watching them play, wrestle on the floor, and hug.

Don't Flush!

By a mom in Maryland, January 2009

When we were on the first night of our first visit in Guatemala, our new six-year-old son was in the toilet section of the hotel bathroom and he wouldn't come out. He was talking very fast and I didn't understand what he was saying, but I could tell he was trying to ask us a question. I used your book (*Adopting From Latin America*) to ask him if anything hurt or if he was sad. Finally, I went to the page in the handbook about the bathroom and realized there was no disposal basket in the stall, and he didn't know he could flush the used toilet paper! I told him I was going to open the door. As I did, he stood there holding up a strip of soiled toilet paper with only his thumb and index finger, and I realized he was using the words *sucio* and *papel* (*dirty* and *paper*). We had to convince him to drop it in the toilet, and then he laughed at us. The three of us stood by the toilet flushing paper for a while to convince him that it was okay.

(Editor's note: The sewage systems in some countries cannot handle paper, so toilet paper is disposed of in a trash can rather than in the toilet.)

Diet for a Cold Climate
By Paul, age 13, January 2008
Snowflake, Arizona

Ever wonder how Russians keep warm in the subzero temperatures? The secret is in their fat-loaded diet. Russian food is a lot different than the American standby, the hamburger or pizza. Their diet contains a lot of fat because Russians have to keep warm. Russians' main staples are soups, meats and sausages, and bread, cheese, and butter. My favorite is sausage. Even before my parents brought me home, I crammed as much sausage into my mouth as I could. I remember (well, I've been told) that at Roald's apartment when the sausage was put on the table, I double-fisted it and crammed my cheeks full. I still do this, but only on special occasions. Another one of my favorite Russian foods is borsch. This soup contains beets, cabbage, carrots, meat, potatoes, and onions. Russian food is not to everyone's liking. So if you don't like fatty things or cabbage and beets, stay away from Russian food. I'll eat it all for you. I think that you are absolutely crazy not to like it! I will always and forever like the Russian cuisine.

Eczema and the Wise Physician
By Pat, December 2008
Louisiana

So at last, we were to take little Caitlyn to be with our family forever! The bundling in snowsuit, stockings, mittens and cap (we're from Louisiana) came first. Next was the big wide-eyed ride to the hotel where we were staying. The job of entertaining a nineteen-month-old, foreign-speaking child in a hotel room for better than a week had begun. We stayed in St. Petersburg for four days with Caitlyn after taking her with us from the Baby Home. During this time, there were some tantrums. She threw herself to the floor or against tables, even bruising herself a few times. We have heard that many of the children act this way.

Then we flew to Moscow, a necessary stop for Embassy paperwork. Very early on the morning that the physician was to visit and give his permission for her to travel, Caitlyn awoke at 3:00 a.m. with a high fever and spots *everywhere*. Oh, my goodness, chicken pox! I was sure that if the authorities or the airline personnel found out, we would be placed in quarantine.

I will tell you that I now know what an anxiety attack is like. I was certainly feeling it as we stripped the burning child and wiped her down with warm water, letting it dry on her hot skin to sooth her. Christine was just coming out of denial; she didn't want to believe that this was happening. And Caitlyn was just sick, poor baby! She finally went back to sleep, and when the doctor arrived three hours later, her temperature had returned to normal. God bless that doctor as he wrote on a slip of paper that Caitlyn had "eczema." I will tell you that he just had to know what we knew – and it was not eczema!

We repeated the wise doctor's diagnosis as we boarded four different flights, always mindful that we just might be spending the week in Moscow, Amsterdam, or wherever, if discovered. I kept putting cover-up make-up on some of the bumps to lessen the obvious look of the chicken-pox blisters. In Amsterdam, the airline personnel were the nicest ever; however, the woman checking us onto the flight kept looking at Caitlyn's face (which was encased in an ugly, hot cap to conceal her spots). I told the woman how terrible it was that most of the kids had eczema, some even worse than Caitlyn's. The airline attendant just shook her head in agreement saying, "Oh, how awful!" Christine and I were actually trembling with fear that we would be found out. And to add to baby Caitlyn's discomfort, many of her first molars were pushing their way through her tender gums. What a trooper that baby was!

Probably because we were trying to be unobtrusive, we were held back in the security area while the airline personnel inspected our carry-on bags. They instructed us to get rid of a bottle of expensive Vodka. I balanced our purses, carry-ons, and the stroller, while Mommy carried Caitlyn on her shoulder (so her head would be turned down and her spots wouldn't be as noticeable). I'll be honest with you, my heart was pounding, and I felt resigned to being discovered.

On the plane, we were so very fortunate that the flight wasn't full and we got a free seat where we could lay the baby down with her head on Mommy's lap. I really felt bad for the gentleman ahead of us for having to put up with the sick tears and crying for the ten-hour flight, and I still pray to this day that he had already had the chicken pox!

Caitlyn became a United States citizen in Memphis, Tennessee, where we first arrived in the good old U.S.A. We felt peace at last, knowing that even if discovered, we were within driving distance to our home. Caitlyn has been at home with her mommy for a month now and comes to visit my hubby and me often. Fortunately for us, we live very close to Christine and our precious new granddaughter.

In Russia, we were told that the baby didn't speak yet, but she certainly does babble in Russian and sings many songs for us. And after just two weeks, she could understand most of what we were saying. She calls out to her Poppi and me, "Bye-bye! *Puh-Kuh!*" saying good-bye in both English and Russian.

Caitlyn enjoys American food, her new toys, and her dog, and she and her mom are facing the usual challenges that come with an almost-two-year-old. The baby is demanding of Christine's time and attention. She has no problem when she is left with her Poppi and me, but when Mom comes home, Caitlyn wants her entire attention. Caitlyn no longer has tantrums, and she shakes her head "yes" and "no" to indicate if she wants something. Of course, she is just twenty months old and still cries when things do not go her way, but her smiles, hugs, and singing show us how far she has come.

Friends who have seen Christine and Caitlyn together always exclaim how much they look alike. And her chicken pox and fever are just memories. So now we prepare to celebrate Christmas, a time for giving thanks for all we have, especially this year.

CHAPTER SEVEN

Language

"The secret of language is the secret of sympathy
and its full charm is possible only to the gentle."
~ John Ruskin

Language and Bonding – Partners or Competitors?
By Teresa, July 2008
Snowflake, Arizona

Many parents lament the fact that their children lose their first language so quickly after adoption. One couple I met had been very eager to help their children maintain their ability to speak Russian. The husband had spoken Russian and English from a young age, and the wife had taught Russian for years.

The family had had some of the to-be-expected challenges that come with adoption of older children and with the adoption of a sibling group. None of those was a new revelation. But when I asked about their experience with language and maintaining their kids' Russian, the dad said that their youngest daughter had refused to speak any Russian at all with him or his wife. They had attempted to communicate with her in Russian many times over a period of weeks, to no avail. Less than a year later, they had given up on the idea of bilingualism for the youngest of their children.

Her refusal to speak Russian convinced the dad that he needed to communicate with her in English. He was sad about loss of the opportunity to help her maintain her language and culture. His wisdom was evident, nonetheless, when he succinctly summed up the situation: "I had a choice to make. I could allow my daughter to lose her Russian, or I could lose my relationship with my daughter. The choice was not difficult."

The Call Home
By Daliah, September 2008
Snowflake, Arizona

In 2003, when I was going to school at the School for the Deaf and the Blind in Tucson, I called home. Katie happened to be visiting for three weeks from Kazakhstan as part of a summer visit program. I was surprised when she was the one who answered the phone. She said hi and added something in Russian. I did not know what she had said, but she handed the phone to my mom after she was done talking. My mom told me the phrase Katie said was, "Brush your teeth." Katie thought it was funny to repeat that phrase on the phone because it was a phrase that was popular around the house at that time, probably because it was easy for everyone to say. (The family had all been listening to Russian language CDs before my brother and sister came home.)

I am glad we had the experience of adopting Katie and our brother Abe because we love them as part of our family.

A Proud Georgia Tech Yellow Jacket
By Charlyn, September 2008
Georgia

My youngest son, Drew, was adopted in December 2005 at eleven months of age. He was very small for his age and ate like a bird. He also had difficulty sleeping at night and when he did sleep, he snored. Yes, snored. Not just a little bit, but loudly, like an old man. You could hear him downstairs when he was asleep in his room upstairs! After consulting with our pediatrician, she referred me to a pediatric ENT (ear/nose/throat doctor) who determined that Drew had problems with his tonsils and adenoids and they needed to be removed. The surgery went beautifully and helped him tremendously. Although still small for his age, he now eats and eats and has finally made it "onto" the growth chart!

As a part of the surgery follow-up and monitoring process, the ENT also regularly tests Drew's hearing ability. A few months after the surgery, I took Drew for a follow-up hearing test with the audiologist. She went through several testing procedures with him and everything seemed fine. Then she put some head phones on his ears and explained that she wanted him to repeat whatever she said to him. He had just begun talking so I was a little uneasy about how this might go, but he seemed to understand. The testing went something like this:

Audiologist: "Drew, say *mommy*."

Drew: "Mommy."

Audiologist: "Good, now Drew, say *banana*."

Drew: "Banana."

Audiologist: "Say *baseball*."

Drew: "Baseball."

Audiologist: "Say *toothbrush*."

Drew: "Toothbrush."

So far, so good.

Audiologist: "Drew, say *football*."

Drew didn't say a word.

Audiologist: "Drew, say *football*."

Nothing. I was getting worried. Still nothing. Total silence. Maybe she had changed the decibel level and he didn't hear her. Then suddenly, he hollered, "Georgia Tech and Buzz!" His daddy would be so proud!

Matryoshka Family Portrait (with Georgia Tech's mascot, Buzz)

Learning My Native Language…Again
By Paul, age 13, May 2007
Snowflake, Arizona

I came home when I was three and a half years old. After ten years of speaking hardly any Russian, my mom and I decided to start up on it again. We signed up at our local community college for a Beginning Russian Conversation course. The first couple of lessons were very difficult. By the third and fourth class it got easier; I was recognizing the alphabet and could read simple words. My parents thought that I would be "programmed" for Russian, seeing as I spoke fluent Russian when I was three. In other words, they thought that I would easily pick it back up. Not so very true. Learning the language again was a big challenge. I had to learn the whole Russian alphabet and a lot of phrases, so I wasn't able to just "blow off" the class.

Our Russian teacher was named Dasha. I thought that she was a great teacher. It was kind of scary because she would pick on me sometimes to answer questions. I had to be on my toes to answer them.

Every time after we went to Russian class, we got to go to Dairy Queen and get ice cream for the way home. Pretty soon I hope to be fluent in Russian and go back to my orphanage to be able to speak the language with my former caretakers.

Small Gesture; Big Impact
By Ray, 2007
Ohio

We adopted two brothers from Russia (Siberia) in the fall of 2002. We prepared by buying your CD for learning basic Russian. My wife tried one listen to the CD and told me it was my job to learn the language. For the next two or three months, I listened to it on the way to and from work. I tried to say each phrase exactly as you said it. On our first visit, we stayed in Moscow with a translator; she said I had better pronunciation than her father! When we first met the boys, I knew exactly what I would say: "Come here," and "Don't be afraid." The orphanage director did not expect us to know any of the Russian language.

In Siberia, we stayed with a host family that spoke no English. Before we left the orphanage with the boys, I asked the translator if most people who stayed with this family spoke some Russian. She laughed and said, "No. You were the first." She said that normally she would receive five to ten calls per day from adoptive parents to request that she translate over the phone, but she never got a call from us. One time I was trying to communicate with the husband in our host family. We figured that he was talking about the garden he grows, which is about a kilometer away, but we weren't exactly sure. When the translator came over, she verified that we were correct. It was an incredible feeling to know that they were appreciative that we took the time to learn some Russian. It may be a little challenging, but it was well worth it.

Music and Language Ability
By Maren, 2008
Colorado

When we adopted our son Tim (three years old), he relished being in the same room with his sister no matter what she was doing. He often sat on her bed while she practiced for her piano lessons.

When he had been home nine months, Tim was eager to show off his musical talents; his sister had taught him a few simple songs. One Sunday afternoon Tim came into Audrey's bedroom and announced that he was going to play some songs for her on the piano.

"First I'll play *Heart and Soul*." (Play, play, play.)

"Now I'll play a scary pirate song." (Play, play, play.)

"Now I'll play *Nakey Doodle*." (He whipped off his clothes, returned to the piano bench, and played, played, PLAYED!)

He has since taken lessons for several years, but now he stays clothed when he performs.

With Our Driver
By Rebecca, 2008
Kansas

Our first trip was just before Christmas, and we had arrived just as a snowstorm was about to hit. I had learned some Russian, and I got very creative with it. For example, when our driver picked us up at the airport, he was holding a placard with our name on it, but he didn't speak English. On the way to the car the driver turned and said simply, "Cold!" obviously trying to relate to us with limited English. Because of words and phrases I had studied, I was able to respond in Russian that yes, it was cold, but it was hot on the airplane. He warmed up immediately and for the next seven hours in the car he and I visited – understanding each other and learning new things – while my husband went to sleep in the back seat.

One Child's Language Progression
By Teresa, March 1999
Snowflake, Arizona

A Few Weeks Home
Sergei seems to be quite gifted linguistically. He is very fluent in Russian for a three-year-old, and he is delighting everyone with his use of English. Paul Sergei is speaking *incredibly* well: "No, thank you." "Watch!" "I got it." and "Good doggies." After getting booster shots at the clinic, he cried in Russian, "My arm hurts." He added in English, "Big time!"

We had placed bets on how long it would take him to begin saying the before-dinner blessing with us. Last night he chimed right in, after just two weeks at home.

Yesterday when I served him lunch, after twenty days home, he looked up at me and said, "Thank you, Mom. You are a good-a *boy*."

Two Months Home
Paul Sergei speaks English very well already, after just two months. He is able to communicate all of his wants and needs. He continues to ask "Why?" at least a hundred times every day; his curiosity surely is one reason for his quick language learning. He even says to me sometimes, "Mom, how do you say _____ in *Russian*?"

Four Months Home
Well, he's now "Paul." We rarely say Paul Sergei anymore. Paul now communicates virtually everything in English. There is rarely any Russian being used anymore, except for an occasional word. We're trying to maintain his Russian, but it is fading.

Eight Months Home
Paul is learning letters and letter sounds right and left. He's even beginning to catch on to the idea of reading, and he has only spoken the language eight months!

Fifteen Months Home
This morning Paul said, "I want to do it like Dad. He's teaching me to be a man. I have to follow my role model."

For the fifteen months Paul has been with us, we have constantly reassured him that we love him, that we are family, and that we will always be together. The other day as he and I were finishing a conversation, he heaved a big sigh and said, "Well, I guess I'm *stuck* with this family *forever*."

The Secret Conversation
By Lora, July 2008
Texas

When we first brought six-year-old Ally out of the orphanage, we had an interpreter, Katya, with us. We had studied some basic Russian before we traveled and we were doing pretty well with understanding Ally. Partly by context, and by catching a word here and there, we were able to put a lot of conversation together. Ally chattered non-stop and she spoke quite rapidly, so there were a few times that we couldn't figure out what she was saying. So we looked to Katya to translate. When Ally realized that we were talking to her through the interpreter, she started to get the idea that we didn't speak the same language. Ally had a puzzled look on her face; it was as if she couldn't believe that grown-ups couldn't speak "properly." Ally waited for her chance to sneak Katya aside. She whispered in her ear. Ally kept looking over at us with a curious expression. Katya whispered back, and Ally shook her head. It was soon translated to us; Ally had told Katya that we would have to learn Russian because *she* wasn't going to learn English. We had a good chuckle, but we did work even harder to speak to her as much as we could in Russian.

About three months after she was home with us, I was trying to say something to her in Russian. She looked at me as though I were insane and said in English, "Why are you speaking Russian? We are American and we speak English!" That was the end of our Russian language learning experience. There are times I wish she had retained her Russian because it's like she has lost even more of her heritage because she only speaks English. Funny thing is, it took Ally about three years to realize that she didn't still understand Russian. She hadn't realized that she switched? Or maybe she still believed it was there, but not being used?

Learning a New Language
By Nastia, age 17, October 2006
Home to Florida 2006

Learning a new language, learning to talk English, was not that hard. I heard how people were talking and I just listened to them talk, but when somebody was asking questions, I didn't know what to say. Reading and spelling are still hard because of the different alphabets and different ways to spell. I guess it will get easier in the next months and maybe I can write well in a year or two.

Did You Really?
By Paul, June 2009
Chandler, Arizona

We've been home with our new daughter, seven-year-old Lilya, for seven months now. A few weeks ago I thought I was complimenting her when I said, "Wow, Lilya, I'm amazed at how fast you've learned English. I studied Russian for over a year before we went to Ukraine to bring you home because I wanted to be able to talk with you in your language. But you speak English so much better than I speak Russian."

Without batting an eye, Lilya responded, "Dad, you must not have studied very hard."

No English? No Problem!
By Kathy, April 2007
In Kazakhstan before Almira came home to Louisiana

Almira, now fourteen, is concerned about school mostly and does not want to get behind when she comes to the U.S.A. We told her today that we want her to keep her Russian and she said she plans to. She said there is no way she can ever forget Russian. Almira said when she comes to school in America, she just won't talk; she'll just do her Algebra, since it is the same in Russian. Then she just laughed.

CHAPTER EIGHT

Coming Home and Early Months

"There's room in the home where there is room in the heart."
~ Danish proverb

Not Exactly Perfume
By Leslie, December 2008
New York

I wrote in an earlier story that Galya embraced every aspect of her new life. I should have said that she embraced every aspect of her new life except one. The second week she was in Buffalo, my older daughter, Jordan, who is an avid equestrian, took Galya to a horse barn. As she sat on top of a pony, the silent tears trickled down Galya's little face again. It seemed as if she was petrified, but thought she had no choice in the matter, so she sat tight. She probably didn't have many choices in her original family or in the orphanage, but I think mostly that she thought she had no choice that particular day with this new family. There she sat, with tears streaming down. Jordan comforted her and did her best to assure her that all would be okay. Galya calmed down and then she did ride the pony with Jordan close by. The rest of that day wasn't very memorable.

Nowadays, Galya, like her beloved big sister, would rather ride horses than do anything else. Recently, she inhaled a deep breath of the scent of horse manure and declared, "I just love that smell! It's like perfume to me!"

Breakthroughs
By Janna, 2008
California

Lili came home just two months ago today. A week ago we seemed to make a breakthrough. Her tantrums are now exponentially less severe and not nearly as frequent. She's able to play for short periods of time alone or with the other kids without needing me right there. We've had some really long days, but overall our days are good now. She's happy and loving and fun. I'm constantly amazed by her. To think of all she's been through it her short little life and yet to see how truly happy and joyful she is; it's by God's grace. Right this very moment she's sitting next to me on the floor as I type, coloring a dinosaur and singing in Mandarin. I have no clue what she's saying, but it sounds happy.

Her English is growing by leaps and bounds, too. One day last week I was in the kitchen doing the dishes, and she came up to me and said, "Mama, Lady drink all gone." Sure enough, Lady's water bowl was bone dry.

Last night I sat down with Lili and explained to her that when Jackson,

Maddie and Justin went to school in the morning I would be going with them and that she would be staying home with Daddy. Her little eyes welled up with tears and she said, "Mama no school. No home Daddy; home Mama." It was so sad. But I knew it would be good for her and Sean to spend the day together and for her to see that when I leave, I always come back. Today was the first day I have worked since Lili has been home. Sean worked from home today to stay with her. I called during my lunch time to check on them. Sean said she cried for about half an hour, but after that was fine. We were mighty glad to see each other when I got home.

Jealousy
By Molly, age 12, September 2008
Snowflake, Arizona

About two and a half years before my brother and sister were adopted, my sister Katie (we called her Katya then) came here for about three weeks, to see what it was like here in Snowflake. Well, while Katya was here, my cousin Leah came over every day to play with me. Katya did *not* like Leah. And it was sad, because Leah had not been (no, *could* not be) mean or nasty to a single soul in her entire life, no matter how horrible people were to her.

Well, Katya was absolutely *awful* to Leah. And I was not an angel either. Don't get me wrong, I loved Leah, but I wanted Katya to like me so that we could be best friends. So I was an absolute jerk to Leah, for Katya's sake.

Well, about two weeks after Katya had been living here with us, I had a dentist appointment. When I got back from my appointment, I went into the house and saw the worst thing that could happen: *Leah was playing with Katya!* When Leah saw me, she said, "Molly, look! Katya likes me now!" I was so mad that I stomped off to my room. After about ten minutes I lost my nerve and went and apologized to Leah and Katya. (No matter how hard I try, I just can't keep a grudge!) All of us have been best friends ever since.

The Snake
By Teresa and Daniel, age 7, November 2008
Daniel came home to Arizona March 2008

One day last summer when Daniel had only been home from Vietnam about three months, he came to visit for an afternoon at our home. Daniel is a very active little guy who doesn't sit still for long, so we spent most of our time outside. We were wandering and playing when suddenly Daniel became very agitated and talkative. He was talking insistently and with great emotion – all in Vietnamese – and gesticulating toward something. Though we couldn't understand the words, we could easily understand that he was insisting that we come with him to another area near the garden. We followed him; he stopped short and pointed at a big bull snake slithering through the leaves near our cottonwood trees. He became rather frantic and gestured that we should kill the snake. By his pointing and charades, we were able to determine that he thought the snake was dangerous because it would climb up the tree. He was trying to tell us that the snake would hurt us if we didn't kill it…that it would drop from the tree and bite us.

We repeated several times, calmly and slowly, that this was a *good* snake, the kind that hunted the mice and other little critters that would eat the vegetables in our garden. Over the next several minutes, Daniel kept a close eye on the snake. When he seemed to understand that we didn't need to kill the snake after all, we got the camera and took a few pictures of the snake. We watched as it made its way to a hole near a big cottonwood tree.

Four months later, yesterday, Daniel was back at our house for the afternoon. I showed him the pictures from the day he had visited in June. Now Daniel speaks some English. He told this part of the story: "The snake doesn't bite. It's okay. The snake goes home."

Lots of understanding and growth have taken place in the last four months for a little boy who has come halfway around the world.

Daniel with a goat, his sisters, and friends

Going, Going, Gone
By Tom, January 2008
New York

Before we adopted Galya, she spent a few summer weeks with us in 2002. At the time I was a news videographer in Buffalo, New York. One day early in Galya's visit, my wife Leslie had an afternoon appointment, and since I had only an hour left at work, Leslie brought Galya to me. A newsroom is a very busy place, but everyone I worked with knew about Gal; we had done a story about her and the other kids from Russia who came to America for a summer visit. One of the producers had a Slinky and showed it to Galya. She was fascinated. How could you not give it to her? She probably had never played with one or even seen one at the orphanage. Needless to say, this was suddenly her new favorite toy.

As I drove home from work that day with Galya, she chirped away in Russian, commenting on everything she saw in this place thousands of miles from the only home she had ever known, accompanied by the *jing-jing* sound of the Slinky. Then she was crying, crying in Russian, pointing out the car window, and no Slinky. The Russian I spoke was, "Do you need to go to the bathroom?" or "Are you hungry?" Asking if the Slinky had gone out the window was beyond me, and her English would not explain where the Slinky went either.

Her new treasure was gone. I pulled over, got out, and tried to find the Slinky. There was no way my little girl was not going to have her Slinky! I searched the side of the busy street looking for what would have probably been a mangled Slinky. I was thinking of the nearest toy store. She was going to have a Slinky that day, maybe even two.

Finally, I gave up the search; I could not find her Slinky. I had failed. I walked slowly up to the car, expecting to see a puddle of tears in the back seat. Instead, I found a grinning six-year-old, with the Slinky going *jing-jing* in her tiny hands. It was the first little trick she played on me, and the beginning of the playful relationship that we have always had since. Maybe I was the first adult she could joke with, maybe the first adult she could trust enough to joke with. Whatever – I am just glad it was me.

I Only Speak English
By Michelle, March 2009
New Hampshire

When we returned home with Alejandro, age five, he only had a few words in English. We got by in the first month. I often had Alejandro on my hip in one arm and my Spanish/English dictionary in the other. Throughout each day, I would teach Alejandro words and phrases, and every night I read him a popular story in both English and Spanish.

He attended a ten-day summer camp at the school where he would be attending kindergarten in the fall. I stayed and helped each day so Alejandro could participate and still know I was with him. The children liked him, and he had fun. He picked up quite a few phrases and words in English.

We had two neighbors who were nearly fluent in Spanish, so we would have them come over to help with language barriers. That summer, we went to a Mexican restaurant each week and asked the staff to speak with him in Spanish. They would translate ideas we were having trouble communicating. Every chance we got, we encouraged Alejandro to learn English, but also to hold onto his Spanish. He worked very hard to learn English and he did a fabulous job. It was clear that he wanted to fit in. By the end of that summer, he was somewhat able to converse.

Soon he began to refuse to speak Spanish and eventually he started to even pretend not to understand it. Once when we went to the Mexican restaurant again, the staff spoke to Alejandro in Spanish. He pretended not to understand them, but they knew he did. He clearly stated in complete sentences in Spanish, "I don't understand any of what you are saying. I only speak English."

Morning Has Broken
By Molly, age 10, March 2007
Snowflake, Arizona

On the first day that my new brother and sister came, I was surprised. I expected them to speak almost as much English as I did, but they hardly spoke any. (Their names were Vitaliy and Katya, but now we call them Abe and Katie.) When we got to our house, it was past midnight. I thought that Katie and Abe would sleep in till 8:00 or 9:00 a.m. the next morning, but no, they were up at 6:00 a.m. Katie was shaking me awake and saying, "Wake up, Moe!" (My name is really Molly, but Katie called me Moe back then.)

"Katie, it's summer, and you're waking up at 6:00. You don't have to get up yet!" I mumbled, but she went right into the kitchen. I groaned and fell back asleep. I woke up again to Katie jumping on my stomach. (By then it was 6:10.)

"Katie, what are you doing?!" I exclaimed.

"Oh, I think that you maybe are not OK, so I try to make better," she said, looking surprised.

"Well, I'm better," I said.

"Oh, goody," she said, running out of the room. (She used to say "Oh, goody" quite often when she first came home. I wonder if she knew what it meant.)

I sighed and then I got up. I was pretty mad, but I tried to be patient. Katie woke me up at 6:00 a.m. for the next two weeks, but soon after that she stopped waking me up, even if she got up early herself. I was relieved.

Reading in English after Barely Two Months Home
By Debbie, January 2009
Chandler, Arizona

Our new daughter, Lilya, age seven, has been home from Ukraine for two months. She has made remarkable progress with English and with expressing her feelings. This evening, my 25-year-old daughter, Kristi, my 18-year-old daughter, Elizabeth, and I were just relaxing, watching TV together and chatting. We noticed that Lilya was "reading" a book in English with much interest. She was following the words left to right, down the pages as she "read" the following sentences:

"I don't want to do it. I won't do it. I don't want to do it. "

This went on for a few minutes.

Kristi finally asked, "Lilya, what book are you reading?"

Elizabeth looked over and said, "She's reading *Twenty Things Adopted Kids Wish Their Adoptive Parents Knew*. How ironic is that?!"

What Was on His Mind?
By Roger and Teresa, 2008
Snowflake, Arizona

We had been home with our son for only two months when we received a letter with some good news from our agency. The director of our son's orphanage, Valentina, would be in Phoenix six weeks later; there would be a picnic and all families were welcome to come visit her. Valentina is a remarkable woman; she is a pediatrician and the director of the orphanage where our son spent the first three years of his young life. She had been very loving and concerned for our son's best interests the whole time he was under her care. He had contracted polio as an infant, and could have been moved to another orphanage where children with physical challenges were cared for, but Valentina chose to keep precious little "Seriozha" in the only home he had known. She had presided over his care and health requirements, being sure that he received the physical therapy he needed. She also made certain that even though money was an issue (there was never enough money for all the needs at the orphanage), she had a special pair of mid-calf leather boots made for our son so that he could learn to walk even though the muscles in his right leg were weak as a result of his illness.

Hearing the news that Valentina would be in our state, we were so excited, thinking, *How wonderful that our son will be able to see Valentina again! It will be a link back to Russia, and he'll know we are interested in being in touch with his "first life" and how much the people there loved him.* The day before the picnic rolled around, and we enthusiastically told our son, "Tomorrow we'll all get to visit with Valentina!" He was eager and smiley. We loaded up the car and headed to Grandma's house in Phoenix so we wouldn't have a four-hour drive on the day of the reunion.

The next morning, we packed our potluck lunch and dressed Seriozha in a cute outfit for the occasion, eager to show Valentina how much he had grown. But our son didn't seem quite himself that day; he was a bit restless. We all were excited, so we imagined that he must be too.

At the park, we searched out Valentina. A few parents gathered around her, visiting, while others waited their turn. When she turned and saw our son, she was obviously very pleased. She greeted him, speaking gently in Russian, complimenting him, and asking him questions. He answered with nods of his head, but didn't say a thing. He could still understand Russian, but already was actively "trading in" his extraordinary language talents in his native language for new ones in English. As he and Valentina visited, he rather shyly clung to us, which was a surprise, because he was normally very outgoing and interactive and loved to visit with everyone. Valentina was curious to know about his medical check-ups, swimming we had done, his pre-school class, and our home life. We updated her on the months he had been with us, offering as many details as we could think of, and then our time with Valentina was up. We all agreed that it had been a great visit and expressed how delighted we were that she and our son had gotten to see each other again. We went on to eat lunch, visit with other parents, enjoy the beautiful spring weather, and watch all the kids run and play in the park. It was a memorable afternoon.

At 2:00 o'clock we loaded up our ice chest and picnic supplies and headed for the car. We buckled up, drove away, and chatted about what a wonderful day it had been. Seriozha, who had been uncharacteristically quiet all day, began to kick his feet, talk away with his big sisters, and sing. He was bubbly, exuberant, and giggly. It wasn't until that moment, when our son became himself again, that we realized that in the days before the picnic and the entire time at the picnic, something had been on his mind.

Had he been worried subconsciously that he might have to leave us? Had he thought that possibly he would be going back to "group-oo" (his name in Russian for his group at the orphanage)? There really was no way for us to know for sure, but in retrospect we saw the very clear change in his behavior when all of us were together again in the car, headed for home. We could only imagine what might have been going on inside of that very bright little mind of his. We're glad we went to the picnic; it was a pleasant day and an amazing opportunity to touch base again with someone who had played such an incredibly important role in our son's life. And when we noticed the immediate change in our son's behavior once we were on the road home, we were more thankful than ever that he was our son. We felt that he was grateful, too.

Just a Little Request
By Elizabeth, age 18, February 2009
Chandler, Arizona

I remember the first time I clearly saw compassion in my little sister, Lilya. It was not long after she arrived in our family from Ukraine and she was seven at the time. After she came with our mom to pick me up from school, she suddenly said, "Mom, you and Dad need to go back to Ukraine."

After being asked why, she told us this:

"I have it one friend who needs a family. He lives at the *dyetsky dom* (children's home) and he is a very funny one boy! Please, Mama; he's such a nice boy!"

"But Lily, Mama already has five kids. That is enough."

Lilya responded that five was *not* enough; Mom needed six kids.

"Lily, we don't have any more rooms at home."

She responded that her room had two beds; she could share.

"Maybe we could have Susan (our adoption coordinator) find him a family in Arizona so you could play with him."

"No! He need it *our* family! Please, Mama; he very funny boy!"

I remember how proud I was of my sister at that moment. She knew that we loved her and she showed that she was happy to be in our family. What made me even happier was the fact that she noticed a need in someone else's life, and tried with all her might to fulfill that need.

What a Beginning!
By Paul, age 12, April 2007
Snowflake, Arizona

After weeks of waiting and hearing about my new cousin from Russia, I was eager to meet him in person. My dad and I went up to my grandma's cabin in Greer, Arizona to visit with my cousins, including my cousin Sergei, the newest addition to the family. I was both excited and nervous at the same time. When we first arrived, I saw my new cousin Sergei on the front porch; he and my Uncle Paul had come outside to greet us when we pulled up in the car. Sergei was rather short and skinny and had teeth like a beaver. After we met on the porch, we walked into the cabin. I was met with the familiar faint smell of peanuts; my grandma always feeds peanuts to the squirrels and blue jays. No sooner had I sat down in the infamous brown recliner (The Brown Chair sends even the most determined night owls to dreamland!) than Sergei came up and promptly spit in my face. Yuck! After a scolding from his mom and dad and an apology to me, Sergei began to wrestle with me. He was really strong and rough. Even though I was ten at the time and he was seven, we were evenly matched. Sergei's strength that day still amazes me when I think about it now, three years later. He was a little warrior! That is how I met my new cousin. Today we are very close and we love to brag about our Russian heritage together. We always agree on the fact that RUSSIANS ROCK!

CHAPTER NINE

First Year Adjustments and Settling In

"True life is lived when tiny changes occur."
~ Leo Tolstoy

Some Adjustments for Elizabeth
By Carole, January 2003
Missouri

Christmas

Christmas arrived less than two weeks after Elizabeth came home, and it was quite chaotic. My three grown stepchildren were here for the holidays, and two of them brought new yellow lab puppies, which Elizabeth loved to terrorize. She gasped as she opened each gift and asked, unbelievingly *"ETT-a my-AH?"* (This is for me?), over and over, and then would run into the arms of the givers to thank them. It was quite a sight and definitely a holiday to remember. In the beginning she ran to the sound of the doorbell and leaped at family members and friends she recognized, such as *"DYEH-doosh-ka* and *BAH-boosh-ka"* (Grandpa and Grandma).

Elizabeth is eighteen months younger than her brother Michael, and he is quite a string bean, so though she was several inches shorter than he when she came home, she weighed as much as he did and was as solid as a rock. She most definitely was not malnourished from orphanage life. She rode Michael's bicycle, bounced his old spring horse across the garage floor, tumbled, flipped, and leaped at us from the top of the stairs, whether we were ready to catch her or not. She loved for us to hold her upside down by her ankles while she attempted sit-ups. She was helping us move Christmas presents, and we didn't realize until she handed one to Grandpa that she had carried a heavy car battery up two flights of stairs!

Sleep Issues

Our only major issue in the beginning was sleep. She didn't want to, and we did! We were told at the orphanage that Elizabeth might sleep better in a room with someone, as she was used to a dormitory-style bedroom with many children. Michael was happy to share his bedroom, so we put twin beds in his room and turned the other bedroom into a playroom for both kids. But Elizabeth still avoided sleep like the plague. I counted one night and she asked me thirty-eight times, *"Nee spot?"* (It's not time for bed, is it?), then burst into tears when I finally said it was. Sometimes the only thing that calmed her enough to go to sleep at first was for me to lie down with her. I started out right next to her, and then gradually moved to the floor, but she was a very light sleeper and woke up crying and in a panic if I was not there. My husband finally took pity on me and added an air mattress to the kids' room, which basically meant the two kids and I sleep side by side.

(Note from 2007: After maybe a year and a half, Elizabeth was sleeping relatively well and was ready for her own room, so that's when we separated the kids.)

Beginning to Read – Not Quite!
By Teresa, August 1998
Snowflake, Arizona

This morning at the breakfast table, four-year-old Paul picked up a tube of Colgate toothpaste. He said, "Mom I can read this. Watch." Then pointing to the letters one at a time, he said, "C - O - I - G - A - F - E."

I was quick to congratulate him on his letter knowledge. I thought to myself, *He has only been speaking English for seven months, and he knows some of his letters. Not bad at all.*

Then he insisted, "I can read the whole thing, Mom. I can *READ*. Watch!" He slid his finger along from left to right underneath all the letters on the label of the Colgate tube and proudly shouted, "Aquafresh!"

Home and Home School
By Ally, age 11, January 2008
Texas

I've been here with my family for almost five years now. It's amazing! I really enjoy being in the family. I love them very much. I love being home-schooled because it's fun and relaxing. It makes me feel like I am being American instead of Russian. I enjoy it because I get to spend so much time with my family. I like playing more and learning what I want to learn without the pressure, and I like to explore with my family, driving and seeing new places and things. I also don't like sitting at a desk all day; in home school I can get up and move around when I feel like it. The rules aren't as strict here and there is more fun and freedom. In Russia we had to sit and be quiet and not bother the other kids. We had to wait until the teacher asked us to talk. Also, the teachers in our orphanage were very strict. To them, taking care of me was just a job. They didn't love me like my mom does.

Firsts
By Teresa, November 1998
Snowflake, Arizona

Our four-year-old son has been home with us for eleven months. We've all had a huge year, exhausting and joyous at the same time. Imagine all the changes our son has been through. We have a new child; he has a whole new world. Here is a short list of firsts he has experienced: first light switch, first flush toilet, first bath toys, first slippers, first crayons, first time outside at night, first train ride, first plane ride, first shower, first pizza (didn't like it), first swim lesson, first bike ride, first visit to the beach, first holiday family gathering (where he met thirty extended family members). It has been an incredible time for all of us.

A big "first" for Paul was Halloween. We talked about it for weeks and weeks before it rolled around. I "spoiled" Paul a bit for his first Halloween (when it came to wearing costumes, that is). I took out the dress-up box that I've maintained for years, and in the two weeks before Halloween, Paul dressed up first as a clown, second as a pirate, next as Zorro, and then as a vampire! He had a great time wearing the various outfits for days at a time and role playing endlessly. The pirate "get up" was the most popular, though, so he kept coming back to that, probably because the costume was complete with eye patch and plastic sword and lent itself to much four-year-old swashbuckling. Trick-or-treating wasn't much of a hit; it was probably too scary for a little boy who hadn't grown up with the idea.

Golden Friendships
By a mom in Connecticut, August 2009

One of the best things we did for our eight-year-old daughter when she came home was to keep in contact with friends she had from her summer program. When she got together with children she had known in Russia, it was really beneficial. Maintaining contact with old friends and observing how they were adjusting and getting comfortable with their new settings, schools, and parents was a real benefit. I am especially grateful to one friend's mother for coordinating her family's schedule so that we can manage to meet and get the kids together two or three times a year. Our daughter's friend, who came from the same orphanage, has a special place in our hearts. Her family, which includes an older brother adopted at the same time, is considered an extension of ours. This past summer we shared in her brother's graduation from high school. I'm so glad we have made the effort to get our daughter together with friends who had been in the same orphanage, as there is no one else in the world who can truly appreciate their shared background and the challenges of coming to America to live with a new family. It was one of the most positive things we did for her as parents to ease the transition for her. The added bonus is that we have made wonderful friends with the other parents who have experienced this fantastic journey.

Sisters

Health Notes
By Ann, August 2008
New Mexico

When our three-year-old daughter came home with us, the pediatrician found her to be very healthy in all regards. She was in the fifth percentile for weight and the tenth percentile for height: small but healthy. I expressed a bit of concern over minor digestive problems she was having. The doctor said that it might take as long as a year for her to become accustomed to her new diet.

Her tummy problems resolved within about six months. And less than one year after coming home, she is now in the tenth percentile for weight and the twenty-fifth percentile for height. Excellent progress.

Anniversary
By Teresa, December 1998
Snowflake, Arizona

One year ago today, we waited at the orphanage in a big sitting room with wooden floors and very little furniture. When little Seriozha walked in, Valentina, the director of the orphanage, asked him if he knew who we were.

"*Da*," (Yes) he said, as he gave one sharp nod of his head. "*Mama ee Papa*."

Just one year later, it has proved next to impossible to maintain Paul's Russian. Several people have asked us lately, "How's he coming along with his English?" That question always makes us laugh, as learning a new language is possibly the least of the big changes in the life of a newly adopted child.

To share how he is doing with his English skills, I'll include a comment he made this morning on the way to the babysitter's house: "Mom, I used to wake up sometimes in the night and come get in bed with you and Daddy when I was afraid. Now I just pull the covers up and tell myself, 'It's not really a nightmare. It's just a *shadow* of a nightmare.' Then I can go right back to sleep."

Shared Roots
By Roger, August 2004
Sergei came home to Arizona January 2004

We brought Cousin Sergei (almost nine now) home with us to spend some time visiting with our son Paul (from Russia, now eleven). They had twenty-four hours together here at home just playing and playing. Those two boys really have a grand old time. The occasional disagreement does pop up, but so far they have worked out any differences very well on their own.

A few days later:

The good times continue! I took Paul to the cabin yesterday so he could have a visit with Cousin Sergei, who was there with his mom, dad, and sisters. We went fishing; I caught a small trout. After I cleaned it, the boys decided to dissect the head. You should have heard the giggles and *oohs* and *aahs*. It was really funny.

Several times they have agreed on something (a like or a dislike or how they feel about something), and then one or the other of them pipes up and says, "Yeah, we're Russian!"

This is fun to see in the short term, and it is very positive for them to have each other to identify with over the long haul.

Overcoming Fear
By Paul Z., age 14, 2006
Taylor, Arizona

As I was walking home from school, I was not scared. I was amazed because I used to be scared of everything. I used to be afraid of being left alone. I used to be scared of someone hurting me, and I was scared of heavy equipment. I was born in Bulgaria. When I was about four years old, my mom took me to an orphanage and she left me there alone. Then the people at the orphanage took me to another orphanage. I had just gotten used to being there, and then the people took me to another orphanage. I was there by myself. They left me there, and I did not know any of the people. I was afraid that the boys there would hurt me.

In the first orphanage, people were a little nice to me, but I also got beat up, and I had to sleep in a room by myself. We were only able to play behind a fence and we could never get out. In my second orphanage, I went to a school and I only learned Bulgarian words and we went on walks, but we were also behind a fence.

In my last orphanage I always got beat up by boys and the boys stuck my head under a car tire and the car was starting to back up. The driver stopped the car and went out to hurt the boys that were trying to get me killed.

In my third orphanage, some people came to adopt me, and I was scared because they were strangers, but I overcame that fear by learning to get to know them and love them. After I overcame that fear, I then knew that those people would not hurt me because they cared about me. There were also other strangers, but I was not afraid anymore because I made friends with them. I was sad when they gave me to another family.

When I was adopted by my forever family, I did not want to be left alone because my parents in Bulgaria had left me. I would not even go to the restroom without someone there. I overcame that fear because my mom helped me by saying, "Paul I will be standing right here by the door. I will sing to you so you can hear me." Then she moved to the couch, still singing songs. Soon after that she moved to the steps. Finally she said, "Paul, it's time for you to go to the restroom by yourself." As time passed, I went to the restroom without having to have people be close by. Now my mom can leave me anywhere and I am not scared of being left alone. I learned to trust that I would be okay.

When I first lived in America, I was scared of people because I always thought that they would hurt me. I always got hurt in Bulgaria by some boys in the orphanage. I also did not want to be with strangers. The way I overcame that fear is by getting to know people. My parents told me that if I am nice to people, I won't get beat up. So I learned to be kind to others and that helped me overcome this fear.

I was scared of heavy equipment because they made loud noises and were big. I thought that I would get hurt. My dad helped me to not be scared by taking me on heavy equipment and showing me how to work on heavy equipment. I learned to not be scared because the heavy equipment could not hurt me. I have even driven backhoes and forklifts.

Now as I walk different places, I am not scared anymore. I feel proud of myself. People can overcome fear if they choose to, but if they don't choose to overcome their fears, they will always be frightened.

Important Communications
By B.J., May 2007
California

In mid-April during a very impressive wind storm, the wind was blowing so forcefully that my van shuddered against the strong gusts. Alek inno-cently asked me what that was. I told him it was the wind. He asked if God made the wind, and I told him I thought so. He asked if we could see God. I told him we see God everywhere – in the sky, the trees, the flowers, in others, etc. He asked if I had ever seen God, and I told him, "Not like I see you." Then he said he'd seen God. I asked where, and he said when he was in Russia at the orphanage.

That gave me pause. We were quiet for a moment. Then he asked me if I had ever spoken to God. I told him I spoke to him quite a bit and that prayers were one way to talk to God. He asked if I had ever heard God talk back and I said not perhaps in the way he and I were talking. I asked him if he knew that feeling inside when he was doing something he knew was wrong. He said, "Yes," and I told him that was God telling him so.

Alek was quiet for another moment after that. Then he asked me if God had a telephone. I told him God didn't really need a telephone. Then he asked me if I knew what his phone number was. I told him, "No," and he very promptly informed me that he in fact knew what God's phone number was. I asked what it was, and Alek, without missing a beat, said, "1-1-1, 2-2-2!" Now, it would help to know that the children in Alek's pre-school class learn their numbers by repetition - they learn 111, 222, 333, 444, and so on. Just a moment later my phone rang, and Alek asked, "Mom! Is that God?"

Adoption of a Teen
By Kathy, 2008
Louisiana

Almira turned fourteen when we visited her in Kazakhstan in April 2007 to bring her home. When school started in the fall, Almira tested at the seventh grade level in Math, but of course her English language skills were still low; she had only spoken English for a few months. She was placed in a sixth-grade classroom, where she excelled, due to her outstanding work ethic and her willingness to jump right in to do her very best even though the language, her family, the school system, and curriculum were all new to her. Almira is a shining example of a successful teen adoption. She was bright and smart; all she needed was a chance.

CHAPTER TEN

The Change in My Life
a book within a book

By Katie Flake

For my family: Mom, Dad, Daliah, Jewel, Shiloh, NaElle, Jayze, Noah, Levi, Molly, Abe, and McKay

Preface
By Teresa Kelleher

Katie, a fourth grader in 2007, told me she wanted to write a book about her adoption, but that she and her parents thought it would be a challenge to get it published.

I told her about my dream of publishing a book of stories *by, for* and *about* children who had been adopted. We decided to work on the project together. Besides, as a teacher I thought, *What better way could there be for Katie to perfect her English than to write about her transition from life in Kazakhstan to her new world?*

I told her, "Katie, this will take a long time. We won't finish the book until after you are out of the sixth grade." She agreed to move ahead, and that's when Katie, my son Paul, and I began our book.

We have written and collected many stories, some from families in surrounding communities and others from afar. Almost three years have gone by, Katie is in seventh grade, and here are her writings; they have become a book within a book.

Katie lives with her parents and ten siblings. She enjoys a variety of activities, everything from school to sports to music. She loves spending time with her large extended family and hanging out with friends. Katie gave me the nudge I needed to begin this wonderful project. It has been a pleasure to work with her. Congratulations to you, Katie, for following through with a commitment you made as a ten-year-old long ago!

In the Orphanage
By Katie, age 10, May 2007
Home to Snowflake, Arizona 2005

When I first came to the orphanage it looked normal, kind of like a house. There were stairs and pictures and all that stuff. It was a plain, two-story, white building. The upstairs had several little rooms. I think there were about seven rooms in our apartment: two bedrooms, a hall, a playroom, a TV room, a kitchen, and a bathroom. An apartment is a house in a building. There were twenty-five kids in each apartment. There was one big bedroom for the boys and another for the girls. There were about five or six girls in my bedroom.

My apartment was a little better than the other apartments. My room was light yellow and my bed was nice. It had a red blanket, and I also had a big brown dresser that was almost as tall as the ceiling. The next room was the kitchen. It looked like a real kitchen; there were tables, chairs, and a tiny room for the mop and a broom. There were five round tables and five kids sat at each table. We could sit where we wanted; I used to sit by my friends.

In the orphanage it was sometimes fun, but sometimes sad. Sometimes if I was sad, I wanted to be somewhere else. I got sad because sometimes people would take my seat. But then I would sit at another table and pretty soon I would be glad again.

In the TV room we had all kinds of things. We had shelves, couches, chairs, and a TV. The TV was a pretty big color TV. On the shelves we had glass china (plates and tea cups). They were beautiful decorations. Sometimes we cleaned them if they were dusty, and then we put them back on the shelves. I liked to put the stuff away. It was fun. Not everyone got to do that.

When I found out I was going to leave the orphanage, I was grateful that I was adopted. I was going to go to a different family and that was cool. I knew it would be a new adventure.

School in Russia
By Katie, age 10, May 2007

In my school in Russia we had grades one through eleven. There was only one school in the town, so it had all the grades. I was in first grade when I was there. What I learned in our school in Russia was math, reading, writing, and art, but we never had music. In first grade we learned cursive because in Russian schools you do not learn to write in print. At recess we would stay inside of the building because it was a rule, but I don't really know why. It also was easy to get to school because the orphanage was right across the street. The building was white and it looked like the orphanage. We sat at desks to do our work. Each student sat at a desk by himself or herself; each of us had our own desk. We did not go home for lunch because the cafeteria people fed us lunch at school. We never went on field trips; they did not have any school buses. I don't remember any of my teachers, but they were probably nice.

I like school better in Arizona because I have made more friends here and learned a different language. I like to have recess and to use the computers. School is better here because I have great teachers and better educational opportunity.

No More Oatmeal!
By Katie, age 11, November 2007

Back when I was in Russia, I hated oatmeal. I still hate oatmeal. Want to hear why I hate it? Because it just does not taste good. The oatmeal I ate in Russia was watery and gooey looking. It did not have anything in it (no sugar, no milk, no nothing!). The texture is gross. That is why I still hate oatmeal. I would rather eat ice cream.

Now I will tell you what I used to do. When my friend would leave the table to go to the bathroom, I would pour my oatmeal into her bowl. When she would come back to the table, I would say, "I'm all done." She would go ahead and eat all of the oatmeal in her bowl. We had to eat all of it. If we didn't want to eat it, we would have to stay in our room until the teacher said we could leave. But I would get away with the trick. I would feel like, "Yes! I didn't have to eat my oatmeal today!"

A Funny Story
By Katie, age 11, March 2008

Have you ever seen a person fall off a chair? Well, one time at the orphanage in Kazakhstan, I was away cleaning up my room. Then I heard everybody laughing in the dining room. I was thinking, "Why are they laughing?"

When I came into the dining room, I heard a friend of mine say that one of the teachers fell off of her stool. One of my mean and "wide" teachers was having lunch at the kitchen table. While the teachers were eating, everyone heard a loud CRACK! Down fell the mean and fat teacher. It was kind of funny.

All the kids laughed, and the teacher was embarrassed. She deserved to fall because she was mean. She always yelled at everybody for no reason.

Well, one good thing about it is I did not get in trouble for laughing. Nobody did. Now I think that she learned not to sit on a stool that wasn't strong. I hope she learned not to yell at everyone.

Snow Tunnels
By Katie, age 12, January 2009

In Kazakhstan there was a lot of snow. It would get up to about five or six feet. The fun part of it was that my friends and I at the orphanage would dig tunnels. We would get dressed in warm clothes and build tunnels to play in. We would find hard packed snow, build stairs, and climb up on top of the snow. Sometimes we would fall through into the tunnels and make a new hole to get out of the tunnels. We would play until we wanted to go inside. I think we played sometimes for as long as three hours. Sometimes we ran inside to get warmed up before heading back out to play. The ladies at the orphanage would help us get the clothes put away. That's a fun memory.

When Mom and Dad Came to Kazakhstan
By Katie, age 10, October 2007

I used to live in the orphanage in Russia. I had been there for two years. I knew I was going to get adopted because the principal told me. First, on the day my parents came, I was going to play outside. Some kids told me there were some English-speaking people there. They were coming out of the principal's office when I was coming out of my room. Then I saw them and they saw me. Mom started to cry because she was happy. I was excited too.

Then we went in the car to Abe's orphanage. I met my brother who was also being adopted. We went to a big park and played for a long time. I was so happy. After the park, we went to Marina's house. She is a woman who helps the people who adopt. Abe and I were playing while my mom was talking for about an hour before we went to bed.

The next day we went shopping. We got to choose our clothes. Mine were very cute. Then we went on a bus and there were lots of people that I didn't know. Finally we got back to Marina's house. The next day we had to go home on the plane. I was sad because I had to leave Kazakhstan, but glad because I got to meet my family. On the airplane it was fun. I watched TV and ate lots of good food, but it was not comfortable to sleep. I had to go on four different airplanes. When I got off the last airplane, I saw my family. I was so glad. It was my happiest day ever.

Trying to Talk
By Katie, age 12, June 2008

For the month my parents stayed in Kazakhstan before they could bring me back to Snowflake, my mom had to learn my language. Well, I will tell you something: sometimes she did not make much sense! When I had to brush my teeth, she would try to say in Russian, "If you brush your teeth now, you'll get ice cream later." But what she really said was, "You don't brush teeth, you ice cream, no!" At least she was trying, and we got along.

For that month, my mom taught me some English. She would point to things and say what they were. I don't know how long it took before I learned what she was trying to teach me. What I do know is that when my dad came back on a second trip to Kazakhstan to take me and my brother home to Arizona, I still couldn't understand much. After about three months, though, I was really good at English. I could understand most of what was said to me. My sister says that when I made mistakes and she corrected my English, I would always ask my mom, just to be sure.

Now, almost three years later, my mom doesn't need to speak Russian anymore. I'm fluent in English now, and I have mixed feelings about speaking Russian. I'm really bad at speaking Russian, so don't try to communicate with me in Russian! It would be hard to speak it much here because there aren't many Russian speakers in my town. I don't really want to go back to Kazakhstan, so I don't think there is a reason for me to learn Russian again unless maybe I go on a Russian-speaking mission for my church. If I did learn Russian again, I don't think it would be too hard for me, though, because I knew it until I was ten and I would probably remember it once I started studying it again.

From Kazakhstan to Snowflake
By Katie, age 10, February 2007

When I came from Kazakhstan to Snowflake, I was so excited because it was beautiful here and the family was so nice. We all went to the park, and the first thing we did was play a game called "Snake." After that, my brother Abe, who was adopted at the same time I was, and I played with cousins. When I saw I had so many cousins, I was excited. My mom told me I have fifty-five cousins, so that's why I shouldn't tell you about them all because it would take all day! I rode horses with my new family and we jumped on the trampoline. And that was just in my first day home.

I now have ten new sisters and brothers. One of my sisters is tall and pretty; her name is Jewel. There is another who is only nine days apart from me in age; her name is Molly. I like to play with her because she is my age. Another sister, NaElle, jumps on the trampoline with me. My other sister, Daliah, reads me books. When I first got here, my brother Shiloh used to twirl me around because I was so light. I didn't like this...I loved it! Another brother, Jayze, helped me wash my dishes when I first got here. My brother Noah teeter-tottered with me in the backyard. Another brother, Levi, chased me around. Abe, also from Kazakhstan, jumped on his bed. My youngest brother, McKay, played sword fights. My mom gave me piggy-back rides and she let me comb her hair. My parents, especially my dad, liked to pillow fight with me.

I remember that the second day I was here, my dad came into my bedroom to wake me up. He looked around and said, "Where's Katie?" I was hiding under my pillow. Then I jumped up and yelled, "Boo!" I hit him on his forehead with my pillow, right where his bald spot is, and he almost fell down. That was funny. Then he said, "Ha, ha, ha!" and he threw a bigger pillow at me. That got us started with pillow fights. As you can see, I have a very large, loving family.

Katie, on the far left, with her family, all wearing caps from Kazakhstan
Front row: Katie, Molly, Abe (on Shiloh's lap), and McKay
Middle row: Daliah, Jewel, Jayze, and NaElle
Back row: Levi, Noah, Pam (Mom) and Shon (Dad)

Learning English
By Katie, age 10, April 2007

I had just gotten here to Arizona and I had to learn English. So I started to learn by listening to people. I had a translator that helped me a lot when I first came to Snowflake, but too bad for me because she had to leave after about three weeks. I was sad. After she left I was a little scared because I might do something wrong. Then it really happened.

One time my sister Molly said, "Can you give me some water?"

I said, "Yes, I could." I thought she said, "Pour the water on me," so I did. She was a little mad at first and then she was giggling at me. I felt a little unhappy because I did a mistake. But then I laughed too. At that time it was summer so it wasn't a big deal because it wasn't cold.

How I Got My Name
By Katie, age 10, May 2007

After I had been home in Arizona for a while, I went to the doctor to get a check-up. I was at the doctor's office for my appointment. When I was there waiting in the waiting room to be called for my appointment, I said, "Mom, can I change my name?" My mom said, "OK," and I said, "Thank you!" At first my name was Katya. My Mom said, "How about Katie?" I said, "Can't I be Jenny? My mom said, "We have too many Jennifers in our family. We have at least four." So I said, "OK," and that's when I changed my name to Katie! It felt good that I got an American name. I'm the only Katie in my family, so I'm glad we picked Katie instead of Jenny. Some people find out my Russian name and call me Ekaterina, but it annoys me.

My New Home and Life – a Year and a Half after Coming Home
By Katie, age 10, February 2007

I want to talk a little about how different my life is here. When I first got here, I did *not* like the food. I ate hotcakes with no syrup. Now I think that would taste nasty. I hated French toast because it had black spots on it. Now I think it's good. It just took me a month or so to get used to the new foods here.

My new house is large. My favorite room in the house is the laundry room. Just joking! I hate folding laundry. My favorite room is actually the front room because that's where we spend time with the family and at the piano. We play lots of games like "Who stole the cookie from the cookie jar?" and "The Animal Game." I love to play the piano because it is one of my two instruments. I play piano and I'm also learning to play the violin. I play the violin in my school orchestra. My special piano teacher is my mom.

I don't like helping with my chores. We have lots of laundry and I hate sorting laundry. I don't like vacuuming or doing dishes either. Even if I don't like it, I still have to do chores to make the house look nice.

Another difference is that here my mom makes me and my brothers and sisters go running every morning. Sometimes it's like, "Yeah, I'm getting out of the house," and sometimes I don't want to leave the house. In Kazakhstan I usually didn't exercise. We didn't have P.E. at school, and at the orphanage we just played outside. Now I love sports. Football is awesome. I play with my friends at school. We also like to hang out and talk.

Even though both Kazakhstan and Arizona are good, I like Arizona better because I have more freedom to do stuff here.

A Christmas Memory from Kazakhstan
By Katie, age 11, December 2007

Christmas is fun except when you're in the orphanage. In the orphanage, for Christmas I would get a broken Barbie or something like that. What I did with the gifts is get the Barbie that I did not want and get the good parts from it (like the head) and stick them in the other Barbie so I could make a whole one. That is what I got for Christmas in the orphanage.

In the middle of the day I would have a piece of candy. We didn't have a tree or lights or anything like that. None of us kids knew what the meaning of Christmas was. Nobody read us any Christmas stories, and we didn't have Christmas songs. I like Christmas better here at home with my family.

Losing Friends
By Katie, age 12, January 2009

I had two really good friends at the orphanage. One was going to go back with her mom. Another family was going to get my other friend. After my mom and dad came for the first trip to Kazakhstan to see me, I spent the days with Marina (the adoption worker). I was supposed to go back to the orphanage to sleep at night, but Marina found a way for me to stay at her apartment. It was huge. She owned the apartment building. I was pretty happy to go away when my parents came back for me, but it was sad not being able to say good-bye to my orphanage friends.

I've lost a lot of friends, but I've gained a family. It's pretty amazing to be with a family that loves you, and it feels good for the person getting adopted. Adoption is great, and if I have enough money for it, I will adopt in the future.

Molly, Katie, Minnie, Abe, and McKay

About Me and My Birth Mom
By Katie, age 12, November 2008

In Kazakhstan my house was very small. It had upstairs and down-stairs. My mom and stepdad and I lived downstairs. Our house had six rooms and all the rooms were little. I was the only kid in the family. I had my own room with a dresser that my mom gave me. It was brown and it was little too. I had a bed that had pink pillows and a pink blanket. I liked to spend time in my room because I had most of my stuff there. I was at my house in Kazakhstan living like a normal person. I was happy and also sad sometimes – like everybody else.

It was a normal spring day for a six-year-old. I was playing all day and having fun. But that night was the saddest night of my life. I was getting ready to go to bed. I said, "Good night, Mom. I love you." I did not know they were going to be the last words I said to her.

In the middle of the night I woke up. I went to the keyhole and looked through. There were about ten people outside my door. I did not know what was happening. I went out of my room. It smelled like fire, and it was hot like it too. Part of the house had burned. Then I saw doctors running all around me. They were there to help my mom. They picked me up and put me in a car. I don't remember if I was sitting there alone or if someone stayed with me. After a while, I fell asleep.

When I woke up in a hospital, there was my stepdad looking at me with his blue teary eyes. In a cracking voice he said, "I'm sorry, but your mom is *dead*."

That night I cried for three hours straight. The next day I was in the hospital, and then I got to go home. When I got home, I was thinking about my mom. I was heartbroken and confused.

My Grandparents' House in Kazakhstan
By Katie, age 12, February 2009

Well after the fire we went home. I stayed at my home for about two or three days. Then my stepdad said, "You are going to your grandparents' house." I was so excited; I started packing right away. I was finally going to meet my grandparents. I was only six so I don't know what side of my family they were (my mom's family or my dad's family). I didn't have to go very far, only about half an hour in a car. But since we didn't have a car, we borrowed one from a friend. On the way there, I was thinking about how my grand-parents' house would look and what it would be like there.

It was daytime when we got there. The first day, right after I arrived, my grandpa took me fishing while my grandma fixed lunch. We went swimming. I was afraid of the lake because of the fish. I still am afraid of swimming with fish.

I remember that they had a big field of vegetables and corn across from the house. Next to the house there was a flower garden. They had a huge brown dog that was so tall when he stood on his back legs. He was taller than me. Well, I am short, but he was big! He was friendly when my grandpa was around, but I was afraid of him when my grandpa wasn't close by.

My grandpa showed me his pigs and chickens, and my grandma showed me the house. In the house there was a shoe room. We had to go through the pantry to get to the bathroom. And there was a fridge in my room because there was only one electric plug in each room. I remember that I played in her front room putting on make-up in front of the mirror and thinking about how pretty I was.

One memory I have is watching my grandpa and some other men butchering the pig so we could eat it. Watching them cut it up was gross, but most of the time I spent with my grandma and grandpa was fun. I was there for a while and it was a good visit. Then I was at the orphanage for two years before I came home to my family in Arizona. What I learned is to get over the hurtful pain. Now I have a new family and friends. That is what has helped me.

"The best medicine is listening, love, compassion, laughter, and play."
~ Dr. Patch Adams

Our Adoption of Katya and Vitaliy
By Pam, Katie Flake's mom, September 2008
Snowflake, Arizona

Meeting the Boys
Finally, in June of 2005, our applications were all approved and we got our visas and passports, and were allowed to go to Kazakhstan to see Katya again and meet our new son. We were met at the airport by the woman who had helped us every step of the way from Kazakhstan, Marina. The next day, we were taken to Kolenshak Orphanage. After a few minutes, they brought in some little boys who came up to us and started singing for us. We realized that these were the little boys we were to decide about. Two of the boys were healthy looking, and very sweet, but there was one boy that caught our attention. He was very pale and thin, so skinny that I thought to myself, *He could crawl through a knothole if he wanted.* We were introduced to the three little boys. Vitaliy was the second one; he was more withdrawn than the other boys. After sharing some of his history with us, Marina told us we had to choose which little boy we were to adopt. She said it was time for us to go see Katya, and that we were to think about which boy to adopt and decide for the next day.

Reuniting With Katya
That afternoon it was time to get Katya. Her orphanage was about a twenty-minute drive away from the first one we visited. (There are some twenty orphanages in Karaganda.) When we went to Katya's orphanage, there were several minutes of formalities, and I found myself wringing my hands during this time. We had been waiting for two years since she had visited us for the summer program, and I was frantic to see her again. Finally, we followed the workers through corridors and around corners, holding our breath, until all of a sudden, there she was! Katya and I threw ourselves into each other's arms, and just knelt there and cried for a while. Shon, my husband, then swept her up into his arms, and it felt so good to see them together that way. She was giggling with delight as he tossed her up in the air, and she kept saying, "You came! You came!" We just stood there, crying out of joy to have our sweet Katya in our arms again, finally.

Then we spent a wonderful evening together, with Katya eating, and eating, and then eating some more. (Apparently, all they had to eat in the orphanages was very thin soup made with vegetables, and occasionally with meat, when they could get it, and rice and bread.) Katya slept in the top bunk, right by our bed, and she just kept looking at us over the top of her bed. Every couple of minutes she would reach down to us, I think to confirm that we were real.

We had another night with very little sleep, though, because we agonized over which little boy to adopt. Whatever decision we made would mean that we would have to leave two little boys behind. We prayed all that night so that we could know which little boy to choose. Every time I closed my eyes, Vitaliy's sweet little face was right there in my mind. By the next morning, we knew which little boy we wanted in our family, and we couldn't wait to go and get him the next day.

A Month Together in Kazakhstan

The four of us lived in an apartment in Karaganda together for a month, where we all got to know each other better. We made many friends while there, and enjoyed learning about Kazakhstan and the heritage that our new kids came from. We went to court at the end of that month, where the judge asked us many questions. Finally, she approved the adoption, which meant that Katya and Vitaliy were officially joined to our family.

Shon and I had to leave them while we went back to America, though. Their visas and passports couldn't be applied for until after the adoptions were finalized, and it wasn't possible for us to stay the additional month that would be required for that process. We just couldn't bear to let them go back to their orphanages, however, so we made arrangements for them to stay with Marina in her apartment. It tore us up to leave them behind, and we counted down the days to when we could have them in our home. Again, we prayed every day.

Bringing the Kids Home

In August, Shon headed back to Kazakhstan by himself to pick up the kids. He thought he might have to stay for a week, but when he arrived, Marina told him she had been able to get their paperwork ready. She had brought Katya and Vitaliy to the airport, and they were eager to go, so Shon changed tickets so that they could leave on the next flight! They headed out and flew for a day and a half to get from Almaty to Phoenix.

After the long flights, Shon, Katya, and Vitaliy walked into the airport in Phoenix. We were all there to greet them: Grandma Beecroft, all of our other children (Daliah, Jewel, Shiloh, NaElle, Jayze, Noah, Levi, Molly, and McKay), and I, all waiting at the airport with banners saying, "Welcome Home!" They were a happy but exhausted group that we hugged and kissed.

It has been amazing watching these two children grow physically, spiritually, emotionally, and socially. How grateful we are to have these two wonderful children in our home. We are blessed!

American Names
By Pam, September 2008
Snowflake, Arizona

The week after Katya and Vitaliy got home, Katya wanted us to start calling her by her American name, Katie. Vitaliy then wanted us to call him by the American name we had chosen for him. I had been reading the biography of Abraham Lincoln while we were in Kazakhstan, and so we had decided to name him after "Honest Abe." So his American name became Abe, and he has been Abe ever since.

Metamorphosis
By Shon, dad of 11, September 2008
Snowflake, Arizona

Katie and Abe are such a major part of our lives now that we have a hard time sometimes remembering when that wasn't so. They're so intertwined into the fabric of our existence now that they are just naturally included in just about everything we plan or do, from family vacations or camping trips to preparing meals to parent/teacher conferences to counting noses as we all pile into the van to go somewhere.

Back when their names were Katya and Vitaliy, though, we were so new to each other that their habits and dispositions included traits that were totally foreign to us. Katya, for example, had been an only child until she was almost seven years old, when her birth mother passed away. Just three months later, she came to stay in our home for three weeks. The language barrier, of course, hindered our communication, but beyond that was the fact that we didn't understand what was going on inside her head, either. We didn't know about her mother at that point, so the sad little girl who smiled only rarely, and who hoarded just about everything she was given, was a real enigma to us.

Even two years later, though, after the adoptions had taken place and Katya became Katie, we still had a lot of obstacles to overcome. In our rather large family, none of our other kids had ever had the chance to be an only child. (Even our oldest daughter was joined by a sister when she was only thirteen months old, so she doesn't even remember what it was like to "fly solo!") It's not that Katie was trying to be mean or selfish – far from it. She's always been a sweet little girl. However, she just wasn't used to thinking of others' needs as important. Saving a piece of dessert for the brother who wasn't going to get home from work until dinner was over, for example, or picking up her sister's side of the bedroom as a kind gesture because of excessive homework that night, were simply ideas that didn't occur to her. We've had many occasions to ask her to consider how she'd feel if the situations were reversed.

Katie has certainly worked hard on this, however. Just a few weeks ago she came home from school and related an incident to her mother that made us realize just how far she's come in this area. A boy at school had said some unkind things to a girl Katie knew, and didn't seem to be repentant about it. Katie confronted him – all four foot eight inches of her, and demanded that he consider how he'd feel "if someone said things like that to you!" She's now an enthusiastic participant in spontaneous acts of kindness, and one of her favorite pastimes is helping to babysit her younger cousins, who love her. (And, just in case you don't remember from your own pre-teen years, babysitting is *not* an activity that can be done well if it is done selfishly!)

Vitaliy's metamorphosis into Abe has been in different areas, however. Until he came to us, he'd lived all of his seven years in orphanages. As he has told us about his previous life, we've gotten the definite impression that he was near the bottom of the pecking order among the children he lived with, and that even the meager rice and soup rations he was allotted were frequently plundered by bigger and stronger kids. His little pinched face and skinny body had us convinced that he was liable to need some major medical attention once we got him home. When I held his hands, I could feel each bone, like they were fragile bird bones, and I felt like I had to take care not to accidentally break any.

During our month-long "bonding time," while we stayed in Kazakhstan, we tried to take advantage of the warm summer weather to get outside every day. It wasn't long before we realized that this was a brand new experience for Vitaliy – he was fascinated by just about *everything*. He'd squat down and study ants and other bugs in the dirt, and go loopy trying to chase butterflies and grasshoppers, but *never* catch them. (He liked to look, but touching was too much!) There was a small playground near our building that included a little slide about three feet tall. He absolutely *loved* it – but not if one of us wasn't there to hold his hand. He had a terrible fear of heights (even heights that weren't as high as he was tall), but also a fascination with them. Swings? There were only two that worked, and if there hadn't been other kids who wanted to use them, and if his pusher (me) had been able to keep going (he had no clue how to "pump" himself), I'll bet he'd still be there!

(Later, after he learned to speak English, we asked how often he and his group got to go outside. The answer? They didn't. They mostly just watched lots and lots of television.)

Just about three weeks after we'd met our new children, Pam and I took Katya and Vitaliy to a community swimming facility. They had a large wading pool with fountains and small waterslides for little kids. (There were also huge waterslides, but we stayed away from those.) Vitaliy had obviously never seen the like before! Marina, our adoption facilitator, had provided some arm floaties for him to use, so even if he'd accidentally fallen in over his head he'd have been okay, but there was zero chance of that. He spent just about the entire time running around the sides, wanting desperately to climb in and join the fun, but scared to death of something that was obviously totally alien to him. At one point I picked him up and carried him out into the water, reasoning that if he could get into it, he'd see for himself how fun it could be. He nearly strangled me out of fear that he might fall – there was amazing strength in those pipestem arms! I never came anywhere close to putting him down, even though the water didn't even come up to my knees. He tried dabbling his toes in from time to time, but I don't think his knees ever got wet.

Now? What a change! The little fearful boy who didn't dare climb three feet now has fun ascending into the rafters of our barn. The other day we went fishing, so Abe went out and caught grasshoppers for bait. He has diligently tried to exterminate several red ant colonies in our yard, and although he hasn't been successful (We won't let him have chemical pesticides.), it's not for lack of digging. And, although we haven't spent enough time in pools to give him enough experience to learn how to swim, he does now venture away from the sides. We knew we had a determined little boy that first time we saw him at the pool, when we noticed that he wouldn't quit trying to overcome his fears and take part.

And, by the way, he's as healthy as a horse. All he needed was food! In fact, instead of the wan, ailing lad we thought we were getting, we actually have a very active, even hyperactive, boy who can do push-ups, run around the block, and do the same chores and tasks as any of our other children.

CHAPTER ELEVEN

Hurdles, Challenges, and Trust Issues

"Success requires three bones –
a wishbone, a backbone, and a funny bone."
~Kobi Yamada

Reuniting Brothers
By B.J., February 2008
California

We adopted two boys from Russia; half brothers, they had been apart for three years in separate orphanages. They had been separated from the time our younger son was four months old and his older brother was about four years old. We were lucky enough to get them at three and a half and seven and a half years old. Unfortunately, we know of some difficult things our older son had to endure at the children's home or *dyetsky dom* which has no doubt had a profound effect on his ability to let people in and take care of him.

At the ripe old age of seven, when we were only home a couple of months, this poor child came down with a fever as kids sometimes do. He absolutely would not let me near him to nurture or care for him. He wanted to do it himself. I felt compelled to step in, but also did not want to disturb this child's sense of capability, so I made myself available, and watched him, but gave him space as well.

Another two months passed and he needed some major dental work (I mean *major* – five root canals, six crowns, three fillings, and one extraction). It took a good two weeks for him to settle in to his new teeth and that came with a lot of discomfort and fever as well. This time things were a little different. He allowed me to rub his back; he lay in my lap; he let me put a cool compress on the back of his neck. He was starting to trust me.

Even now, a full two and a half years later, while he now willingly hugs me tightly around the middle every night before bed, there is still some mild distance he keeps. But about six months ago on a snuggly Sunday, we were all in bed (six of us, including the two doggies), and a random tickle-fest broke out. Out of the blue, his guard went down, and he just hugged me tightly and said, "I love you, Mom." It was the first time in the two years he'd been my son that he actually said it. In fact, it was the only time. But knowing from whence he came and how difficult it has been for him to let down his guard, those words spoke volumes.

I realized our kids adore us even if they don't feel comfortable or know how to show us. They love us as we love them. Never ever forget that. As a mom I longed to hear it from him, but never forced it – and knowing how randomly it came, it was all that much more authentic and meaningful.

So, I guess the point of sharing this story is that we, as parents, want to know our kids love us – we want to hear it. At least I did. And if he never says it again, I'll always know. It was truly a lesson for me that what is said isn't always about me – it's about them – and while his words gave me great comfort, if he never says it again, I'll still know.

The Complexities of Saying Good-bye
By Teresa, December 1997
St. Petersburg, Russia

This afternoon we took gifts to the orphanage and finished saying our good-byes. Sergei's best little friend, Misha (also almost four years old), hugged and kissed him; they smiled and said good-bye. So sweet – it's doubtful they have any comprehension of the permanency of their words. Sergei called each of his caregivers by name and told them good-bye. He even sang a prayer with the orphanage director so we would have it on tape. Lots of tears and many thanks were shared. Sergei had a very special care-taker at the orphanage; he called her Mama Zoya. She was so delighted for him to be adopted, and at the same time she must have been heartbroken. She and her husband had considered adopting Sergei at one time, but realized sadly that they couldn't afford it and that even if they adopted him, he would have a tough future here in Russia. We left in the van, possibly Sergei's first time outside at night.

The First Day Home with My Family
By Paul Z., age 17, March 2008
Taylor, Arizona

When I came to my new house I thought that they were going to be mean because other people in Bulgaria had been mean to me. When I first moved in with them, it was hard because I did not know them and I did not know what they were going to be like. When I walked in the door with my new dad and mom that first afternoon we were together, I had lots of brothers and sisters. Most of them were married with kids. They talked to me and welcomed me into the home. Yevet, my new mom, showed me around the house. She showed me my bedroom, and then it was time for dinner.

That first night at the dinner table I was scared because my dad was very strict and so was my mom. They said, "We have manners and we expect you to use them, too." They said that if we talked about rude things, then we would have to go outside and eat. If we ate before our dad said to go ahead then we would have to leave our food on the table and go outside until we were called back in. Then we would finish our food…if we were civilized! That night my manners were good, and I didn't have to leave the table. As a matter of fact, I've never had to leave the table. Their rules at the table seemed strict at first, but now I understand that they helped us all to behave.

At the dinner table that night they asked me questions. When they asked me how I was treated in Bulgaria, I did not want to tell them because I thought that they would mock me. I did tell them, though, what it was like to live there, and I also told them how I was treated. It was hard for me to talk about it, but I did so they would know what my experiences were. After they got to know me a little bit that night, then we did some chores in the house to make sure it was clean, and then we went to bed. That night when I went to bed, I hoped that I would be safe in my new family.

Caught Red-Handed With the Green
By B.J., October 2007
California

Zackary and Alek, both adopted, keep track of who has what birthday party to attend (which really drives me batty), and yesterday was no exception. Zack has very few orphanage behaviors he still exhibits, but one reared its nasty little head yesterday.

We're working very hard to instill in the boys a sense of responsibility and pride in their things. To that end we don't just go out and buy them something new when they break a toy by playing with it inappropriately, or by just not taking care of it. Yet they want and want (as children do). One of many things we have *not* broken down and purchased as of yet is a video game set. First, all Zack would do is play with it, and second, we don't believe they've earned it yet. So, Zack had a bowling party yesterday for a school friend. He asked if he could bring a few dollars to play video games. I said, "No." "No" because he was there to play with his friend and bowl, not go off and play video games. He got upset but accepted the decision.

As we were readying to leave yesterday, though, I popped back into my room to get my shoes, and there stood Zack – Dad's wallet in one hand, dollar bill in the other. BUSTED!

He first told me he was bringing the dollar to his dad. I looked at him thinking, "You must really think I'm empty headed." But then he went and told his dad that he'd taken a dollar. We told him all he had to do was ask, but that we'd already explained he was not going to the party to play video games.

So, as we finally readied ourselves to go, I asked Zack to empty his pockets as he was not to have any money on him and we had a trust issue now. He said, "No," so I told him I'd check his pockets for him.

He rolled his eyes and said slowly, "Ooooo, Kaaayyyyy" and proceeded to pull another dollar out of his pocket. Off to Daddy we went for yet another confession. I was livid. Rick and I had looked at each other the first time and admitted we didn't know what to do...then this. Then Rick mentioned that his quarters have been dwindling. At first Zack swore up and down that he had nothing to do with it. I asked him to look me in the eye and say that and, sure enough, he admitted to taking Rick's quarters. At that point I said, "Your trust is pretty much in the toilet now, Bud. You're getting searched." He started to protest, but I was too quick and I found... YUP! A THIRD DOLLAR IN HIS @#$*^ pocket!

After lots of talking, Rick and I decided to let him go to his party. Once we collected ourselves we realized that had we kept him home he'd have been focused on how angry he was at us for keeping him home from the party and not the reason why. We decided to do two things that would hit him where it hurts – his integrity. First, when we got to the party – late – I made him tell his friend's mother why he was late. (He had to tell her he was caught stealing money from his dad.) Second, after the party, I made a stop at the sheriff's station. Rick and I shared with Zack that when grown-ups steal they go to jail. Our goal as parents is to instill in our kiddos an understanding of respect not only for their things, but for others, as well as for the law. This topic – respect – is probably one of the most difficult lessons to teach. I really wanted Zack to understand the seriousness of his choice to take something knowing full well it was wrong. I wanted to let him to see the result of allowing his impulse to have the better of him. The deputy was kind enough to spend time with Zack and have a real heart-to-heart talk with him about the importance of the law.

Today was a better day – and we look forward to even more "better days." I know Zackary is being nine. I know he has more street smarts than most adults. But I also know Zack is a beautiful boy with a kind heart and a shining soul. Each day I see a glimpse of that soul and it lingers just a bit longer than the day before. Every day I rise, thankful on some level for the richness these boys bring to our lives. Some days we get frustrated, other days we might raise our voices, but the joy of watching these kids grow... there just aren't words.

(Note: I asked Zack if he would be OK with sharing this story. We talked about what he thinks might help another child who is new to America and who might be scared like he was when he first came here. He said he doesn't remember much about when he first arrived, but that he's glad he has food to eat. That was powerful. He also told me he'd be OK with sharing stories about him as long as it helps someone else. I'm glad about that because it shows he's learning empathy and that he has compassion for other children in the same situation.)

Handling Differences
By Patti, 2009
New York

As adopted kids get older, it's important to help them deal with seemingly incessant comments about differences. I've talked to friends and other adoptive parents who have had people comment inappropriately on their children's differences and challenges.

We agree that stares and questions from curious people have been the norm. The best way to handle staring seems to be to ignore it, and the best way to deal with questions is to give a brief response and move on. Most parents model positive reactions by calmly responding in a general way without sharing information of a personal nature. Then we change the topic. That works pretty well most of the time.

I know that most people make observations or ask questions "innocently." Kids are straightforward with their remarks; teens and adults are often awkward and uncomfortable. They don't mean to be abrupt or rude, but they sure can be insensitive! Most of the time, our kids are able to take unsolicited questions and comments in stride. When they get tired of people pointing out their differences, they sometimes find it best to ignore questions or say, "That's just the way it is," and keep moving.

It does seem particularly odd – and even annoying – that people ask personal questions of parents as if their children weren't standing right next to them. After all, why would someone ask *a parent* a question about *a teen* that is obviously old enough to answer for herself or himself? Some

S

people just don't "get it." Generally people mean well and their curiosity is natural, but it would be nice if they would *think* first before asking intrusive questions.

I remember an article I read some years back (written by a social worker, as I recall) in which it was mentioned that sometimes people need a reminder that just because a difference is visible does not mean it is "open season" to delve into someone else's personal matters. It's not rude at all for us or our kids to give a second or two of lag time before answering. It gives everyone a chance to think before the conversation continues. Most "offenders" realize very quickly that they may have overstepped their bounds. By reacting calmly we can help people realize that their curiosity is normal, but that they should "back off" before invading our children's personal space. If we remain composed, they can back off gracefully. And as parents, it's important for us to remember that whatever our reactions, our top priority must be to protect our children's needs and their privacy. If we can do so without making the situation difficult or awkward for our kids, so much the better. We can also deflect questions or change the subject when we can tell that our kids have had enough.

As time goes on, though, our children must determine the "just right" way to handle the inevitable questions. They are the ones who will handle people's remarks and inquiries over the long haul, and most kids with differences or obvious challenges have learned to be resilient and strong. Our son has weathered quite a few storms in his life. We know that he'll persevere and do well because he's like a salmon; though he is at times swimming upstream, he keeps on swimming! We are very proud of him.

A Big Bonding Challenge Meets "The Car Cure"
By Teresa, March 2008,
Snowflake, Arizona

For our first two months together after our three-year-old son came home to our family, he pushed me away, physically and emotionally. If others were around, our son did not want to have much to do with me, treating me the way I think he probably treated the caretakers at the orphanage. He came to me and told me when he was hungry, he asked me for toys or other items he wanted, he let me know when he needed the bathroom. He often ignored me or even told me to go away when anyone else was available to him. He even "commanded" me to do things for him!

It was frustrating, exasperating, and emotionally painful. There were many happy and positive times, too, but I sure didn't want to allow this hurtful behavior on his part to continue. I could feel myself getting frustrated to the point of feeling angry with him at times. And, of course, since he was three and I was forty-three, I determined I was the one who had the responsibility to initiate a positive change. I wanted to be his mommy, so I was ready to try any idea I could think of in order to make the bonding "click."

What our son finally responded to was what I call "The Car Cure." Every afternoon I got into the car with him, a picture book, and a snack. First we sat facing each other and talked for a few minutes. Then I read the book to him while he sat next to me and looked at the pictures. Next we ate our snack and talked about the pictures and story we had read. After that, we drove to the park to play or we stopped at the river to throw rocks into the water. After only three days of "The Car Cure," there was a remarkable difference in the way our son interacted with me. I was relieved and my spirits lifted.

From my journal, April 1998, three weeks after starting our car time: Paul Sergei and I still do our "talk-read-snack-play" time each day after I pick him up from the babysitter's house. Yesterday a cute event took place. I wanted to get home quickly to make a phone call, so I didn't make our usual stop on the way home. Sergei kept insisting, "Stop here. I want to talk! Stop the car!" I made my phone call and then we sat in the car – in the driveway – to have our special time alone together. He likes the one-on-one time, has been more affectionate with me, and is now spreading his time around more evenly among the four of us.

A note from March 2008:

The Car Cure was the key to beginning the bonding process that my son and I needed. We both loved our ritual and continued it for three months, until the end of that school year. I look back on those afternoons as the experience that helped us turn the corner in our mother-son relationship.

Last week – ten years later – my son and I went back to the wash. He didn't want to get out of the car when I parked near the wash. You know, at thirteen, it's not cool to throw rocks with your mom. But after a minute he joined me on the sandy beach beside the rocky bank. As I tossed a few rocks into the water, I mentioned to him about how we used to come throw rocks into the river when he was little. Before long, he was picking up flat rocks and skipping them expertly across the water. It was pretty neat to reflect on the ten years of life that had passed since our first visits to the wash.

When it was time to leave, just like ten years ago, he said, "Just a couple more, Mom. Watch this one!" Then he added, "I'll skip it all the way across. Look!" A few seconds later, he continued his plea, "Wait! Just one more before we go. This will be the best." When we got back into the car, we agreed that our visit to the wash had been fairly entertaining. We talked about how we both looked forward to skipping rocks again when we would go camping at the lake over Spring Break the following week. The car + the book + the snacks + conversation + the rocks = quality time together for us – ten years ago and now.

The Whole Truth
By B.J., May 2007
California

We've waxed and waned on behavior issues, and most recently Zack got written up for lying at school. He was just playing around, but he got caught red-handed by the Play Yard Supervisor in a lie. As trust is a critical lesson we've been working on, when I got the message that his teacher had called, I knew something was up. I turned to him and asked him how his day was at school...

"Why?" he said a little too defensively.

I next asked him if something happened that day at school.

"*What*?!" he responded as his eyes fell quickly to the floor. At this point I knew something was up. I asked him if he deserved the treats he'd already received that day. Still holding his gaze to the floor he muttered, "Nooooo..."

I told him I was giving him an opportunity to tell me what happened that day at school before I returned his teacher's call. He pretty much 'fessed up to everything, and then added that he lied to the Play Yard Supervisor because he was afraid he'd get in big trouble. I explained that while he'd be in trouble either way, he would have been better off had he come clean from the get-go. He probably would not have been written up at school, and probably would not have lost his swim date the following Saturday. He broke his gaze with the floor and looked at me with eyes the size of saucers. I didn't say anything, and then he burst into tears. The thing that totally amazed me was how completely calm and unthreatening I was handling this. I asked him if he thought he deserved to go to a swim date and he said tearfully, "No." I explained that I understood that he was afraid to get into trouble, but that the situation was made worse when he wasn't up-front with me. Had he explained what had happened before accepting treats, we could have worked it out together and perhaps had a less drastic consequence. We possibly could have salvaged his swim date with his friend, too. He understood, and it was a great opportunity to have a valuable conversation about this very important issue.

Trust had been a little shaken, but it gave me an opportunity to confront the issue with him in a non-threatening way, let him know his behavior was not OK, but that his dad and I were always there for him – through good decisions and not-so-good decisions. We are teaching that the punishment is more a conscience-related consequence and not physical. Physical punishment may have been all he knew in his prior life. It is probably the most valuable lesson, in my opinion, that a child can learn. Those who strike their kids don't teach them anything about honor, character, or integrity. What a tremendous opportunity we gained together by sharing this circumstance.

The Hurtful Memory
By Gina, 2008
Adopted in Arizona as an infant

My much, much older sister, who was not adopted, has always complained that she was never spoiled like me. I admit it. I came along at the right time in my parents' lives. I was spoiled and I loved it! I miss it.

My college days were in the sixties: Vietnam, Flower Power, and Hippies! I was a "wanna be" hippie for about a minute. I came home one weekend with a long dress on, sandals, and flowers in my hair. It didn't last long because soon I was into something else.

Many years later, in a "Do you remember when…?" conversation with my sister, we talked about the "hippie" weekend. She said, "You really upset Mom and Dad. Dad asked me if I thought he should disown you." I don't remember anything that was said after that. Disown? A knife in my heart!

How could this father – who taught me how to ride a bike, a horse, and how to drive a car, who was always there when I needed a shoulder, and who always made me feel like I was the light of his life – not want me?

Over the years, my sister has said other hurtful things, referring to my being the adopted daughter. It has taken me some time, but I now realize that she was just jealous. My dad would never disown me. His whole life was spent showing me how much he loved me, as was my mother's.

My sister is now in her eighties, and I enjoy visiting her and spoiling her as much as possible. Several times now she has told me how glad she is that I am her sister. It only took me sixty years to hear that!

Adoption and Race Issues
By Christie, mom of 12, 2007
Oregon

Race for most people is a subject on talk radio or a protest carried out by someone else. Race for us is a two-sided coin. On one side, it's a little girl's dark skin shining in the sun next to her bright yellow sundress or a little boy's beautiful black hair that, when the rain catches the tip of each corkscrew curl, makes his whole head shine like glitter. Our family photo at Christmas is so rich in color! Yet on the other side of the coin, race is prickly, like walking barefoot on gravel or reaching a road with two turns and not knowing which way to go.

In our hallway hangs a piece of art (one of the few on our walls not made of crayon and colored paper) framed in wood under soft-glazed glass. It is a picture of four intertwined hands, one white, one tanned, one brown, and one black, all holding each other, strongly, together.

I have to admit there are many sides of racism I never knew or could have understood without my black children. Now I truly understand why ignorance is such a huge part of what we fight. Why can't we just live together equally, like the hands in the picture?

CHAPTER TWELVE

Lessons Learned and Giving Back

"A child needs love most when he deserves it the least."
~ Erma Bombeck

Learning Charity
By B.J., January 2008
California

Back in September we celebrated the High Holy days (Jewish New Year and Yom Kippur). *Tsedakah* is Hebrew for *charity* and is a big theme in Judaism, particularly during this time of year. Our Temple collects all sorts of canned goods and donates them to the local food pantry for those in need. They provided a kids' service, and one of their projects was a Tsedakah box to collect money for charity. Zack, now nine, is very money-oriented these days, and not in a giving way – more like in a taking way. Anyway, Zack was able to get some loose change for the Tsedakah box and decided his "charity" was himself!

Zack felt that no TV for a week was a good punishment for his behavior. He came up with that, and we accepted it as a consequence, telling him we would get back with him about an appropriate punishment for stealing. After much thought and conferring with our life coach/counselor, we decided that for a time, Zack needed to be removed from anything monetary. No allowance for a while, and nothing to do with raising money. Consequently, he would be unable to participate in his school's fundraiser. He cried and was really upset initially, but if he learns that he may not steal from *anyone* then it's all worth it, and the pouting, the crying, and the tantrums will all be for a greater good. It's so important that we nip this behavior in the bud.

We're being really careful, though, to ensure the punishment fits the crime. I think one of the biggest errors some parents make is trying to take away everything because it makes *us* feel better to take away from a child who is being ungrateful. But what does the child learn if a parent is only acting in the interest of making himself or herself feel better? It's a fine line to walk, so Rick and I are working hard to be sure we're being consistent and making discipline decisions that fit the offense. We don't want to overdo it. In talking with other parents of nine-year-olds, I found out that this is a learning thing, too, and that stealing is not so uncommon for this age group. There could also be some latent hoarding behavior from his previous life, but I'm not so convinced it's that. We are being careful to keep everything else the same: we play, we laugh, we work on homework together, and we read. I'm working really hard to make certain my attitude with him is consistent, and that I continue hugging him (which he now lets me do at will) and letting him know I love him.

Now, months later, when a behavior issue comes up and we remove a privilege, the upset is short lived. If Zack complains, we need only ask him if he knows why he's being deprived and he stops for a second, looks down, and then says, "Yes." He's actually quite good-natured about it, considering. He's taking it well, and what is amazing is that he seems to be getting it.

Today I went to his school for my regular volunteer work and stopped by the cafeteria to speak with the woman who runs it. There is a "red cart" there where kids can buy snack items. Part of taking away Zack's privileges included not being able to buy from the red cart. In fact, he told us that buying snacks from the red cart was his reason for stealing change in the first place.

Rick and I have both done some major soul-searching in this area and it has helped us with our patience and in keeping our calm. We realized that getting upset tended to soothe us more than anything, but it wasn't doing the boys any good. Remaining calm has been a nice change and the boys have shown a change as well. When we show them respect, they'll start understanding its importance and will show it back to us, and others. All the same, kids will be kids, and we know that. We understand more and more that five- and nine-year-old boys will be five- and nine-year-old boys. We don't want to overreact and we look forward to having more adventures with our boys.

Coming Home Day
By Teresa, 2009
Snowflake, Arizona

I've always liked the name we chose to celebrate the anniversary of our son's arrival to his new home and family. It has a cozy ring to it. Everybody likes coming home to a place of warmth, comfort and love. We revisit that day every December.

On Coming Home Day we eat Russian food, watch the video of the first time we saw our son (and brother), look at photo albums from our trip to Russia, and reminisce about our early days together. Those were some crazy times! Our little whirling dervish settled down, fortunately, within the first several months home. Trust me, there were some days when I thought he never would.

For our first Coming Home Day celebration we had borsch made with fresh beets, exactly the way Natasha had prepared it. We complemented the traditional soup with black bread, cheese, tomatoes and cucumbers – *ah-goor-ETTS* in Russian – I love the sound of that word. For some reason it fits the vegetable it names better than the word in English. Of course there was sour cream as a garnish for the vegetables and plenty more to drop by dollops into the steaming bowls of borsch. We talked at the table about how Paul, then Seriozha, ate and ate and **ate** when we had shared the same meal in Moscow with Roald and Natasha.

Coming Home Day has evolved for us a bit over the years. When Cousin Sergei joined the Big Smith Crew, we gathered for a larger celebration with twenty or so members of the extended family. The menu expanded, too; we were introduced to pelmeni (meat dumplings) and enjoyed authentic Russian sausage in addition to borsch, bread and cheese. The Russian cousins boasted about their heritage over the meal – before they took off to play international war games in the back yard and to tussle with their cousins on the trampoline.

Now it's time for a new Coming Home Day celebration. Lilya joined the ranks last Halloween. We'll have to determine just how the three will want to carry on the Coming Home Day tradition. They're all old enough to have their say. And they're all thoroughly modern. It will be fascinating to see what ideas they come up with. If I had to guess, I would say it is likely to include Facebook, e-mail, and texting in the planning stages and possibly some video games and iPods in the celebration. I hope that we moms can convince the kids that the traditional and familiar Coming Home Day menu still has its place in their diet.

Game Boys

The Eyes Have It
By Tina, 2000
Texas

During our preparations for travel to bring our son home, I expressed concern to my sister about my graying hair. I wondered aloud to her if I should dye it before we left for Russia. I thought my silver locks might give the impression that we were too old to adopt. My sister said, "Leave your hair alone; they'll see the sparkle in your eyes."

Approximately six weeks later, we were in St. Petersburg at the Adoption Center (the office where a panel of people gives the final "thumbs up" or "thumbs down" to prospective adoptive parents before the actual court date). After we had been talking to the members of the Adoption Center group for about five minutes, the director of the team, Ludmila, turned and commented to our adoption coordinator, "This little boy will do fine with them; they have kind eyes."

Colorblind
By Christy, mom of 12, 2007
Oregon

Somehow our children grew up colorblind – or at least with their own definitions of race and color. They refer to themselves as brown, tan, and caramel; they also don't seem to have any grasp of how others might perceive them and their siblings as not looking the same. They don't live life as if every wall has a mirror. They think of their brothers and sisters simply as one family, which happens to have lots of kids.

They even have an acceptance among themselves that race is not a politically incorrect subject. They joke about tanning, about being colored rich like dark chocolate, about my Caucasian daughter dating African-American boys. There just don't seem to be *prickly* feelings about race inside our walls. For example, one day our nine-year-old son heard us talking about the upcoming delivery of Jason and Alyssa's second child, a little girl. He excitedly reaffirmed, "So, it's definitely going to be a little girl?" I confirmed this. He then asked, "So, what color is she going to be?" "She'll be white," I told him, to which he responded, "Oh, too bad. The black babies are even cuter!" I think it's fascinating that he didn't correlate Jason and Alyssa's color to the ultimate color of their baby's skin.

Extending Relationships and Friendships through Adoption
By Sheryl, 2009
Illinois

One of the things that I have found amazing in the process of adoption has been the relationships that have formed. It turns out that Claudia had a godmother in Iowa, only three hours away from us. Her godmother, Katie, was a missionary from here in the U.S. who went to the orphanage many times to help with children and to visit Claudia. Katie had first met Claudia when she was only two months old. She had taken pictures of Claudia as a baby and toddler because she knew that someday a mommy and daddy would love to have these pictures. She was right! I can't thank her enough for foreseeing our needs. It is an amazing gift to have photos of Claudia from throughout her early years. We have a special relationship with Katie and will always have her in Claudia's life.

Several other families have adopted some of Claudia's best friends from the same orphanage. From Seattle to Texas to Chicago and in rural Illinois, we have found new friends and family because of the relationship that Claudia and her girlfriends have. It is really a blessing to have these friends of Claudia's and their families in our lives.

Unintentional Hurts
By Jenny, 2009
Taylor, Arizona

I would have to say that the most challenging issue to deal with in adoption is that sometimes children and even adults say things to adopted kids that may hurt their feelings. I've experienced this situation from both sides.

When I was young, before I even had children, I knew a lady who adopted children and then later had two biological children. One day in the store, very innocently, I asked her, "Which ones are yours?" I had no intention of hurting her or her children's feelings; I just didn't know the right words to use. In response she said, "They're all my children," and I immediately realized my mistake. Of course I knew they were all her children and all were equal, and I felt bad, but there wasn't anything I could do at that point to change my words.

Years later, after my husband and I had adopted kids, I began to understand more fully. I have now been in the opposite situation when people have said similar things to me or to my daughters. I don't want my daughters to feel sad when people ask questions that can be misinterpreted. When it happens, I just want the words to go away.

Fortunately, my girls are very strong and they always deal with comments or awkward situations very well. Life is hard for all kids; I'm proud of my girls for being strong and positive about adoption and for letting people know what a great thing it is. They explain to others what we have as a family. If I could say anything to people who haven't been involved in adoption, I would tell them that I am glad my family came together the way it did and that adoption should be experienced by everyone.

Nothing but the Truth
By Tom, January 2008
New York

Adopting an older child from Russia presents some interesting contradictions. Older children know things, they are mature, and they can remember events accurately, but they don't speak English well enough to explain many of the thoughts and feelings they have. A few months after we adopted Galya, we were driving around doing errands with Galya, and Gal in her new English said, "There is Mommy's doctor's office!"

Imagine how proud I was of my little girl, speaking in English, remembering where she had been, and telling me about the visit to the doctor's office. But what she was pointing at was not the doctor's office; it was the Town Court Office of Tonawanda, New York, a suburb of Buffalo. I said, "Honey, that is not the doctor's office. It's Court. You know, like the place we went with you in Russia, where the lady there made us sign all the papers after you left the orphanage."

She looked at me in the quizzical way that I had seen so many times before. In her head she knew but she couldn't explain. And my wife was looking out the window not saying a word.

"Leslie," I asked, "did you bring Galya to Court?" Silence.

Then Galya was emphatically telling me, "Daddy that is the *doctor's* office. Mommy told me it was." OK, here was my dilemma: did Galya have things confused, or did my wife get yet another speeding ticket?

"Leslie, did you tell Gal that traffic court was the doctor's office?" I asked, and I saw the silent nod while she studied the curb. Now what? Well, I told Gal that mommy went to a very *special* doctor. My wife knew all too well how I felt about her driving.

Galya is a couple of years older now, her English has a Buffalo accent, and she definitely can't be told anything that she knows is not true. Not anything, no matter what. This is the gift of adopting older children: the lighting-quick process they use to become who they are, and the fact that you make it possible.

Giving Back
By Sandy, 2008
Louisiana

Our Russian adoption story does not end with the arrival of Misha at our home in Louisiana when he was three and a half years old. We are forever connected to his *babushka* and his brother, Evgeniy, who reside in Russia.

While we were in Russia, we became very close to our translator and the lady known as his babushka, who gave Misha extra care after he arrived in the orphanage. We decided that, through these contacts, we wanted to give back to Misha's orphanage by raising money to provide a fabulous Christmas for them. So we created a hot chocolate stand in front of our house during the Christmas season. That's all it took!

We began receiving phone calls from people wanting to donate to our fund for the orphanage. In the first year, we raised $7,000! After speaking with Babushka, we wired her the money to buy food (so all of the children's stomachs would be full), medicine, toys, and any other needs they had in order to spread the Christmas cheer.

The second year our hot chocolate stand earned profits of $14,000! Babushka hired contractors in Russia to design and build a play center outside for the children that Misha once played with. They love it!

We have had several angels on our side since the beginning of our adoption process. We knew that we didn't want our experience to end with simply having Misha in our lives. We wanted to continue to help the children at his orphanage and his brother.

We are forever indebted to the Russian people for allowing us to have Misha in our family and also to all of those who have donated money for the benefit of the orphanage.

Misha's Story Continues
By Sandy, 2008
Louisiana

Through the assistance of two pro golfers from Russia and their father, we were able to find Misha's brother, Evgeniy, and communicate with him and his foster mother. Misha (seven years old) realizes that Evgeniy (eight years old) is his brother. Their first conversation began with Evgeniy telling Misha that he loved him in Russian and Misha repeating the same phrase to his brother in English. They stay in touch through Skype on the computer, and they see each other with a web camera. Also, our Russian golf sisters help us three-way call every couple of weeks.

Last year, we were successful in helping get Evgeniy, his foster mother, and his babushka visas to come to Louisiana and visit Misha. That reunion was the first time the brothers had seen one another in two years. It was quite the homecoming!

It was one of the most incredible experiences we have been through. They said they had literally been pulled apart from each other when they were younger. So to see them reunited was awesome! We had Evgeniy's foster mom, sister, and our translator, whom we befriended in Russia, visiting us.

During their visit, we did everything you can imagine in the days we were together. We swam in the back yard every day, went to the zoo, explored the Children's Museum, visited the Duck Camp, went fishing, and did skeet shooting. Then we went down to the beach condo on the Gulf Coast and went boating. We had some excitement, with dolphins almost jumping into the boat, and there was even a manta ray on the water one day. It just kept getting better and better! It was a lot of fun for a boy, who up until this time, had not been out of a five-block radius from his home.

Evgeniy and Misha played together nonstop: Legos, skate boarding, jumping on the trampoline, and on and on. They held hands as they walked along, and even planted a cheek kiss a time or two. They sat together every night and put their arms around each other. It was these tender times that just tore our hearts out!

Evgeniy warmed up to my husband David so much; he would light up when David walked in the door after work, wanting to play and play. He had never had a man in his life before. Evgeniy's foster mom said she had never seen him come out of his shell like he did around us.

After spending time with us, Evgeniy's foster mom made an incredibly unselfish decision. She came up with the following idea: she would like to terminate her rights and allow us to adopt Evgeniy so that the brothers can be together. We were terribly excited to hear this; it was an answered prayer. However, since Evgeniy is almost nine years old, we feel it must be his decision. The only life and security he has ever known are with his foster mom. For now, he is torn. In time he will be able to make that decision, but we will all be patient and put it in God's hands. We do know one thing for sure. We love him so much, and he will always be part of our family.

Childhood Memory Gives an Insight
By Jenny, February 2009
Taylor, Arizona

Once when I was a child, my sister and I had an argument. Jokingly, my sister told me that I had been adopted. Well, I knew it wasn't true, but her words went straight to my heart. Aside from years of information from my parents to the contrary, it was also a fact that my sister and I looked almost exactly alike. And yet I clearly remember that in that split second after hearing my sister's words – "You're adopted," – I wondered about it. Those words set me back into deep thought for a brief moment but one that had a big impact. In that split second I had questions and doubts. That experience left quite an impression on me.

Years later my husband and I adopted. I have thought back to that time when my sister told me that I was adopted and how it made me feel to hear it. In a small way, I think the questions and doubts I felt then helped me understand the feelings that some adoptees might have. I think God was preparing me for the future. That experience was God's way of helping me understand my daughters.

A Blast to the Past
By Teresa, March 2008
Snowflake, Arizona

Yesterday was an eye-opener. My husband, our son, and I met Lori and Mark's newly adopted kids. They brought home their new children nine days ago: Lena Trinh, a nine-year-old, and her seven-year-old brother, Daniel Long. We walked into their dining area and suddenly I felt I was "back in time" ten years to when we brought our son home from Russia. Their new kids were buzzing around with total high energy, grabbing first one thing and then another. One project was begun and held one child's rapt attention for two minutes and then was abandoned suddenly for a new one. Insistent requests were made urgently in a language that no one understood. Pointing and gesticulating filled the air. "No...NO!" was repeated again and again as dangerous or fragile items were moved out of reach. "Let Mom do it," was used more than once as one and then the other child reached to grab a knife or to turn on stove burners. Everything was happening in fast motion, and all adults were focused on what the "new kids" were up to every second. Noise filled the air: TV, pets, reminders, questions, conversations, calling of names to attempt to get the kids' attention, etc. were all taking place at once. Lori and Mark looked tired.

I distinctly remembered that feeling of exhaustion in the first weeks at home; for me, it had been sort of a busy "numbness." I thought back to ten years ago when our son came home; everything was moving at "warp speed," and our energy level didn't come close to meeting the immediate needs of the new child or the kids already in the family. One step at a time. One meal at a time. One day at a time. One nap at a time. Hanging on until the next level of language comprehension caught up with the next level of need and the next new experience.

Yes, being with Lori and Mark's family yesterday felt alarmingly similar to what it had been like in our home ten years ago when we brought our son home from Russia. And here we were, my husband, our son Paul, and I, at Mark and Lori's home to meet their new kids and to give them a break from Lena and Daniel for a few hours so they could rest and catch their breath.

After we ate a quick lunch and had a short visit, it was easy to see that the kids were comfortable enough with us to have us take them to the park. We loaded up in the car, quickly moving everything out of reach that the kids might grab and destroy. We hurriedly fastened seat belts, said quick good-byes to their mom and dad, settled in, and pulled out of the driveway.

Once at the park, the kids jabbered and played, ran and jumped, flew from the swings to the monkey bars to the jungle gym, giggling and speaking to us and to each other in Vietnamese without stopping, seeming to think that we could understand all that they were telling us. After an hour and a half we crossed the street to the lake, where we threw rocks in the water, played in the sand, and were too slow in chasing Daniel. Before we knew it, he was up to his ankles in the chilly March waters of the lake. We played only a few more minutes there, realizing that though he didn't express any discomfort, the little guy must be cold. We headed back to the car in two "waves," first my husband and Daniel, followed by the rest of us. We wrapped Daniel's feet in a warm jacket, buckled up, ate a snack, and drove for a while. Just as Lori had predicted, it was only a few minutes before the kids dozed off.

An hour later we took them home and popped in a DVD movie to watch while Lori and Mark finished their project (moving Mark's office upstairs out of harm's way). Another hour passed, our "respite care" stint was up, and Lori and Mark were back downstairs to join us. Big sister Anna was home from shopping with her friends, and there they were, all together again as a family. The kids, now rested, were busy – zooming, actually. Once again, both parents were actively involved, keeping an eye on the kids every second, helping them.

I could relate to their wonder, their joy, and their exhaustion. Our son remarked, "I was never THAT wild, was I?" We assured him that he *had* been that energetic. Those first weeks at home can be a crazy busy time. When we were in the middle of that intense post-adoption period of adjustment, I remember wondering if life would ever be on an even keel again. Yes, life does settle down fairly quickly for most, and yes, the family does find a "new normal."

Common Traits
By Ronda, November 2008
Snowflake, Arizona

I was adopted as an infant decades ago. After starting our family of biological children, my husband and I adopted a child. Later, I worked as a school secretary and made it sort of a hobby to keep an eye on children who were enrolled in the school who had been adopted. Over time, I began to see some characteristics and personality traits that adopted children had in common. The most noticeable was that they seemed to seek attention more than most children. If they could get it in a positive way, through sports, music, etc., they seemed to be happy and well-adjusted.

Ten Commandments for Adopting Families
By Pam, mom of nine bio kids and two adopted, 2008
Snowflake, Arizona

1. Thou shalt keep thy sense of humor through runny noses, lost lunch money, or even spilt grape juice on thy new carpet!

2. Thou shalt place no child before another. Thou shalt not choose favorites. All thy children shalt be treated equitably and fairly.

3. Thou shalt not take the name of thy children in vain, even if thy beloved ones have just broken thy kitchen window while throwing rocks at one another, even after thy thousandth lecture NOT to throw rocks!

4. Thou shalt be prepared for thy dentist bill, doctor bill, grocery bill, repair bill, and know that just about every other bill on this earth shall increase.

5. Remember to love thy children, through hours of homework, history projects, and last-minute reminders that thou wast to bring six dozen cupcakes to the class party in thirty minutes.

6. Thou shalt never say *never*.

7. Thou shalt expect the unexpected.

8. Thou shalt not covet thy children's love for their birth parents.

9. Thou shalt snuggle, hug, embrace and give endless affection, even when thy child has warned thee that the principal shall be calling thy home.

10. Remember, oh remember, thou shalt enjoy thy adventure.

A Practically Normal Life
By Jim, age 14, January 2009
Snowflake, Arizona

I was born in California and spent time pretty much right away in foster homes. I was adopted when I was two and fell in love with my family right away. My big sister Amber was sixteen when I came home. She babied me and carried me around like I was her baby boy. I don't think that I have been affected that much by my biological parents because I've been with my adoptive parents since I was so young. I don't remember my biological parents; I don't even remember knowing them. In fact, when I was three or four, I told everyone that I came from my mom's belly, and she played along.

Some people still don't think I could be adopted because I look a lot like my parents. When we moved here, we wouldn't tell new friends about being adopted when we first met them. Later, when they came over to our house, I told them I was adopted. They usually said, "No way! You look just like your parents." It's kind of funny because we still trick people occasionally and it's interesting seeing how people react.

Right now, as I'm getting older, I'm curious about my biological parents. I want to know what I'll be like when I grow up; I'd like to know how tall I'll be, for example. I'm planning to find them and get information. Even though I'm pretty sure they were drug addicts, I'm still curious about who I'm related to and who is in my family tree.

My family now is like all families; we have our ups and downs. We have each other to play with, talk to, and go to in times of trouble. My sister Amber still spoils me today. She invites me to come over to her house to spend the afternoon. We make treats and watch movies or something. I still have a special place in her heart, I guess.

Adoption for me has been a wonderful thing. It has let me have a practically normal life. I would like to adopt when I'm older because there are many kids out there who need that same chance, just to have a normal life.

CHAPTER THIRTEEN

Muriel's Stories

One hundred years from now, it will not matter
what kind of car I drove, what kind of house I lived in,
how much money I had in my bank account.
Nor what my clothes looked like.
But the world may be a little better because
I was important in the life of a child.

~ adapted from a poem
by Forest Witcraft

Little Ones to Care For
By Muriel, December 2008
Taylor, Arizona

In The Beginning

When I was growing up, my mom would always help someone in need. My grandma was the same, so I think that is why I always wanted to be a nurse. When Jim and I got married, I was planning to attend nursing school, but plans changed. We moved to Los Angeles in 1958 and had two babies. My second pregnancy and birth were difficult. We would have liked to have more children, but it wasn't an option.

A neighbor told me about the Bureau of Adoptions. It wasn't long before they began bringing us foster children. I had worked with them as a foster mom for about two years when I heard about the possibility of having a medical foster home. That was somewhat along the same lines as being a nurse, so I applied. I was approved and licensed to open a medical foster home that served infants to six-year-olds, all with major medical needs. Many were very ill or severely disabled, and some were not expected to live long. Some had been abused, so they were taken away from their parents. Others we just kept for short periods so their parents could have respite care.

When we started in 1969, we had two kids to a bedroom. Our own kids were ten and twelve years old at the time. The need was great for this kind of foster care, so as soon as a baby moved along, another was there almost immediately to fill the empty bed. There was always a waiting list. Back then it was fine to have a nursery with six to eight beds. They don't allow that anymore; now kids are placed in foster homes. Before long, we turned half of our house into a nursery and added an extra bathroom with a high tub so it was easier to bathe the babies.

Babies Galore – Our Daily Life

Our two biological kids, David and Jennifer Lynn, grew up seeing and helping with all the little ones that we took care of. My kids often took turns holding all the babies. Our son David treated the kids just like siblings. Jennifer Lynn helped with feeding, holding, and bathing the babies, but she didn't want to change diapers; that was my job!

We took babies with every kind of problem – no exceptions. We never turned down a baby. There never was a child that was hard for me to take care of. My motto was, "Bring that baby!" Once or twice we had to put in another crib just to make room for all the babies that needed our care. Most of them were newborns. I would get calls regularly to see if I had an opening. I think I might have been first on their lists to call because I rarely had a vacancy.

I took care of the babies twenty-four hours per day, seven days per week. I started my day at 5:00 a.m. Whether they were sick, crying, or just needed attention, I was up with all of them. There were some that had to be fed at night. Sometimes I'd sit in my rocker and sleep with the babies in my arms. My old rocking chair got a lot of use. If I got four hours of sleep at night, I was doing well. And this went on for years!

We just lived all as one family. When the kids were big enough to start school, there was a lot to do to get everyone ready. Everybody got along. There weren't very many times when everyone was crying all at once. But then, noise doesn't bother me a bit; I probably didn't even notice when it got loud.

I kept all the doctor appointments for all the children; sometimes there were three appointments a day in hospitals all over Los Angeles. If the kids needed surgeries we took them to LA County Hospital or Children's Hospital. If they needed heart surgery, they went to St. Vincent's Hospital. (Over the years, we had three children who needed open-heart surgery.) Once, I took Baby Vannia first to one hospital, and they told me they couldn't do anything to correct her shunt problems. I took her home, turned around, and took her to another hospital. The second hospital corrected the problem. I nursed her back to health, and that little child was adopted about a month later.

Over the years, I was trained by doctors to do many complex nursing procedures, and the doctors trusted me with the care of the children. I was able to change gastrostomy tubes or reinsert them if they came out of a baby's tummy. I routinely cleaned and bandaged wounds after surgeries. When a baby had a cleft palate, we fed him through an NG tube, a nose tube. A few children had cystic fibrosis. We helped drain their lungs by cupping our hands and pounding their backs to clear their chests. Sometimes we helped with physical therapy that different children needed. The babies needed various procedures, and the doctors trusted me with their care. That training by the doctors allowed me to help the babies without taking them to the doctor or to the hospital quite so often. Emergency workers got to know me over the years because of the times when I had to call for their help. They were supportive of our efforts and understood that some of the children and babies were at risk because of their serious medical conditions. And of course if there was ever something that I couldn't handle, I took the children to the hospital.

Social workers were welcome to show up any time. They never found any problems or anything wrong. I never had a bad report. I feel good about the fact that I had an absolutely clean record. I am proud that I always gave the best of my attention to every single child that was under my care.

When kids left us, they went to various places. Some went to other foster homes, some were able to go back to their parents, some ended up going to institutions for long-term care, and some were adopted. It was always so wonderful when the kids got adopted. I loved those babies; I would have adopted all of them if I could have.

Vacation – What's that?

One time, our older kids convinced us that we needed a vacation. Our oldest daughter, Jennifer Lynn, came to stay with the babies in Los Angeles so that we could leave for five or six days of vacation. We were going to go to Arizona to visit my dad because I hadn't seen him in ten years. We packed and loaded up the car and headed off. We made it about as far as Indio, where we got hit by a woman who had been drinking. Fortunately we weren't hurt, but the car was damaged. It had to be towed for repairs. In Indio, we caught the bus back to LA and Jennifer Lynn came to pick us up and take us home. That was the end of our vacation. We never did end up taking a vacation. I don't know what a vacation is, that's for sure!

Our Adoptions

A funny thing happened, and it got us started with adoptions. It involved our Alan. When we got Alan, he was just a little bag of bones. Besides having Down syndrome, he had little skinny legs and was being tube fed. With all of us working together, we got him on the bottle and he was never tube fed again. He grew and filled out. He had to have several surgeries, including an open heart surgery. Sometime later, a social worker was visiting our home. She commented, "He's mighty cute. I think we can put him up for adoption." My first thought was, "No! We can't let them do that." After all, Alan had been with us since he was just two months old. Jim and I talked about it and decided to start the adoption process ourselves. We completed his adoption when he was five years old, but in the meantime, there were other adoptions.

Our First Time Adopting

A little girl we had been caring for since infancy, Lisa, was five years old. An older girl named Antoinette, who was also in our care, was helping me bathe Lisa. As Antoinette bathed Lisa, she commented to her, "You're a foster child, too, just like me." Lisa gasped, "Not me!" Then she turned to me with a look of shock on her face and practically pleaded, "Mom, I'm not a foster kid, am I?" Well, of course she was a foster child, but I didn't have the heart to say that to her. I said, "I've had you since you were a baby. You're mine." To this day, she comments that there's no way she can be adopted. In so many ways, she is just like her dad. When she was little she would even say, "I must be your daughter, Dad. Look at our backs. We have matching moles!"

We finalized Lisa's adoption eight years later, when she was thirteen years old. At the same time, we adopted little Vincent, who was then eight years old.

Goldenhar's Syndrome

Vincent had come to us when he was one month old. He had Goldenhar's syndrome, which is a condition that usually affects one side of the face, with facial differences, ear and hearing challenges, and sometimes involves the need for surgeries to correct craniofacial, ear, and hearing problems. Vincent also had only one side of his body fully developed. He was born with one lung, his heart was "flipped over" and in the wrong side of his chest, and he had a hole in his esophagus. When Vincent came to us, the doctors said he would only live for about three months.

We just did with Vincent what we did with all the babies: we took care of him and gave him all the love and attention we could! He required special care, of course. Doctors surgically repaired the hole in his esophagus and put in a gastrostomy tube. For over three months we had to take him to the hospital each week to have procedures done so that his esophagus would not fill up with scar tissue. If scar tissue closed up his esophagus, he would not be able to eat. His father or mother had to sign for him to have medical procedures in the beginning. A little while later, his mom allowed us to have guardianship of Vincent so we could make medical decisions. We had a very open visitation schedule, and his mom used to come to visit regularly, about once a month. She was a good person and she cared very much about Vincent. It became difficult for her, though, because she had another child at home and she lived far away.

When Vincent was little, he had issues with balance. Over time he adjusted and overcame the challenges. He liked sports and played sports, but he didn't choose to be involved in organized leagues or teams.

His mom's visits tapered off over time to just birthdays. It got harder and harder for her to come because of the distance and the expense. After years of taking care of Vincent, we brought up the idea of adopting him to his mom. She said that as long as she could see him whenever she wanted and always have visitation rights, she thought it was the best thing for him. So we started the adoption process when he was eight years old, and his adoption was finalized that same year. Special needs adoptions were pretty fast in general, but they were especially fast for us because we had already been caring for the kids for years.

Because of the Goldenhar's syndrome, Vincent's eyes were wide set, but not so much that any medical procedures needed to be done about it. One side of his face was smaller than the other, and on one side he barely had an ear. At age twelve he had his first surgery to build up his ear. Then he had another surgery of the same type when he was fourteen. The doctors used his own cartilage to build up his outer ear, but he doesn't hear from that side because there is no ear canal. I used to cover up his little ear by keeping his hair kind of long. I guess I was being too protective, though, because one day he said, "I want a haircut!" He got his hair cut and he has worn it short ever since. Having one smaller ear was never a problem for Vincent. He always did well socially and had plenty of friends over to the house all the time.

Vincent was very gifted academically, especially in Math. He took all the advanced classes in high school and did very well. We moved to Arizona when he was fifteen years old. You might think that would be a hard age for him to move and make new friends, but he managed just fine. He made friends, went on lots of double dates, and went to all the dances and proms. He ran for office and became the vice president of his class. In all his growing up years, I only remember one time when someone said something ugly to him, and believe it or not, it was an adult that said it.

Vincent graduated from high school and went to college in Phoenix. That's where he met his wife. He now teaches Special Education at a middle school and he coaches football and basketball. He and his wife now have children and are also foster parents to two others. Vincent is doing well in everything. I guess we proved the doctors wrong!

Two More Adoptions

We adopted Jennifer Jo when she was seven, after caring for her since she was two. We called her Jennifer Jo because our oldest daughter was also Jennifer. We had two daughters, both named Jennifer! We thought we were finished adopting. In 1986, though, little Jovan came to our home, weighing in at only four pounds. He had Down syndrome, but he actually was quite healthy overall. Many Down syndrome children have heart problems, but Jovan had a healthy heart. He only ever needed one surgery, and that was when he was two.

When 1989 rolled around, I decided to retire from the medical foster home business so we could move to Arizona to be close to my dad. I had given it twenty good years, twenty-four hours a day, seven days a week! We had guardianship of Jovan by then, but since we were moving to Arizona, we thought it best to leave him in the care of a good friend (who was also a foster mom) so he could stay in California. We moved to Arizona in June of that year. By July, I was missing Jovan terribly. By August, I just couldn't handle it without him. Jim was going to travel to California on business in September, so we arranged for him to bring our boy back to be with us where he belonged.

Jovan is now twenty-two years old. He has been very healthy his whole life. In fact, after starting out at four pounds, I thought he might be small. To the contrary, he now weighs in at a whopping two hundred thirty. I don't know what I would do without him. He helps with unloading groceries and he's good about helping me with whatever I ask him to do. He wants to take care of his dad, and he really watches over his brother Alan and looks out for him. I've told my husband that if anything ever happens to me, these two boys must stay together!

Believe it or not, when I retired in 1989, I felt lost. I still had five of our kids living at home, but it was a different feeling; I wasn't taking care of babies any longer. I missed them, that's for sure, but I do have a lot of memories. And I also have something else to share that gives me a lot of satisfaction. About three years ago, our daughter Jennifer Lynn decided to go back to school to study nursing. She was tops in her class and was hired even before graduation. Now she is an Emergency Room R.N. and is working towards specializing in trauma care. I'm so proud of her! She has come around to being like all the generations before her. Her great grandma, her grandmother, and her mom all dedicated themselves to caring for others, and now she has chosen the same path. Here she is helping people in the same way all of our family has done through the generations.

Jennifer Jo Knows
By Jennifer Jo, January 2009
Adopted in California over twenty years ago

I was two and a half when I came to my mom's medical foster home. I have been with my family ever since. My parents officially adopted me when I was seven years old. I have a better environment because I have a family. I have what I need and want. And, yes, I am a little bit spoiled!

To people who have not been adopted, I would say, "Find someone like my mom and dad." Find a family; find a home. Stay off the streets.

I'm an adult now. The most challenging adjustment for me was moving out of my parents' home. I live in a group home now where I have my own apartment. Switching to my apartment was difficult at first, and some things have been hard for me to deal with.

I've been working for the last ten years for a bulk mailing company. I can use American Sign Language, so I translate for the deaf people I work with. I also make arts and crafts (clothes and beds for dogs and cats). The sales of these items benefit Second Chance, a facility for helping stray animals. I also like music; I play keyboard and bongos.

I would like to adopt someday. The most incredible thing about adoption is when parents take in a child because it's the most amazing and wonderful thing they can do for her. My mom and dad adopted me, and I'd like to adopt just like they did.

CHAPTER FOURTEEN

Adoption is...

"There is no greatness where there is not simplicity, goodness, and truth."

~Leo Tolstoy

Adoption is...

fun. ~ *Stephanie*

a good thing. ~ *Elizabeth*

very special because it helps give children homes to live in. ~ *Tasha*

great because kids get homes. ~ *Galya*

wonderful and extraordinary. ~ *Daniel*

good because it helps the kids get healthy and fun because it helps the family grow. ~ *Natalya*

loving others no matter who they are. ~ *Arona*

my great story to tell my friends. ~ *Elise*

when your parents can't take care of you and you get lonely... and then you get a new family. ~ *Sergei*

a new chance for a good life. ~ *Paul*

awesome because you get to stay with a family that loves you. ~ *Katie*

a road to a new life that includes family, home, love, and care. ~ *Irina*

the key to happiness. ~ *Chris*

CHAPTER FIFTEEN

A Place to Write My Story

Use friendship for strength,
Courage for protection,
Beauty for healing,
And all of the above
For love.
~ Sheryl Eaton

Adoptees: The following blank pages are provided so you can reflect on your own adoption experiences and feelings and write notes here about your adoption if you wish. Your notes may become a story (or stories).

"Those who wish to sing always find a song."
~ Swedish Proverb

"I am not afraid of storms for I am learning how to sail my ship."
~ Louisa May Alcott

"Spirit can walk, spirit can swim, spirit can climb, spirit can crawl.
There is no terrain you cannot overcome."
~ Irisa Hail

"How wonderful it is that nobody need wait a single moment before starting to improve the world."

~ Anne Frank

"How far that little candle throws his beams!
So shines a good deed in a weary world."
~ William Shakespeare

"Dare to reach out your hand into the darkness,
to pull another hand into the light."
~ Norman B. Rice

PART TWO
For Teen and Adult Readers

CHAPTER SIXTEEN

For Teen and Adult Readers

"Everybody, my friend, everybody lives for something better to come. That's why we want to be considerate of every man – who knows what's in him, why he was born and what he can do?"

~ Maxim Gorky

The Shovel
By Paul Z., age 17, April 2008
Taylor, Arizona

When I was about eight years old, I got hit on the head with a shovel. I remember that after I had been in the orphanage for a while, I started to get beat up. There were a bunch of kids, boys, and they were all bigger than me. They hit me because they didn't think I was worth anything. I wasn't able to protect myself. The big kids would sometimes take me into the bedroom of one of the other boys. The adults, the caretakers, were friendly, but they thought the kids were playing.

The boys that beat me up with the shovel were about seventeen years old. They carried me off to their room and then they threw me on the ground. I had a big cut across my head. There was blood all over the floor where I got hit with the shovel. Then a couple of hours later I had a two-inch-tall bump on my head. After that, some of the adults there sewed my head up.

When I found out I was going to get adopted, I felt good because I knew I wouldn't get abused anymore. When I met my adoptive parents, I thought they were taking me to save me from the orphanage.

A Very Early Childhood Memory
By Gina, 2008
Adopted decades ago in Arizona

"You're adopted," taunted a neighborhood bully.

"No, I'm not!"

"You are, too, because my mom told me."

I ran to my dad's office behind our house. With tears in my eyes, I asked, "Am I adopted?"

Dad lifted me onto his lap and with his arms around me asked, "Who told you that?" I filled him in. Then he filled me in.

"Yes, you're adopted, and that makes you very special! You see, some mothers can have babies, and some can't. Mothers who can have babies may want their babies or they may not. But a mother and a father who adopt a baby always want them. It's hard to adopt a baby, and it takes a lot of time and work. So, if you're adopted, you know your parents really, really wanted you. We are so happy you are our daughter! We love you so much!"

Satisfied and a little gratified, I said, "Do you think _____'s mother wants him? He's not very nice."

My dad just smiled.

They Needed Us
By Donna, 2006
Pennsylvania

From the day my husband and I received photos and a video of two-year-old Danil, I began to imagine what our first meeting would be like when we went to Russia to adopt him. I wondered if his eyes would light up like the stars. I wondered if his smile would stretch from ear to ear. I wondered if his hug would warm my heart like hot chocolate. Would he be talkative or quiet? Energetic or calm? Excited or scared?

I imagined different scenarios of our first meeting over and over in my mind. And then, there we were in Russia on our way to finally meet him... traveling down dirt roads, avoiding as many potholes as possible, and breathing in the dust that filled the hot summer air. Our director pointed out his dilapidated orphanage, surrounded by overgrown bushes and weeds. Together we climbed the broken concrete steps to the second floor and anxiously made our way down the damp corridor to his room. With only a few more moments to wait, some final "I wonders" flooded through my mind. I prayed, as I had done so often before, that the Lord would calm our hearts, and Danil's, too, as the moment had finally come.

When we entered Danil's room, we immediately noticed the group of toddlers scattered throughout the small space. Upon seeing us, all the children came running, pulling on our arms and legs, grabbing for the Meeshka bear that we brought for Danil, calling out, "*Mama ee Papa! Mama ee Papa!*" (Mama and Papa!) But as I glanced through the children who were crowding us, I did not see him. Where's Danil? Where's our son?

And there, across the room on a sofa, away from all the commotion, sat Danil – alone. I gently began to pull away from the crowd of attention-seeking children and slowly moved toward him. Danil, however, did not share the others' enthusiasm. Instead, he screamed, cried, and buried his head into the sofa. I knew in an instant that we were strangers in his limited world. He had only ever known his orphanage caregivers all his little life, and he would need time to feel safe with us as well. So we g-e-n-t-l-y approached him with the Meeshka, being so, so careful. To our relief, Danil stopped crying and relaxed the rest of his body within a few minutes, and we began to breathe again.

We were convinced that it was not our gentle approach with him, the gift we brought him, or the interpreter's comforting words that gradually changed his spirit from being fearful to being calm. It was the Holy Spirit working in his little heart... and the lollipop from our backpack!

Slowly he allowed us to play bubbles, bear, and ball with him. We moved away from the other children where we could play quietly, and we could see him becoming more and more at ease with us. Eventually, we even got him to smile and giggle a little when we tickled him. *That* was my dream come-true. *That* was the moment I had been waiting for. It took a little longer than I had anticipated, but it was worth it!

His gray eyes did not light up the sky, his smile disappeared as quickly as it came each time, and his touch came simply from his hand (not yet from his heart), but it was enough for me. I knew that in God's perfect timing he would take this small seed of love and grow it into something beautiful!

The Best Adoption Ever
By Robert, age 17, January 2009
Hawaii

I was born in California, but my biological parents were unhealthy and had lots of problems. Alcohol was a problem. There were three of us: my brother, my sister, and me. I am the oldest, and my brother and sister are a few years younger. I did what I could to take care of them. I used to have to take stuff so my brother and sister would have food. I was even stealing food from stores so they would have food to eat.

One night I got in trouble for no reason; my parents got angry with me and I was in the corner with my hands tied, as punishment, I guess. My parents left me there tied up and left with my brother and sister. Later, my parents were in jail. We were in foster homes for a long time. It seemed like I was in a billion of them. We were all together at first. Then we got separated. Most of the foster homes I was in were nice. Some were awesome; I got neat toys and play guns. I got in trouble some, though, at home and at school, so I would get moved around a lot. I was naughty some.

My brother and sister were adopted together. My mom had to look for me for a while. It took her a few months to find me. I was reunited with my brother and sister when our parents adopted me from Utah when I was six.

There were some tough times. It was a huge adjustment. I had some problems. Living with my parents and our family is fantastic because I have a family and I get the freedom to do what I want. I want to say thank you to my mom and dad for taking care of my needs. They treated me the way a person wants to be treated, helping me to see a better way. They got me the medicine I need and they are helping me learn better behaviors. Otherwise I'd probably be in jail by now. Stealing was a very difficult issue to deal with. I can deal with life better now.

Now I'm a junior in high school. I participate in a program that helps me know how to act when I'm looking for a job. The training will also help me find a job. Having a real family helps, and being back with my brother and sister is important and makes me happy.

My goal is to become a trauma doctor. I want to help people who have had big challenges in their lives.

Conflict
By Tasha, age 14, March 2007
Home to Snowflake, Arizona at age 4

My biggest conflict in life was going from home to home, trying to find somebody who wanted me. My biological mom did not want to take care of me, so she left my two brothers and me by ourselves until somebody found us. We were by ourselves in a house. My biological dad was into drugs, so he got arrested and put into jail. When somebody found us, they put us into foster homes, splitting all of us up into different families. It was a very hard time for me because I did not even know who my mom and dad really were. I was only about two or three when this happened. I did not know who I loved or didn't love.

I was put into a foster home with a relative while my brothers were just put into other homes of people who they did not even know. My foster home was the worst place I have ever been in my whole life. My foster mother thought that I was an ugly child in glasses, so she would not even let me wear them at all. There were about five other kids in the house. Some were foster kids like me and the others were the kids of the foster parents. I had to sleep in a bed with a girl that I did not even know the first night I was there. She purposely pushed me off the bed and made me sleep on the floor, without a pillow or blanket, the whole entire night. Trying to live in that home with other children, not being able to see, bumping into walls, and crying until I finally fell asleep was a horrible experience that I never want to have happen to other children.

I have a letter from the foster parents saying that they would have adopted me had it not been for my parents adopting my brothers. The adoption people wanted us all to be together, so my parents adopted all of us. I'm happy about this because it allows me to be close to my brothers. Also, I'm in a family who loves me the way I am.

Adoption Questions
By Anna, age 16, December 2008
Arizona

I have had a pretty rough life for a sixteen-year-old girl. I was adopted when I was a baby, I've experienced the death of my adoptive sister, we have recently adopted two kids into our family, and I've been through depression. This has not been an easy life, and somehow I'm still alive. I never would have thought that my sister would have died or that we would adopt two kids.

Going through depression dealt with the loss of my sister and not knowing where I came from. I know some information about my birth parents, but not enough. It's still really hard for me to not know where I get my looks and talents from. I have so many unanswered questions that I wish could just be answered right now! I've been in the process now for almost two years to try to find my birth mom. And I have always wanted to go to Korea and see the country and if I find her, maybe even meet her. I keep telling myself that if I don't find her, I won't go to Korea ever. I don't think that I would be able to walk down the streets wondering if that was her. The process has taken so long that if I don't find her, I don't think I could put myself through so much pain.

So many questions fill my head and there's no way to get them out! I want to know where I get my looks from. I want to know what her personality is like; I want to know the woman who gave birth to me! Does my birth father ever think about his daughter? Or does he even remember he has a daughter? Or did he move on with his life and have a new family? Do my birth parents still talk after sixteen years? What if they got married and started a new family? Was I just their mistake in their life? Or did my birth parents break up before she knew that she was pregnant with me, and so would they have gotten married if they knew she was having a baby?

Sometimes I feel as though I was an accident baby. If I ever find her, would she want to meet me? I wouldn't want to be wasting her time or to be a trauma in her life if she's happy. I pray that she is happy wherever she is and whatever she is doing with her life now. I don't know if she even thinks about me. Am I just a chapter in her life that happened and is forgotten? If only I knew the answers to my questions. Maybe if I had a picture of her... Would that help at all, or just make things worse? I guess all I can do for now is wait and pray that something will happen and I will have contact with my birth mom.

Being adopted has its ups and downs – that's for sure. But I guess my life here in America is way better than it would be in Korea. It's better here than being raised in Korea by a single mom. In the culture there, a single mom and her baby would probably be shunned. It would be difficult to find work and there would be poverty.

I'm grateful and I feel blessed to have loving and caring parents, but it's still not easy at times. Everybody has their own story, and here is only half of mine. There is a lot more to my life, but this is one part of it.

In the Nick of Time
By Marilyn, January 1999
Texas

Did you happen to see *20/20* last Wednesday night? A story was aired on the show about children in Russian orphanages. It was very sad. It sure made us glad we adopted before Mia's fourth birthday because she would have been destined for a very rough future had she gone on to an orphanage for older disabled children. Some of those places are pretty brutal and pathetic. I hope Russia continues to allow adoptions out of the country.

(Editor's note: The Russian government has sponsored advertising and education campaigns to encourage adoptions over the past three or four years. Consequently, more Russian orphans are finding homes within their birth country.)

Adoption Poem
By Tasha, age 14, April 2007
Snowflake, Arizona

I have never had an easy life without challenges
Always wondering where I was going to end up next
Not knowing who my real mom and dad were
Living a horrible life, being pushed onto the floor
Missing what I was to experience in life
Being scared and lonely with no comfort,
Until a miracle came and took me to the right place.
My mom and dad that I now live with
Someone who cares about me and loves me for who I am,
Not caring whether I wear glasses or not,
Just how I look on the inside, not out
Bringing back my brothers so we could be reunited,
Giving us what we really needed
With loving brothers and sisters to take care of me along the way
Always feeling welcome and never scared
Giving me hugs and kisses … that cared.
Growing up as the person I should be
Not having to worry about not getting enough to eat.
Taking me in when not even having to.
Adoption is something that I will now want to do, too.

Adoption – A Calling
By Debbie, 2005
Chandler, Arizona

My name is Debbie and I am the mother of four children. Three of them grew in my womb for nine months, and one of them grew in my heart for thirty years. When I was thirteen years old, my mother went back to Ohio to take care of a friend dying of cancer, and there she met another Debbie. That Debbie was also thirteen years old. When Debbie was nine years old her mother had taken her to an orphanage and left her there, telling her she was too much trouble and the biggest problem of her four children. I remember praying and praying for this other Debbie who must have felt so much hurt and was in such need of a family. I never met Debbie, but my prayers for her forever changed my young life. While asking God to help her, I heard him tell me that he had someone for me and that the child would be there one day, and that I just had to wait. Waiting for years was my job. I wasn't quite sure what this all really meant to me or for my life, but I waited.

Time went on, and I grew up. I dated, fell in love, married, and had three children, but I never forgot my call to adopt. I returned to college and got my teaching degree. When I brought up the topic of adoption, my husband would say that as a teacher I adopted each child in my class-room each year. He said he was tired and that we had been blessed with three beautiful children and we should be thankful for that. I was thankful, but something inside my spirit was still calling, and I knew that someone needed me and that I needed that child.

Then one day in 2001, as I was watching the news and folding laundry, I saw a news story about a group who brought orphaned children from Russia for summer camp in the U.S.A. They were looking for families for the children. My heart felt the call stronger than ever and now the waiting became more difficult – but more waiting was required.

In the spring of 2003 I received several signs which showed me that this was the time that a new child would come to our family. I went to Paul, my husband, and shared my thoughts and paused for his response. He said he wasn't sure about adding more to our lives. After all, our children were twenty-two, nineteen, and thirteen. We didn't need babysitters any longer; we could finally run errands without worrying about who would watch the kids or who would be home when the school bus arrived. It made no sense in "the standards of the world" to adopt right then, but in my heart I knew it made "God sense." After weeks of this strong, intense feeling of "this is the time," I looked at Paul and asked him, "If we can't adopt, what do I do with this hole in my heart and this call on my life?" He looked me in the eye like he'd seen me in some new way and said, "Let me go to God in prayer about this again. He would not call you to this and not tell me the same thing." Two days later his response was, "Let's go for it." I connected with the group who sponsored the children for summer visits and let them know of our interest.

Later, that July, we lingered with other families in the parking lot of a Catholic church not far from our home. A bus pulled up and thirty-three children stepped off the bus, all gathering in a group. Well, all but one little guy. This straggler was swinging his backpack around and around, watching planes fly overhead, and staring with interest at the bugs in the grassy area between the children and the waiting families. My girls motioned to the little bug boy and said, "Mom, I bet that one is ours!" They were so right. He indeed was ours, and we knew it from the moment our eyes saw him. He spent three weeks with us for the summer camp program and brought joy to our hearts. This was the child God had for us. And to think, it *only* took thirty years.

Insights for Adoptees
By B.J., March 2008
California

One discovery I made that may be important for parents of older kids to know is that, even though these kids are smart as whips (both of ours are scary smart!), there are still subtle bits of information they miss in our culture by not starting out in America. Zack learned to speak English within six months of coming here. That just blows me away. But he also forgot Russian. That left him kind of in a 'limbo' place – there are subtleties in our language that we take for granted. For example, when Zack had a meltdown and I said, "Get a hold of yourself," what did that mean to him? It's an expression, an idiom, and his meltdown turned into a discussion about what I meant when I said that. It made me think. His school has also begun an after-school intervention program for ELL kids – there are a few other ELL kids, too (from Korea). So while Zack is very bright, his vocabulary and comprehension still need beefing up. He is very literal minded. I'm not sure if that is a normal thing for kids in his situation, but if it is, it may be a very helpful thing for parents – and even older adoptees – to know in order to give them some perspective and awareness.

My Life in Kazakhstan
By Michael, age 11, December 2008
Home to Georgia 2007

I was born in Kazakhstan. My birth mom didn't take good care of me, and when she told me to go to school, I would go halfway, and then I would go to my friend's and I would stay at his house and play with him until school was over. Once my birth mom was walking with her friend past my friend's house and we were playing outside. My birth mom saw me and then

I got spanked. But still I didn't go to school after she spanked me.

My birth mom was named Natasha. She yelled a lot. She had a man friend, and a lady friend. They drank vodka until they got drunk.

We usually slept on the floor made from cement. It was hard and cold even in summer. I went to bed before she did. She was often gone when I woke up. There was nothing to eat. I almost never went to school. No one wore uniforms at that school.

When we did have food, it might be a banana or dry or cooked spaghetti. One time she put bread in the vodka for herself. To get money, she sold our window glass and roofing.

I don't know what happened to her now.

I used to have a brother. His name was Sasha and he was seventeen years older than I. He was tall and thin and darker than me. He had dark and curly hair.

Sometimes, when it was warm outside, he would take me swimming in a pond. Sometimes my birth mom took me to the pond to take a bath. The water was cold in the morning. It was more fun when my brother took me.

Sasha took me to his girlfriend's house when my birth mom was drunk. Sasha's girlfriend's son was my friend.

My brother was put in jail twice. We went to see him and stayed there with him for three days. It made me very sad when my brother died.

Later, police came and took me away to the orphanage. The woman took me to The Shelter before the orphanage. It was boring. When toys came and other things, the adults took what they liked, like flashlights and other things.

Once I got sick and I had to go to the hospital. When I came back from the hospital, the people let kids go outside, but not for long, like for thirty minutes. If anybody did anything bad, everybody had to go in and do push-ups.

Later, they shaved my head and gave me a shower, and gave me clothes. Then, in a police car, they took me to the Regional Orphanage. When I got there, it was a big place with two hundred kids. At first I was scared, but then I got used to it and I had lots of friends. The orphanage was divided into twenty-five families and I was in Family Nine.

(Note: Michael was adopted in April 2007, when he was ten years old. He now lives in Georgia with his mom, sister, and granny. Michael is an excellent student and enjoys bowling, tennis, watching TV, playing videogames, and playing with Coco, the dog. His mother, Dee, writes a blog called *The Crab Chronicles*.)

One Teen's Views on Adoption
By Stephanie, age 14, 2009
Home to Arizona 2004

I want to say that in adoption, there will be hard times and it's not always like a happy ending. Don't think that life is always cool because it's not. There are bumpy roads along the way. I thought when I was first adopted that I would get more of what I wanted, but I've learned that kids should work for what they get. There have been some "un-cool" times. There are arguments – with my brothers and sisters and with my parents. It's hard when your sisters take your stuff. When my older sister yelled at me for something I never did, it really hurt me inside. My parents and I have argued about going over to friends' houses.

I went to my first foster home when I was six or seven years old. I cried a lot and I almost wish that I had hidden in a corner and not gone to school that day. The placement people came to school and I got taken to a foster home by them. I guess that even if they hadn't taken my sisters and brother and me from our mom that day, we still would have been taken away. It was because of neglect. My mom wasn't taking care of us. My older brother and sister had to take care of us, getting breakfast for us and getting us ready for school. We were in the first foster home for about a year and a half.

Then we were at another foster home until I was nine years old. Lucky for me, I was always together with my sisters and brother. My older sister always wanted us to stay together. That helped because we might have ended up in different cities or states if we had ever been separated. She was pretty strong about that – keeping us together.

When I was almost ten, we came to this family. My parents adopted me and my brother and sisters in 2004. Like before, it was pretty hard to call my mom "Mom" in the beginning. First of all, a foster mom is not your biological mom, and when you have gone from home to home, you really can't say she's your mom; it's too hard. For the first month, I called my new mom by her name, but then I got kind of used to calling her "Mom."

There are still times when I wish we hadn't gotten taken away from our birth mom. But even though it is tough, I do feel like you should act your age and try to get along and set an example as best you can. Your younger sisters or brothers can see what you do. You are the older sibling, and if you don't set a good example, they will do bad things too. If you are a teenager, you should be expected to do more. You should do your chores and do your share. It's important to be a role model to your younger siblings.

Working out problems with other kids, at home and at school, has been tough for all of us. It is sometimes easier than before, but it's still hard sometimes. My nephew and two other friends are who I hang out with at school. Having just a few good friends is fine. Sometimes I have to have my own time, too; I consider myself a loner. I like being by myself part of the time – it just depends on how I'm feeling and what kind of a day I've had.

If I could say anything to adoptive families, I would say to be sure to have family time together. You can have some good times and it is amazing that there is some fun that comes with it. I like going to stores to get what we need. Family trips and family reunions definitely are good memories. It's always fun going Christmas shopping, too. For family time we rent a video, go bowling or to the movies, or visit people. If I have had a rough day, spending family time together calms me down and I'm not disgusted anymore if I was upset about something.

It's kind of weird, too: if I eat something sugary on the wrong side of my mouth, it tingles, and my teeth on that side of my mouth feel weird for a while. I've been to the dentist and I don't have cavities. My dad and older sister helped me figure out something: I get angry when I eat too much sugar. If I eat too much sugar, it's pretty certain that I will be in an angry mood the next day. I guess I'm just very sensitive to it, so I am careful not to eat too much of it at once. It helps me to know not to overdo it with sugar.

I've learned to get over it if my parents won't let me go where I want to go whenever I want. I know that my parents want what is best for me. Adoption has helped me in my life. It does make your life better because at least you find out that your true family is the people who take care of you. My family loves me and I love them. I've been with them for four and a half years, and they have given me a good life.

Adoption has also helped me to find what I want in life. I want to graduate and go to college. If I don't get married, I will go on a mission for my church. I want to teach kindergarten or first grade. That's the age of kids I like because they are fun and I can play with them. They are sweet and easier to handle than bigger kids.

Foster families are good because they might give a kid a chance to be adopted, and everyone ought to have that opportunity. At least if you are adopted you won't be passed around town and from door to door anymore like a wild monkey! I think I'll adopt when I get older because every kid deserves to have a family.

My New Life
By Irina, age 16, July 2008
Home to Florida in 2006

I was born in Russia in 1992, in the city called Serpukov. I had a normal family life for only three years. My mother started using alcohol when I was three years old, and my dad left home because of that. Even though it happened, I loved my mother so much and as a matter of fact, I still love her. My dad tried to take me with him but she wouldn't let him. Of course I still saw him, but not often. Going through all of that I had to have someone to trust in my life and that was Jesus. He was the most important part in my life after all of that happened. He did a lot to help me to go through things in my life.

God gave me an angel! That angel was my grandmother. She always took care of me by feeding me, dressing me, giving me a lot of love and care, and of course, taking me to church. She was the person I could always trust and love.

One time my mother left me at kindergarten at night and I had no idea where to go. All of a sudden I felt Jesus talking to me and it felt like he was taking my hand and taking me somewhere! I ended up at my grandma's house. My grandma went through a lot of things in order to save my life. I am really thankful to her and of course Jesus Christ. She saved me while I almost froze to death, while my mother tried to kill me, and while my mother tried to drown me. Literally, she was always there for me no matter what happened.

I was seven years old when I wrote a letter to my school teacher: "Dear teacher, I can't live with my mother anymore and I would like to live in the orphanage."

The next day my grandmother came to school and talked to my teacher, so all of us decided that I should live in the orphanage. There are a lot of orphanages in Serpukov, but my grandma chose the best one for me. My grandmother went to court and asked them if she could adopt me, but they said no because of her age. My grandma and I were really disappointed.

Finally my orphanage life began. I was shy when I first got there and I cried a lot because I missed my grandmother and especially my mom. Then a year later I knew that I was safe, and I found a lot of great friends. I really enjoyed living in the orphanage because it was like a big family, and all the kids became like brothers and sisters. The director was like our mother. Finally my grandma came to visit and she took me every weekend to her house to visit. I really loved it when she would take me or just visit me.

I lived in the orphanage for eight years and I found two best friends. One was named Alyona and the other Masha. They meant a lot to me because they were like real sisters to me. We had a lot of fun together. Every summer the orphanage would send all the kids to different camps and three of us would always find new things, new adventures, and of course, we were the troublemakers.

One day Masha flew to America and that's when we found out that she would live in America in a very good family. We were really happy for her and it was very, very hard for us to say goodbye to her. After that, I only had one best friend, and two years later they had to send her to a different orphanage.

Later on I found out that I was going to fly to America for some kind of camp. Finally, I got it. The director told me that I was flying to America to meet a family that might adopt me and to see Masha! I got there and I saw Masha running toward me with her hands ready to give me a hug. We hugged each other and we both cried from happiness to see each other. I met my family, and I had a lot of hope that they would adopt me.

I got to see Masha almost every day. Then I got to meet MaryLee and Roger Lane, the owners of Hand In Hand Adoption Agency. Their house was amazing. They had all kind of animals and I loved it! I loved MaryLee and Roger right away because they are very loving and caring people who try their hardest to place orphans in the best families.

Then, unfortunately, I had to go back to Russia and wait for the family to adopt me. I didn't hear anything from them for a year. Then I got a call and found out that they couldn't adopt me and that someone else wanted to adopt me. I asked the translator: "Who?" and she told me the director of Hand In Hand. Then I figured it out and without thinking, I said yes. Roger and MaryLee came to Russia to work on papers and when I saw them I recognized them right away and I called them Mom and Dad.

We spent a lot of time in Moscow going places. They brought me a gift every day, and then they brought me a photo album with all the pictures of their family and their animals which I became part of. The day I saw them, my hope came back and I knew that God gave me the best family in the world! Of course it was hard to leave my country, my friends, my orphanage, and especially my grandmother. I am thankful to all the people in Russia that helped me throughout my life. Now I feel really special, and without any doubt, I know that I am loved, cared for, and accepted in my new family. I love my family and I have almost met everyone. I am glad when I meet more and more people in my family. They accept me with love, kindness, and I feel special.

I am still calling to Russia to talk to my grandma and my best friends Lena and Alyona. I see Masha a lot because she lives only two hours away from my house. I love my new life in Florida. That is so much fun. I still trust Jesus because he has been the biggest part of my life, and he still is! I am thankful to my friend Masha for telling my parents about me. I am also thankful to my grandma who has been an angel in my life. And of course I am thankful to Hand In Hand and my lovely parents, MaryLee and Roger Lane.

Making Adjustments after a Challenging Beginning
By Arona, age 18, April 2008
Snowflake, Arizona

I was born in Hawaii. Before being in foster homes, my brother and I stayed with my biological aunt and cousins. They weren't that great to us. I don't want to dwell on or even think about some of the experiences I had before coming home with my mom and dad. My bro and I were in several foster homes before we were adopted; most of them were in Canada. I'll mention a few memories I have from two of the good ones.

I remember being at one foster home when I was four or so. They spoiled us a little bit. We used to love peanuts, so this family kept a big bucket of peanuts in the shell for us so we could eat them whenever we wanted. That was quite a treat. On the other hand, there were also lots of spiders in the back yard at that house. I don't know why I remember that. Maybe it's because I wasn't afraid of them then. Anyway, I *don't* like spiders now.

Another foster home we were in – the last one before we were adopted – was good, too. The family had lots of kids. There was a huge bedroom down in the basement where the four boys in the family slept. To make room for me, they divided that one great big room and made a little room for me. They put in a wall to split it up, and so I had my own little bedroom. That was pretty cool. I remember that they also had a little playground in the back yard.

One day when I was about five years old, all the boys played a trick on me. I was outside playing, and they wouldn't let me back in the house. I tried all the doors, but they had locked them all. They still wouldn't let me in, and I ended up crying. Finally, I went next door crying to the neighbors' house. I remember sitting in their house eating soup. Maybe they gave me soup to calm me down. When my foster parents got home, they couldn't find me. They were worried, of course, and began looking all over for me. When they came to the neighbors' house looking for me, there I sat, eating soup.

I was six when my bro and I were adopted. I don't remember too much about that, except that it was dark outside when I went with my new parents. That first night they took me to my aunt's house; I guess she was eager to meet me. I was excited to be with a new family, but I don't know if I even understood that they would be my family forever.

When my parents adopt a new kid, they take us all to Disneyland. We have done this every time they have adopted. I was seven years old the first time we went, and we have gone three more times after that. When we came home from the first trip, I kept on asking, "When are you going to take us back to our other big house?" Mom had to explain to me that that was just a trip, and where we had stayed was a hotel, not where we lived!

When I was adopted, I had some faults. When my mom was cleaning out the fridge, I panicked because I thought we weren't going to have food anymore. My mom had to explain to me what she was doing and that we would still have food. Another experience Mom told me about was that when I was younger I would always ask what was for dinner; I was making sure that my bro and I would get food. I didn't like to share my food either, which is a habit I had to break away from. It took a while for me to understand that my mom and dad would always provide enough food for us.

The best thing about my home and family is that my parents had a big heart, big enough to adopt more kids. Adoption has changed my life and my possibilities for the future. Having a mom and dad and siblings has helped me a lot. Having a family means I always have friends. Even though I had a difficult start, my parents have made it easier for me to have a better future.

Viktor
By Carla, July 2006
Texas

When we began the adoption process, it wasn't because we had any grand plan to solve the problems of the world. We were aware of the plight of children in orphanages in many countries, and yes, we understood that family life certainly must be better for a child than years in an orphanage. But we didn't set off with the idea that we were saving a child from an atrocious life. We started our adoption process because we wanted another child (already had two bio-kids), and because we felt that providing a home for a child who didn't have a family was the right way for us to add to our family.

Well, the adoption journey itself was a long and rocky road, but after two years of "false starts" and unforeseen challenges, we were matched with a handsome three-year-old boy. When we were "introduced" to our son on video, we received information about him from the day of his birth. He had some medical problems, but nothing that we couldn't help him handle. Paperwork behind us, court date ahead of us, we flew to Russia, anxious to meet our new son.

We were met with greetings that surprised and confused us. Every single person that we met in Russia that had anything to do with adoption – from the adoption coordinator, to the caretakers, to the orphanage director, to the workers at the offices we needed to visit, to our hosts in two cities – practically fell over themselves thanking us for adopting Viktor. We kept responding that we were happy to be adopting him and that he would fit right in. One afternoon, after yet another round of "thank-yous," we asked our adoption coordinator, Boris, to please explain the reactions we were getting from everyone. He stated that though our son's care had been good in the Baby Home, he would really have no chance of being adopted in Russia. He added, "When he moves up to the Children's Home, well, it will be difficult." He could probably see the baffled looks on our faces. He went on, "The *detsky dom*, where the kids go when they are four years old, is not the same as the Baby Home. And later, in the home for older children, this boy would face problems." He explained that because of physical differences, our son would not receive services that healthy children would. He would be the last in line for everything. Boris continued, "It's very difficult. It's like...um...how do you say it?" I interjected a question: "Like a boarding school?" "Well," said Boris, "not exactly. It's more like...more like a *prison*."

Our hearts sank. At that point we were more glad than ever that we were taking Viktor home with us. We realized then that adoption of a child with a physical or mental challenge is, in essence, saving a life.

Orphanage Adventures
By Irina, age 16, July 2008
Home from Russia to Florida 2006

My two friends and I got into a lot of troubles when we were in the orphanage! We had three ways to walk to school, and the director told us that we can walk only one way because the other two ways were really dangerous. Did we listen to her? Of course not! The three of us had to walk the most dangerous way. The road was mostly grass and it was really dark outside. We were a little bit scared but we still went on and on. It took us about an hour to get to the orphanage and our caretaker was really mad at us because we were late. Anyways, nobody knew about it except the three of us. The next morning was regular until all of a sudden the director called us in her office. That was scary! Somehow she found out that we were walking the wrong way and she was yelling at us and telling us how dangerous that way was. Later that day we found out that her daughter was living there where we were walking, and she told the director that she saw us. Since that happened we never went that way to school again. Other troubles happened mostly in summer camps: boyfriends, friends, non-orphan kids, etc... But all of them are kind of embarrassing to share!

Lessons from My Journey
By Barbara, 2008
Massachusetts

All people are a sum of their parts – a mix of genetics, environment and life circumstances. These are the things that make us who we are. For children who are adopted, especially those with closed adoptions, we enter the world with missing pieces to the puzzle.

I was raised in a loving home with two adoptive parents. Most people did not know I was adopted, and it wasn't often discussed. My adoptive mother did allow me to talk about adoption if I brought it up, and supported my searching for my birth mother when I was old enough. She gave me the information that she had and never made me feel like I was a mistake. She really did the best she could with the information she had – especially in the 1960s when adoption wasn't talked about as openly and there were not as many books on the market on how to give adopted children what they need. That being said, my adoption still seemed to have more of an effect on me than my environment and life circumstances.

It is hard for a non-adopted person to understand the longing that some of us have to find our biological parents and the circumstances of our births. The thought that you always want what you cannot have is really true for some of us. Children who are not adopted take for granted knowing their family history, extended family members, and their sense of belonging. That sense of belonging seemed to rule most of my life. Despite having a loving family, I always felt I needed my own "real family." I wanted to have a child to have someone who shared my "blood" and who would look like me.

Having four children of my own did give some sense of comfort in that area. I was married, divorced, and then married again. The need for family seemed to be the driving force in my life. I wanted to start my own family traditions. I wanted my children to have close relationships with their cousins, aunts, uncles, and especially grandparents. I wanted to give them everything that I longed for. I also wanted them to have so many people in their lives that they would never feel unloved. I feel that I have succeeded in this area, yet I still had this void in my life that nothing seemed to fill.

In 2004, after many failed attempts to find my birth mother, I hired an agency that not only located my birth mother but also gave me information about her entire family background. I finally knew some of my roots. On our first phone call, she told me the name of my birth father. I was able to contact him the next day. We confirmed his paternity with genetic testing and he welcomed me with open arms. I am a biracial woman and had many questions about the circumstances of my birth and my mixed heritage. I was able to learn about all of my history and able to meet in person all of the relatives in my father's family. My birth mother wasn't willing to meet me or share my existence with her family, except her husband and one of her children. This bothered me a great deal at first, but I found comfort in being grateful for the blessing I was given instead of focusing on what I didn't have. How you deal with any situation in life is a choice. I choose to live by the serenity prayer, which says, "God grant me the serenity to accept the things I cannot change, the courage to change the things I can, and the wisdom to know the difference."

I cannot change the circumstances of my birth, nor how any of my birth family responds to my existence. I cannot change my genetics, or my past. I can, however, make choices on how to deal with the life I have been given and move forward. I am a nurse and an educator, so I try to focus on educating myself and healing my mind, body, and spirit. I was not able to face how adoption drove my life until I sought therapy. Therapy helped me to identify my strengths and weaknesses. Reading has helped me to see adoption from many different perspectives. I learned that many of the feelings I had all of my life are very similar to feelings of other adoptees. The Internet is full of adoption web sites. I have been able to seek advice from others in my situation and chat with those who have been where I am. It is very important to have some type of support group, whether it is from friends and family, or even if it has to be from complete strangers you find at a site like Adoption Forums. The validation, advice, encouragement, and support I have received have been invaluable.

The greatest lesson I learned in my search and its aftermath is that I was a complete person all along. My faith has taught me that I was never an accident. God loved me all along. My adoptive family loved me. My friends loved me. My children and husband loved me. I had to learn that I was deserving of such a love. I had to love myself. We all go through trials and tribulations. That is inevitable. We must try to learn from each life experience in order to grow. We also must share what we have learned in order to help someone else. Some adoptees may never find their birth families. Some may find them and then be rejected. Some may find them and have wonderful relationships. We must remember that what we want may not be what they want.

Whether to search or not is an individual decision. I have met many people who chose not to. I have met some who have found success. We must be realistic about what we want and what to expect. We need to learn to help ourselves. We need to get help when we need it. Mostly, we need to realize that we are deserving of love. I am appreciative of those who have welcomed me into my biological family. I also have to accept those who have not. My greatest gift was realizing that I had people in my life all along who have always loved me. I discovered I was very much like Dorothy in *The Wizard of Oz*, wanting to see what else was out there for me. At the end of my journey, I was happy to click my heels and say, "There's no place like home!" I had what I needed all along. I just didn't see it.

The Best Gift!
By Tasha, age 16, September 2008
Adopted in Utah at age 4

We all face challenges and trials throughout our lives. Some are harder than others, but all can be overcome with support from family and friends. Our trials are what make us stronger and better people. They make us more understanding, grateful, and loving, and they help us know how to fix a problem if it comes up again.

Trials make us more understanding of what others have to go through. We have all experienced many difficulties and know what it is like. People need to be more understanding of others' feelings. We have all faced personal challenges. Teens have faced normal daily challenges, those associated with dating, for example. Some have faced being adopted.

I was adopted at a young age, so I never really knew who my biological parents were. I heard many stories about them but never knew which ones were true. I have heard that my biological dad was in jail for drugs and that my biological mom used drugs too. I've heard that my mom abandoned us. My brother wants to find out more info about our biological parents, but I would rather focus on other things. I don't want more stress right now. I don't really want to know them. By finding them, who knows what relationship they would want with me? It would possibly cause problems. I am content. I don't need anything else to worry about. I prefer to take a load off myself and not contact my biological parents. By doing so, I will not have to worry about pleasing both sets of parents!

I have people come up to me all the time (kids at school, for example) and tell me how sad it is that I do not know who my real parents are. It really hurts to have people tell you that and to feel so sorry for you. They think it's sad that I don't know my biological parents or know my family heritage and that I don't know my parents' qualities or about their health history. They don't understand how my parents who adopted me did not even have to adopt anyone or take children into their home. It was out of the kindness of their hearts that I even have a family that I can call my own.

Most children that do not get adopted when they are young never get a home or a mom and dad. It's harder to place kids once they are older. They've had more challenges and may be scarred by their experiences. Being adopted is not at all something that I regret or bring myself down about. It doesn't make me sad at all; in fact, it's uplifting. It taught me to be grateful for what I have. I might not even have a family if my parents hadn't adopted me.

It is hard for kids and even harder for teenagers to be grateful for what they have been given. Sometimes they think the world revolves around them. I am so grateful for my family. They are the best thing that ever happened to me. They love me for who I am and would never trade me for anything. They gave me everything I now have: material things, teachings, self-esteem, confidence, education, love, and acceptance. They took me from a bad living condition, cared about me, cared for me, and made me into the person I now am.

I don't know where I would be right now if I did not have them. I probably would have been adopted by my foster family if my mom and dad had not adopted me, but that would have been horrible. I would have been separated from my biological brothers. Getting adopted by my foster family would have taken away the chance to be close to my brothers. I might not even know them! I would have missed their lives, so they would be like total strangers.

I have learned something else from my family, too. My family is all different colors and races, and we all love each other. It means so much to have my parents tell me that they love me. In the future, I will probably adopt children. I will consider adopting no matter what race the children are. Color doesn't matter; support for each other is what matters. We need to all love and care for one another.

The next time you go and decide to fight with your family members, think about what you would be or where you would be without your family. Your family loves you so much. I know that about my family and I know they always will love me. My mom used to say that we were not born in her tummy but in her heart. I really do believe that my parents love me. When life gets tough, they are always there to back me up. For example, my parents have come to my classes at school and at my Sunday school class at church to explain to other kids about adoption. Sometimes they don't want me to talk about being adopted because if I don't mention it to people, they won't judge me. I think my parents want my feelings to be protected. But I prefer to share my feelings and to tell people about my adoption. Then people don't ask as many questions.

I love to know that I am loved. Having a family that understands me and that is thankful for all that they have, and who cares about me so much is truly the best gift ever. My parents are a gift that I was given and am so thankful for them that I can hardly explain it. It means so much. I love them and always will, forever and ever!

CHAPTER SEVENTEEN

Deciding to Adopt and Finding a Match

To laugh often and much
To win the respect of intelligent people and
    the affection of children
To earn the appreciation of honest critics and
    endure the betrayal of false friends
To appreciate beauty
To find the best in others
To leave the world a bit better, whether by
    a healthy child, a garden patch or
    a redeemed social condition
To know even one life has breathed easier
    because you have lived
This is to have succeeded.

                       ~ Ralph Waldo Emerson

A Big Family Considers Getting Bigger
By Pam, mom of 11, October 2008
Snowflake, Arizona

We had nine biological children, and for a long time, we wondered if we were done. We started making friends with people who had adopted children, and we began wondering if we should add to our family in this way. I pondered over it for about a year without saying anything to my husband, Shon.

We thought especially hard about it once we met a family who had adopted eight children. We got to know them and visited with them for several hours about what adoption was like. I finally asked Shon, "What would you think about us adopting children?" Shon answered, "I wondered how long it would take you to ask me that!"

We talked and prayed about it and we decided that if Heavenly Father wanted us to adopt children, he would have to show us how, both financially and spiritually. We left it up to him. We already had nine children and trying to live on an educator's income was very tricky. We knew adoptions could be expensive and we weren't sure how we would be able to swing it. We also knew that bringing children with different backgrounds into our family would change things quite drastically, and we wanted to feel confident that we were up to the challenge. The very next Wednesday, I got a call from a friend who had also adopted two little girls from Russia. She told me that there was a little girl named Katya who was supposed to come to America, and she asked us if we knew anyone who could sponsor her for her three-week summer visit.

I was amazed during this phone conversation because it had come so soon after our first real discussion about the topic of adoption. I told my friend that I would talk to Shon about it. I called him right away, and he was very surprised that this opportunity was dropping into our laps so soon. He and I agreed that we should fast and pray about it for the rest of the day, and then we'd have a family meeting with the rest of the family that night, because if we were going to do it, we had to send the money the next day so they could buy plane tickets in Kazakhstan. When we had our family meeting with all of the children, every single one of them agreed that they wanted us to try to adopt. It was a wonderful family dinner and meeting with a long prayer for Heavenly Father to make this happen if it was right. We also decided that we didn't want to adopt only one child; we wanted a girl and a boy to join our family.

We started the process, filling out many forms and paying required fees. We kept thinking we were almost done, and then there would be someone else that had to approve our applications. There were even a few times that we were rejected by different judges because of the size of our family.

A Journey Spanning Thirty Years
By Sheryl, November 2008
Illinois

Our adoption story actually began over thirty years ago. My father began a business relationship with a gentleman from Guatemala, when they were on the Board of Directors together at Liberty Fund, Inc., a private educational foundation established to encourage the study of the ideal of a society of free and responsible individuals. The Foundation develops, supervises, and finances programs to foster thought and encourage discourse on enduring issues pertaining to liberty. This Guatemalan, Manuel Ayau, was a prominent businessman who served in his country's congress from 1970 to 1974 and even ran for President in 1990. My father, T. Alan Russell, and Dr. Ayau are still friends and business contacts today.

Dr. Ayau's family had started an orphanage in 1857. It was taken over by the government for many years, until the family was finally allowed to take back the orphanage about ten years ago. Now Dr. Ayau's daughter, Mother Ines Ayau, runs the Hogar Rafael Ayau in Guatemala City. The orphanage is an Eastern Orthodox-based home and day school for orphaned children.

Adopting a little girl had always been a dream of mine. Chris and I have two biological sons, and adding a daughter would complete our family. My father and our oldest son, Grant, 8, had visited the orphanage in August 2007 while on a volcano-climbing trip. Grant told Mother Ines, "My mom said that I needed to pick out a little sister to take home." We decided that we wanted to work exclusively with Hogar Rafael Ayau because of the connection between my family and the Ayau family. I knew we would be treated well, and we were. We were not Eastern Orthodox (normally a requirement for adoption); fortunately, Mother Ines overlooked that requirement.

We explained to Mother Ines that we wanted a little girl under the age of six. This was a time in Guatemalan adoptions that was extremely volatile and there was the threat that adoptions would cease. We were cautioned about the great possibility that the process could end with us not adopting a child. Despite the risk, we decided to go ahead, feeling that no matter what happened, we would at least be treated with respect and consideration because of our connection with the Ayau family. I really felt that God had inspired the relationship with my father and Dr. Ayau all those years ago because one day we would want to adopt a child. It just seemed too coincidental otherwise.

We got our referral very early in the process, probably because Mother Ines knew my father and had great respect for him. We were matched with Claudia Jeaneth, age five, in October 2007. When I received the phone call from our attorney, there was little information and no picture. I scoured the Hogar Rafael Ayau web site looking for anything that might give me a clue about Claudia. I found her on a page that was devoted to sponsoring a child. I quickly e-mailed Mother Ines asking her if that was in fact our Claudia, and it was. I couldn't turn back now that I had seen her face. Because of the impending closing of all adoptions, we had to speed through all paperwork and the home study to make the deadline.

Grant and my father had a previously scheduled trip back to Guatemala for a second volcano climb. I wasn't about to let them meet Claudia before Chris and I did! We also wanted to secure her visa, which required both parents to have seen the child before the finalization process. My father, Chris and I, and the boys traveled to Guatemala the week before Christmas to meet Claudia. We had not received our USCIS approval for the adoption yet, but again, Mother Ines had faith in our family. On our last leg of the trip to Guatemala City, on the plane, I was very emotional. I couldn't believe that I was actually going to meet my little girl, the one I had been dreaming about all my life. But I was also scared that she may not like me and I wouldn't be her dream of a mother. What a scary thought! If that were the case, then what would we do?

The next morning we headed to the orphanage. I remember Claudia walking down the stairs and then through the door to us. She was shy, but gave me a big hug. We spent the afternoon together and she blended with our family as if she had always been with us. She got along with her brothers very well and loved her daddy. We were invited to Dr. Ayau's house that afternoon for their Sunday family dinner, and the best part was that we got to take Claudia with us. She seemed so at ease with us that I no longer had fears of her not liking me.

During this trip, I also made a visit to Universidad Francisco Marro-quín, the university that Dr. Ayau started in 1971. I attended a lesson in Guatemalan culture so that I would be better able to help Claudia keep some of her culture and understand her heritage.

While our paperwork was in the process, I made another trip in April to visit and spend some time with Claudia. Mother Ines allowed her to go to the hotel and stay several days with me (by then, we had our USCIS approval). It was girl time: painting nails, coloring, and swimming in the pool. Many people at the hotel pool thought that she had already been adopted because of how well she adapted to me. We had fun getting to know each other even through the language barrier. She didn't speak English and I didn't speak Spanish. My father was also in Guatemala during this time because he was working on fixing up the orphanage's woodworking shop. He completely revamped the shop and got all new equipment for it. His hope is that the older children will be able to learn a skill to carry them through life when they leave the Hogar. During these visits by my father, Claudia spent time as her *abuelo's* special assistant. Of course she loved her "job," because it included having her own bag of Reese's Peanut Butter Cups and getting out of school.

We thought that we were going to get Claudia in March of 2008, but because of the way the process was going in Guatemala, it didn't work out. In June, we again thought that we were going to get her. When that timing didn't work out either, we decided to take another trip to visit her. My sons and my mother and father and I traveled down to Guatemala to see her in the summer. We were there during a tropical storm (rainy season), so it was a little hard to entertain three children in a hotel for four days. Once again, the time together we spent with Claudia was perfect. At one point she put on a bathing suit that I had brought for her and strutted out, as if to say "I have arrived." Claudia's personality lends itself very well to change.

We were told that Claudia didn't begin speaking until she was at least three years old, and that when she did speak, which wasn't often, she was extremely quiet and hard to understand. The staff at the orphanage felt sure that she would need speech therapy. What is so ironic about this is that after she had arrived home with us and had been in school for approximately a month, she got in trouble for talking too much. "Big is God" (a saying that is used often at the Hogar, similar to us saying in English "God is great."). He took a shy little girl and turned her into a beautiful social butterfly.

We brought Claudia home on October 4, 2008, thirteen months after we started the process. We snapped a picture of her when she stepped off the plane onto United States soil, becoming a U.S. citizen. What a moment that was both for us and for Claudia. She has been with us now for just six weeks and you would never know it. She is learning English rapidly and we are learning more Spanish. She has assimilated extremely well into our family and her school. We are more than blessed to have Claudia *Faith* Jeaneth as our daughter. She is a beautiful, sweet, and easy-going little girl. I can't imagine our lives without her. It took a lot of *faith* in God to get her into our arms.

Claudia stepping off the plane with her dad

Second Chance Children – the Story behind the Movie
By Thomas Vetter, 2007
New York

I feel compelled to tell you how passionate I am about the subject of adoption of older children. My name is Tom Vetter. I live in NY with my wife Leslie and our eleven-year-old daughter, Galya, from Russia. I have been a news videographer for twenty years and have been fortunate enough to travel the world and see history unfold before my eyes. I have been in orphanages in many countries and have been touched by what I have seen. Once I saw the orphanages first hand, I knew I had to do what I could to try to make a difference. Most people in my line of work and travel bring home souvenirs such as t-shirts from their journeys; I brought home a seven-year-old girl. (Actually I just brought home a lot of paperwork; we went back later for our daughter.)

Working in television, I knew I could use the power of the TV camera to get others to understand the tough road many kids have had to endure. I have spent many years producing TV specials and documentaries, so when I became aware of the lives of children in orphanages, I did what I knew best and made a short documentary of my travels and how visiting orphanages affected me. The piece is called *Second Chance Children*. The response has been great on the local level, and the movie has won several national awards. It's a view through my eyes of how I feel about children in orphanages. If you are thinking of adopting, it will put you over the edge and convince you of the need.

Our daughter Galya has been here for four years now and is adjusting well. She's excited about writing stories about her experiences if it will help other kids like her to get a family. Thanks for letting me help get the message out about adoption and children's and families' adjustments to their new lives.

(Editor's note: Take ten minutes to watch the video on YouTube. It is very moving and definitely worth sharing. Go to YouTube.com and type in *Second Chance Children*.)

From Lisa's Journal
By Lisa Finneran
President, ArkAngels for Russian Orphans
Virginia

August 14, 2002 We've decided we definitely want twins. Heather, with our agency, tried to discourage us; said twins are rare. But I know that one out of every eighty-eight births in Russia is twins. I looked it up on the Internet. So it's not that rare. I just don't know what to think. One minute I'm excited to know that we could get a call any minute. But I'm also trying not to get my hopes up. And that leaves me terribly conflicted. I'm excited. I'm afraid to be excited. I'm afraid. I'm not looking forward to going through this for the next four, five, six, nine months.

August 27, 2002 Got a call today. Heather said they got word there might be a pair of twins available in October. Healthy infants. Ten months old. Boy/girl. From the northern reaches of Russia. A two-hour plane ride from Moscow. I don't know what to think, what to feel. I need to keep a level head. I need to remember this may not work out. So hard.

October 17, 2002 Understand that in this region of Russia children move from the baby home to the older children's home when they are four years old. In the baby home odds are fifty-fifty they'll be adopted, given a loving home and loving parents. Once they move to the older children's home, chances drop to one in ten. Can you imagine that birthday party?

November 11, 2002 Video, photos, information arrived first thing this morning. So odd. Fed Ex – our stork – came to the door just before 10 a.m. and left me standing there with a red, white and blue envelope. I knew what was inside. And yet it seemed so odd, so impersonal, to meet our children like this. Didn't know what to think when Igor first appeared on my TV screen in his fuzzy blue blanket sleeper. He was sitting on a rocking rooster, smiling, laughing, making sounds with the grown ups on the tape. Expected love at first sight. But no. First thought: abject fear. What am I thinking, doing? I know nothing about this child. I have nothing in common with him. How can I love them just because someone across the globe put my name on their file?

Video starts with Igor. At first he's just sitting there, perched on a rocking rooster (imagine a rocking horse in the shape of a rooster). Eventually he starts rocking. Then he smiles. His eyes are very expressive. When the caretaker makes noises, he responds with similar noises. He blows bubbles and does raspberries. And he's a bruiser.

Lina's in a pink fuzzy blanket sleeper (Like we might not be able to tell them apart.). She too is seated in a rocking toy. She starts out just sitting there. But then she too gets it rocking. Then all of the sudden she smiles and laughs. Next the caretaker slides them together. They rock side by side. He reaches out and holds her rocking rooster. And they laugh. I expected them to be delayed. I expected hollow eyes, no emotion, gaunt. I didn't expect so much animation.

November 13, 2002 I wonder how many boys have worn the blue blanket sleeper. How many girls have worn the pink one? Do they put all the children in these suits for their American videos?

November 14, 2002 Imagine the shock today to learn that the one in the pink is the boy and the one in the blue is the girl. Igor is Lina. Lina is Igor. Our little girl is a bruiser. Sent the video and other information to a doctor who specializes in reviewing this information for adoptive parents. He discovered the switch.

I know I said it wasn't love at first sight. The still photos were grainy. Watching the video for the first time was almost shocking. But now, after looking at it again and again, after seeing them smile with their eyes, I am falling in love. Igor is Nicholas to us. Lina is Elena.

February 11, 2003 First trip to Russia. Anna and Luba picked us up just after 9:00 this morning and took us right to the hospital to visit Elena, finally. Felt like we walked in a back door to the state-run hospital. There's no lobby, no information desk, just a set of stairs. We climb three flights. The first thing I notice is the lighting. It's like they ran out of light bulbs a decade ago. Once my eyes acclimate I see the walls are multicolored, with huge patches of paint peeled away and showing the old colors underneath. I'm afraid to touch anything. Scary. It looks like the '40s era Stalinist Russia I expected. And everywhere there's that smell of cabbage.

So we went to the orphanage and picked up Nicholas. He came to us in the same red fleece pajamas, same green tights, same red hand-knit socks as he was wearing yesterday. I wonder how long they wear the same clothes. We brought him back to the hotel and rolled the ball on the floor with him again. And now Mike is trying to get him to take a nap. If we were at home I'd probably just put him in his crib and let him fall asleep on his own. But we don't have a crib here, so we have to get him to sleep before we put him on the bed so he doesn't try to crawl – or fall – out.

We're told their schedule is they wake up between 7:00 and 8:00 a.m. They eat breakfast and then play. They take naps at 10:00 (for about an hour) and 2:00 (for about two hours). They eat lunch at noon. They have a snack each time they wake up. They eat dinner at 6:00 and are in bed by 8:00.

Did talk briefly with one of the caretakers. Confirmed that Nicholas walks only with assistance. And they said they call him Goshen – "Little One." One the way to the hospital noticed an incredible statue of Lenin in the town square. He's several stories tall, a man rising out of a slab of black granite. I thought that after the fall of the Soviet Union they removed all these statues.

Things I would recommend other first-timers bring with them: sippy cup (while the orphanage has them drinking out of real cups, all the hotel had was glass) and plastic spoons, paper plates (the hotel only had china). Also baby lotion and diaper cream (all the babies seem to have dry skin, and we couldn't find diaper cream in the market). More toys. Board books. Small stuffed animals. Plastic nesting cups (fun to stack and build with, and good for pouring water in the bath.). Cars and trucks. Finger puppets. Nicholas loved the beach balls. He could roll them, throw them, chase them, kick them. We think he even started picking up on the English – when we told him to go get the ball, he did.

Went to the hospital to meet Elena. First talked to the doctor. Said she has pneumonia (yesterday it was bronchitis and the flu). Also milk allergy. Doctor elaborated in English – "cow's milk."

Doctor said Elena needs to be in the hospital for two more weeks. Said that the blotches on her skin are from the milk allergy. Said we could do tests in the United States ("Cost just $5." How did he know that?) to determine exactly what she is allergic to. Doctor said she's a great girl. Said she'll do great in a family. Then they took us to a room where Elena was sitting in a crib. We had to wear hospital masks.

She's wonderful! We know she is not quite herself because she's sick. But she enjoyed being held more than Nicholas. She also enjoyed walking between us (unlike Nicholas). She also liked to point to things – out the window, in my eye, etc. She's bigger than Nicholas. And dressed in rags – including a Cossak-like blanket tied around her waist. I couldn't tell if she was wearing a diaper. And one of her layers was crudely stitched down the front.

When we got back to the hotel room Nicholas was napping on the couch. (Anna had arranged a babysitter for us.) This time when he woke up he didn't seem as confused. I picked him up, put him on the floor, and he started playing with the ball again. He's great with the ball. He laughs. He bats it with whichever hand is free. Mike even taught him to kick it.

Within two minutes today he said his first English words. I was going to the bathroom and I waved and said "bye-bye." He waved back and said "bye-bye." Then when I came back he said "ball." So exciting. The first of many firsts to come.

He also started to explore more, opening and closing the door, acting more like he might try to stand, walking a little more (with assistance). We are also starting to learn some of his signals. When he's getting close to going to sleep he slips one or two fingers in his mouth and starts to suck. When he wants his diaper changed he lies on his back and puts his legs up in the air.

February 12, 2003 Another amazing day in Archangelsk. Anna picked us up at 9:30. Went right to the hospital to spend the morning with Elena. She is so wonderful. She loves to snuggle. Every so often she laid her body against mine and sighed. I think somehow she knows we are different from the caretakers who have spent time with her. Somehow she knows we are for keeps.

When we first got to the hospital, she was wet. All the way down one leg. Mike went and found a nurse. She brought in a fresh pair of tights and a folded up baby blanket, probably once white but now gray. She took this blanket, put it between Elena's legs, put the clean tights on and then used a second blanket to wrap around her waist and secure the two ends of the blanket that would act as her diapers.

Got to spend two hours with her. We played with stickers, the ball we brought, and the toys she had there. We looked out the window.

A nurse came in and gave Elena a massage. She hated it! They thumped on her chest. We assume that was to break up anything in her lungs. Afterwards the nurse asked me if I wanted to dress her. I did. But I didn't get the belt quite right, so when she was walking the tights were dragging in the butt. I tried again.

Later the doctor came and told us to bring "your daughter" and follow him to a "treatment." They took two electrodes, put them in a wet towel and tied them to the front and back of her chest. She had to sit there for ten minutes, one turn of the egg timer. Mike held her through that. She wasn't thrilled, but she sat. We also managed to have a bit of a conversation with the nurse. She asked where in the U.S. we live, and we told her Virginia.

Before we got there I wasn't sure what we'd do for two hours. I thought we'd be bored. But before I knew it, Anna was back for us and it was time to go. I couldn't help it. I cried. Anna told me not to, that there was nothing to be sad about, Elena would be mine soon. And I just couldn't tell her. I couldn't tell Anna that I couldn't stand to leave Elena in that place. That would seem like a put-down. But that was what made it so hard.

The kids are all dressed in rags. Nicholas was wearing tights (with a hole in one butt cheek, the one he tends to scoot around on). No diaper. No underpants. An old faded plaid shirt. Many of the kids had on crude one-piece overalls that tie at the shoulders. And I think the nurses knit socks when the babies sleep. They're all wearing the same heavy knit socks that are so stretched out they are falling off.

February 14, 2003 Onboard the plane – heading home after the first visit. There are four babies on the plane with us. Three-and-a-half-year-old Natalia. Thirteen-month-old girl. Two boys. So far no one is crying. All the babies have a similar look on their faces – fear? Eyes wide. Catatonic. The orphan babies are easy to identify. Next time that will be us.

I have been thinking recently that when we started this process I was somewhat disappointed that I didn't get pregnant. I really thought I wanted to experience a baby growing inside of me. But now, now I wouldn't dream of having children any other way. What we're doing is the perfect thing for us. I so much like the idea of rescuing two children who otherwise would have little hope.

Archangelsk orphanage houses one hundred fifty kids between the ages of newborn and four. Which means they have an average of thirty kids in each age group. Dr. P. said last year they sent fifteen kids to the older kids' orphanage. Which means at best these kids have a one-in-two chance of getting a family. Fifty-fifty.

April 21, 2003 Second trip – I can't believe the weather this time. We actually have the windows open. It's like a crisp fall evening – blue sky, light clouds. From my bed I can see a horizon of churches. But one – the Church of Christ the Redeemer – stands way above the crowd. Its white stone, gold domes tower over the rest of the skyline. Subtle lights from below make it appear to glow in the night. Light extends from the corner stone to the gold gild of the onion domes. So beautiful.

As we sat in the window tonight I asked Mike if he ever imagined twenty years or so ago that one day he'd be in Russia to adopt twins.

"No."

"Did you ever think about being a parent?"

"Not until you mentioned it on Mother's Day."

And here we are. Every day is one day closer. And today there is only one day left. I'm not sure I really believed this day would ever get here.

April 24, 2003 It was a little after noon. I was thinking about lunch. I may have even said something, but I doubt Nicholas and Elena could have heard it or understood it. But yet Elena went right over to her stroller, dug out a bib and came to the middle of the room, holding it up as if to say, "I'm ready." Then she went and got Nicholas' bib and he dipped his head for someone to snap it around his neck.

Tonight our group took all the kids to the hotel restaurant. Russians like to talk and drink before eating, and the restaurant served in the Russian style. So we waited more than an hour and a half for our meal. Well, it was a bit much for the kids, so we all got up and walked around with them. At one point the music started and Alena came over to Elena; they joined hands and started dancing. So sweet. And it was obvious they had done this together in the orphanage.

April 25, 2003 Positive decision! We knew we'd get it. We knew court was really just a formality. But we were nervous nonetheless. But now it's done and today will forever be Adoption Day for Nicholas Peter and Elena Marie!

Tatiana and Anna prepared us well for court. We both knew exactly what to say. Judge was a younger man. Black robe, dark brown hair. Very Russian. Sometime during Mike's statement it seemed like the judge wasn't paying attention, but the truth is he had already made his decision, even written it up before we appeared in court. There's just no way he wrote a two-page ruling in the six minutes he was out of the courtroom.

The judge did ask Mike several questions. Most now a blur. But I did listen to what he said to see if I could pick out any words. I did hear a couple: "*toh-ahl-YET.*" "*KAH-kaht.*" Toilet. Poop. All the while, the judge was snickering. He wanted to know how Mike would handle toilet training.

The head nurse from the orphanage and our adoption coordinator urged the judge to grant us a positive decision. She noted that the twins' mother never visited them, that the last time she saw them was when she left the hospital after giving birth. So sad.

Positive decision on our petition to adopt Igor and Lina and change their names to Nicholas Peter and Elena Marie. Positive decision to waive the ten-day waiting period. Mike cried. I think it's the first and only time I've see him cry. I can't believe that just after 3:30 Moscow Standard Time I became a mom, twice.

Mom of Twelve
By Christy, mom of 12 (3 bio and 9 adopted), 2007
Oregon

I love everything about being the mom of a large family: the noise, the activity level, the chaos, the energy, the laughter, the give and take, the closeness, and the spontaneous creativity that erupts out of a group of enthusiastic kids. I see people watching us and hear them saying things like, "Must be some kind of pre-school," or "I guess they're having a party." When I see them smiling with curiosity, I'm never quite sure whether they are wishing they were part of our special group or else thanking God that they're not! But I know that I'd never want to be any other place; being together and creating a stir (as we often do) are some of the blessings of a big family. And when I watch the kids sleep, five or six together, as they do every night, or when I see them nurturing each other, sharing with each other, and laughing with each other, then I think, "Can there be a better way to grow up?"

Just Plain Special
By Lindsey, 2009
Arizona

I remember the first time I saw Wen's picture. The orphanage had listed him on a separate "Waiting Kids" web site with other children who had special needs. You had to click on the photo to discover each child's medical condition. There were kids with heart problems, blindness, cleft palates and lots of serious diseases. The expression on his face was so lost and sad. I remember thinking, *I hope he's not really sick.*

So I held my breath as I opened his file. When I read that he was born without a right forearm, I quickly scanned the text, looking for something else. Surely that was not the only reason this adorable three-year-old had not been adopted! But it was. Part of a limb was missing. Both my husband and I thought the same thing: *How inconsequential! Not a big deal at all.*

We had no idea how right our instincts would prove to be. It is only after living with Wen these past three and a half years that we have come to appreciate what a remarkable kid he is. He truly has no special need. He's just plain special.

I honestly believe it was a blessing that I didn't give birth to Wen, because I would have coddled and smothered him out of guilt and pity. Instead, Wen came to us as an independent and capable boy. We could see how important it was to stand back and let him do things for himself. He expertly tucked small things under his short arm, used his chin to help balance a bigger load and manipulated objects so he could operate them with one hand.

We are amazed every time he smacks a baseball farther than anyone else on his team. He skis like a rocket, gliding down the hill with pure glee. He's a killer tennis player and a strong swimmer. He even won the wheelbarrow race at Boy Scouts – flying across the lawn a little lopsided, but still lightning fast. He rides a bike, climbs monkey bars, types one-handed, plays video games just as well as his two-handed brother, and does all the same chores – from scooping dog doo to making his own bed.

Because his brother Seamus, who is the same age, expects him to keep up, there is no limit to what Wen believes (and, for that matter, what Seamus believes) he can do. Wen is the kid who unwraps his friends' cheese sticks for them at lunchtime. He holds the stick against his chest with his short arm, and peels it open with his other hand. His little buddies are too young to realize the significance of the fact that what they can't do with two able limbs, Wen can do with just one. But through those little actions, they learn he is completely functional just the way he is.

In China, people with disabilities are shunned and kept hidden away. We were horrified when passers-by would point and stare and chatter rudely at us during our trip to bring Wen home. We used our bodies to block our new son from their view. My husband shook his finger to shame them. We couldn't wait to take Wen home to Arizona, where he would be treated according to what he accomplishes in this world, not for the way he came into it – which was, of course, no fault of his own. That's not to say people here don't sometimes stare, but it's out of curiosity, not disgust. And when they ask him what happened to his arm, he's learned to answer, "Nothing's wrong with it. This is how God made me."

It never takes more than a minute or two before children who have just met Wen are lost in play right along with him, completely oblivious that he looks different. Wen carries himself with such confidence and he is so athletic, it's rare for anyone to even notice his short arm. The first question many adults have is how we managed to adopt a boy from China, which is culturally predisposed to favoring sons and usually has more girls available for adoption. When we explain he was probably abandoned because of his arm, they look shocked and go find him to see for themselves.

The week before we left for China to adopt Wen, I went to the pre-school class he would be joining to tell the kids we were bringing home a little boy who had a "special arm." It was a well-intentioned act by a still ignorant mommy-to-be, trying to pave a smoother path for her new son. But after his first week in that class, one of the little girls ran up with wide innocent eyes to ask me a question. "Miss Lindsey," she said, "is that Wen's special arm – or is it the other one?"

In that moment I learned something very powerful. What had I been so worried about? Wen teaches us every day that we are all unique, in both our challenges and our gifts. And, however we may look on the outside, we're perfect on the inside. I know that is true because God doesn't make mistakes.

Future Adoption Options
By Lora, mom of four, 2008
Two adopted in the U.S.A. and two from Russia
Texas

Ethan was riding home in the van with his mom and brother and sisters. We were talking about growing up and having a family. Ethan said he wanted to get a Jeep. He also said he wanted to have two boys to ride around with him so that they could go and do fun things together. He said he didn't want to get married, so he would adopt his children. "Besides, that's the best way to become a dad anyway," he said. All of the other children agreed and started talking about their plans of when they would adopt and from where.

Making a L-O-N-G Story Short
By a mom of 21 (17 adopted), March 2009
Arizona

This is the quintessential "long story short." There is no way to tell about our adoptions of seventeen children without writing a book, and I simply don't have time! Here's a brief outline of our story.

We had four biological children and wanted more. A friend had adopted from Moldova and we were impressed with her sons. In May, 1997, we adopted two toddlers from Russia. While traveling to bring home a two-year-old and a ten-month-old, we saw the huge numbers of older children who absolutely had no future. It made quite an impression. We decided to adopt again.

Our second adoption was of two children, ages eight and nine at the time. Finances were a huge strain, and because of some very unusual circumstances, we thought that we wouldn't be able to complete the adoption. Then, because of a minor miracle, we were allowed to bring the kids home anyway and to pay off our adoption over the course of the next two years.

Their grandma was an absolute angel. She loved these kids enough to offer them a chance for a better life. Their grandma's allowing them to be adopted is a story of the true love of Christ shining through.

Our third time adopting came about because I had connections with a Canadian agency that sponsored summer programs for orphans. One ten-year-old girl couldn't be placed permanently with the family who had sponsored her, so we decided to adopt her. For our next adoption, we were helping another couple with their adoption when we became aware of a sibling group of one brother and one sister. We decided we wanted to bring them into our home. Well, it turned out that there was another brother. That information had not been divulged when we first traveled, but after hearing about him, how could we *not* go back for him?

Our fifth adoption experience came about because I was doing humanitarian work at an orphanage. A little girl there "locked onto" me, and I couldn't bear to leave her in what was truly a horrible orphanage. I had been in quite a few orphanages by then, and most were good, but this one was not. This was a home for children who were determined to have severe problems and therefore could not be adopted. The needs were evident and enormous. Even though we were told this little girl had significant problems, I was not willing to leave her behind. She has been home with us for six years now and has made incredible strides.

We love adopting older kids. It gives children without hope a new chance at life. We have adopted seventeen children and teens, and I can easily say that their whole lives have changed for the better. Yes, there have been challenges. And I will tell you the truth: there have been struggles, difficulties, and some heart-aches. We have found that it's best to adopt two kids at a time so they have someone to share the experience with. And out of the seventeen adoptions we have completed, only three children have ended up with major difficulties.

Two of our adoptions were truly miraculous stories, so I'll mention them briefly. The first involves birth order. Much of the literature about adoption says not to disrupt birth order and not to adopt children older than those already in the home. One of our biological sons felt that we should not adopt anyone older than he was. Well, as circumstances would have it, we did adopt a sister and brother, both older than this biological son. The miracle is that as much as he had been against the adoption of children older than he was, these two additions to our family were soon my son's best friends. Our biological son later died of brain cancer. His death was devastating for our family, of course, but we didn't let the death of our son keep us from adopting more children. We wanted to give a chance at life to more of the older children we had seen on our travels.

Our most amazing miracle took place so we could bring one of our daughters home. She had been adopted to the U.S. by another family. When the adoption did not turn out perfectly for the adoptive mom, the girl (a teenager) was taken back to Russia. She was left without hope or home and no resources of any kind. Can you imagine? When we heard about this, we searched for the girl. We were desperate to help her because she had been the best friend in Russia of one of our adopted daughters. She ended up back at the orphanage where she had been before. The orphanage was actually quite kind and compassionate in taking her back; since she was sixteen by this time, they did not have any obligation to keep her or care for her. Because she was now a U.S. citizen who had been abandoned in Russia, she essentially had no rights; she was no longer a Russian orphan and was not any longer a ward of the state. The circumstances were highly unusual and the situation was quite unclear and confusing. With the help of the American Embassy and the Russian Department of Education, over time, we managed to get her papers straightened out so that she could be adopted. That in itself was a major feat.

The plan was then for my husband to travel to bring her home. The day before he was supposed to fly to Russia to get her, he was in a near-fatal car accident. Could things possibly get any worse? Here I was, at my dying husband's bedside, figuring that the adoption effort would have to be given up. From his hospital bed, my husband kept repeating, "Go get her. Don't leave her. Bring her home." I was not about to leave my husband in his hour of need; I stayed with him while he recovered. Somehow, connections were made with another couple traveling to the same region to adopt. Miraculously, they were able to be contacted, and fortunately for us and for our daughter, they were willing to escort her back to the U.S.A.

C H A P T E R   E I G H T E E N

For Prospective and New Adoptive Parents

"In bringing up children, spend on them half as much money
and twice as much time."

~ Dr. Laurence Peter

Reservations about Adoption
By Laurel, April 2004
Ohio

Here's a journal entry I wrote eighteen months before we brought our son home. I think it gives insight into what kids already at home wonder about when the family is in the middle of the adoption process.

Our daughter was seven years old at the time I wrote this, we had been in the process for over a year, and we still were not matched with a child. Now, four years later, we're all settled in and our two daughters can't imagine life without their brother!

Today Kate and I went for a picnic. We talked while we ate and continued our conversation after lunch. I don't know exactly how we got on the subject of adoption, but I think it started with Kate saying, "When the new child gets here…" Anyway, a whole conversation ensued, and while she sat on my lap, the tears flowed. "I feel like you and Dad won't pay attention to me and Erin when we have a new child."

I promised her that we would still gave plenty of attention to her and her sister – that we would still read together and have tea parties, and that we would still make time to do things alone together. We talked about how in big families there is plenty of love and attention to go around. I asked her if it felt scary for her to think about the adoption.

She said, "I'm not scared. I feel worried."

I added that maybe it was hard because it was taking much longer than we had expected, and that waiting so long made it seem like it might never happen.

She asked, "Do you think it will happen? Do you think we will get a child?" I sensed a bit of hope in her voice that maybe the adoption *wouldn't* take place after all. I responded that I thought we would adopt a child, but that since we still didn't have a timetable, I didn't know when we would bring our new child home.

She also expressed concerns that, "The new child might not like me," and added, "I don't know if I can love an adopted child or if I'll love him as much as the rest of the family." I reassured her that even if she felt that way, it wasn't a problem…that it was good that she was sharing her feelings.

Near the end of our conversation she sighed and summed up her feelings: "It makes me sad to talk about it sometimes, and sometimes it makes me feel better. But even when it makes me feel sad, I still want to talk about it."

I was impressed with how articulately she expressed herself and her willingness to do so. This process is a challenge for everyone in the family; I hope we have news soon.

Interesting Connections Observed
By Dee, January 2009
Georgia

My two kids, both adopted, are teens. I've learned – over time – something they have in common that might be of interest to others. Low blood sugar seems to be the likely trigger for behavior and health issues.

My daughter was recently suffering from a lot of headaches, some migraines and some not. The migraines were terrible and she took medication for them. I noticed that sometimes what she thinks is the start of a migraine, isn't. The routine now is that if she feels a headache starting, she eats a snack, takes acetaminophen, and waits fifteen minutes. Sometimes that takes care of it, so I suspect that it's just low blood sugar causing the headache.

My son sometimes has some defiant behavior problems and they are almost always tied to one of two things, either low blood sugar because he didn't eat enough at school, or fear. I am trying to train myself (and my mother) that when he refuses to do something, to step back and question him about when he has eaten. Often a good snack like cheese or something with protein will restore him to a cooperative place.

Other times he is really fussy due to simple fear. Before he went to camp last summer, he was really grouchy for several days. When I left him at the camp bus and kissed him goodbye, he acted as if he were going on the Bataan Death March! When I picked him up a few days later, he was all smiles and wanted to go back. Sometimes the fear is of a much smaller thing, though, such as something he hasn't done before. The other day we were going to the eye doctor, a new experience, and he was terrified despite our reassurances.

Sometimes my daughter overreacts to something small, and I have learned, with the help of a therapist, that sometimes small things trigger memories of abuse and it causes the overreaction. For instance, one night she panicked because her younger brother was playfully jabbing a butter knife at her. It triggered a memory of seeing her birth mom slash her grandfather's face and she freaked out and started screaming and crying. The great thing is that with therapy, she has started to understand what triggers her reactions.

For some adopted kids, anything new is scary, and you will see acting-out behaviors. Try to take a deep breath, be patient, and coax them into the new thing. They will usually relax when they experience it, if you are reassuringly close. I have learned about these connections the hard way. If you see your child wildly overacting to something small, seek the help of a trained therapist. The web site for Nancy Thomas lists therapists in every state.

P.S. I'm offering this information because it might be helpful, but of course parents will want to ask their children's doctors about it before giving any medicine.

Our "Onion"
By a mom in California, 2005

One thing about our son is that he has many layers, like an onion. The onion analogy works well when we refer to him. We've been able to peel back the thick, protective outer layers. He trusts us and knows he is loved unconditionally, but he doesn't talk much about his earlier life. He claims to remember little or nothing of Russia; whether that is by choice so he does not have to talk about or recount things, or unconsciously, we may never know.

Many older children who have suffered abuse from very young ages before finding their forever families tend to develop those layers. It has taken a *very* long time to peel back some of our son's thicker layers, and nearly three years later, we're still working on it. Some kids might feel like they have to be tough and resist the urge to let their guard down. We honor that with our son and give him space when he seems to need it. We generally see his gentle side toward other kids when he thinks we're not looking.

When I see these moments of tenderness from our son, I am greatly relieved because I know that tenderness is there and can be nurtured and eventually brought out. It also forces me, when I feel angry with his behavior, to put that emotion aside and just love him. He sometimes comes to me and puts his arms around my waist to say he is sorry, or just for the sake of a hug. I have vowed that, no matter the circumstance, I will never, ever turn away a hug. Not ever. We feel, as parents, it is our job to teach our children the ways of life, but what a blessing to be open to what they can teach us!

The onion analogy may provide somewhat of a label for an otherwise intangible experience for some kids who did orphanage time. It may also give parents a glint of hope as it does us.

My Story for Katie
By Susie, 2004
Florida

The Decision

In September 2002, when Christina was eighteen and Kellie was eight, your dad and I decided that we wanted another little girl to love. Once we decided we wanted to adopt from Russia, we worked very hard for one year and saved enough money to find you. We worked extra hours and cut out extra spending. There was so much paperwork to fill out! When we finished with that, it was time to wait for you to find us.

On your dad's birthday in November, I got a call at work telling me about a little girl for me to see. I was so excited and so was everybody else. It seemed like forever for your picture to be downloaded from the e-mail. Then, finally, there you were! You were so beautiful. I called your dad and Nana and told them, "Katie has found us." We watched the mail every day, and a video of you finally came on December 3. We saw a perfect, sweet, and beautiful little girl, almost three years old.

The First Trip

Nana and I flew out on January 26, 2004. We were nervous and excited. You were so far away that we had to take three planes to get there. Three days later we finally got to meet you. To our surprise, you had green spots all over! You had chicken pox and so did all your friends. (It was a good thing that my mom and I had both already had chicken pox because we were told that they seemed to go around often in the baby homes.) The spots made everyone look funny, but you were still so cute – and shy. You didn't speak to us at all and you didn't want to be hugged or held by either of us. Nana and I got to stay with you until lunchtime. We did bring a small photo album for you to see; that interested you. We came back after your nap and played with you again until dinner time.

We came again the next morning and afternoon to see you and play with you. You waved goodbye to us as we left. You were so young; we didn't know if you would understand what our visits meant. We were sad to leave you, but we knew we would be back soon. We flew back to Moscow the next morning and flew back home the next day. Everyone was glad to see us, but they were more excited to see the pictures and hear about you.

The Second Trip

On our second trip, Dad and I walked upstairs, and I went into the reading room to find you. I opened the door, and our eyes met. You ran over to me and called me Mama and hugged me. I couldn't believe you remembered me! You then uttered ever so softly a word in my ear; it was "*kishka*." You were looking out the window into the snow-covered playground and trying to show us a cat.

I walked you out to meet your dad. You were so shy that you wouldn't look at him. I held you and played with you until lunchtime. The caregiver and the interpreter talked with you and told you that we were going to be your mommy and daddy. You were a little afraid of your dad at first, but that ended after he climbed right into the ball pit and played with you. Your dad and I came back after naptime, and this time you played with me for a while and then warmed up to Dad. You were running back and forth between us and hugging us. When it came time to leave, you wouldn't let go of your dad's neck; it made him so happy.

Our court date came on March 31, which was your sister Kellie's ninth birthday. Your dad gave a speech saying why we wanted to adopt you. In the courtroom, there was a nice lady judge, a prosecutor, a social worker, and a representative from the baby home. I'm not certain what the prosecutor's job was there in the courtroom; I think maybe she was the representative of the Ministry of Education. She listened and then asked questions about us, our home, and our plans for childcare. The hearing lasted about one and a half hours. When the judge granted our petition to adopt you, everyone cried. We were so relieved. The next day we went to the baby home to get you. We went in to see the director, Nina, who was also the head pediatrician, and we all cried again. She was so happy that you were finally going home to be with your family.

We found you in the reading room and you were still very quiet. We changed your clothes.(Parents bring new clothes for their children so that the clothes at the orphanage can stay there.) We said good-bye and left the orphanage. We were so excited and anxious about being able to take you home. You were very quiet during the short ride back to the apartment; you just sat on my lap looking out the window, taking in the sights and sounds.

The Week in Russia

For the week we stayed with you in Russia, we kept you on the same orphanage schedule for eating and sleeping. You started picking up English really quickly, and you told us when you were hungry and had to potty. You loved bath time, brushing your teeth, and your Minnie Mouse pajamas. It was a good time for us to get to know each other. You were already calling us Mama and Dadda after the first night with us. You absolutely understood that we were a family.

Then we hit a snag – the Russian government could not print your American name on your passport – and Dad had to go back home without us on April 7. He had to leave to take care of your sisters. You cried as you watched him leave from the kitchen window. It was clear that you were beginning to understand that we were your parents. You cried all that morning for your Dadda after he left for the airport. You kept saying, "Dadda, *machine-a*." (*ma-SHEE-na* means *car* in Russian.)

The Flight Home

I finally got your passport a few days later and we flew out of Tomsk on Easter Sunday morning. At the Tomsk airport they don't start to warm up the jets until passengers are loading. When the engines started, the loud roar really frightened you and you started to pull away from me. A nice Russian man behind me (who didn't speak much English) asked me if it was OK for him to carry you up the stairs and into the plane. I was so grateful for the help because I was carrying a diaper bag, an overnight bag, and your paperwork. (I was scared to death and did not want to lose your paperwork, so I carried all the important papers in my hand.) You cried nearly the entire flight – you were scared of the noise of the plane. You finally calmed down some when some nearby women talked to you and I pulled out our photo album and your toys.

The flight from Moscow to Zurich wasn't as bad since the plane wasn't as loud inside as the Tomsk plane. The flight from Zurich to New York was even better; the plane was huge, relatively quiet, and we could even walk around. Plus, we were lucky enough to have two open seats in our row so we could stretch out to rest.

I didn't know very many Russian words, but since we had been together for more than a week already, we could communicate some. Plus, by now, you loved hugs, so we hugged for most of each flight. When you did go to sleep, you slept right on my chest, snuggling close to me.

We finally got home the next night at 11:00. It had been a long trip, but when you saw your dad waiting at the luggage area for us, you ran into his arms. We all hugged and cried. You met your sisters out in the van, and when we got home we all fell, exhausted, into bed. We were finally home.

Postponing School
By B.J., March 2008
California

Our second son was severely developmentally delayed when we first got him. He's doing great now, but suffered from the effects of neglect. One of the areas that was delayed was his speech (at nearly four years old he still wasn't speaking his own language), so sometimes he says the sweetest things. While we were in Las Vegas, he kept talking about wanting to go see the hotel 'You Nork, You Nork.' I'm still giggling about that. Another time as we were reading a book together before bed, he randomly took my face in his hands and said, "Momma, you delicious!" That still makes me tear up. So sweet.

I think language is a big issue for older kids coming here. And with that said, I'd offer to parents not to be afraid to hold their kids back a year in school if they feel so moved. We could have put our first son in second grade, but I'm so glad we decided to keep him in first. Socially and academically it was a good decision for him. At first I worried that it would be bad for him to be with younger kids, but it really seems to be OK. As he prepares to enter fourth grade at ten years old (most of his peers are nine), he sometimes asks why he's so much older than the other kids. We tell him it's what has worked for him, it's nothing to be concerned about, and he is just as smart and capable as his classmates. Beyond that, we don't put too much energy into comparing where he is to where others are. I have reminded him that few kids come to first grade as he did: adjusting to a strange new culture and living condition, and speaking a completely different language. I reiterate his accomplishments since he has been here and how proud he should be of himself.

We worried as well about our second son, but he, as one of the older kids in his class, also seems to be doing very well. He still has moments of frustration searching for ways to vocally express himself, and our lesson here has been with patience; we let him work it out and find his words rather than try and finish for him. Just be patient and attentive. While we do gently correct language, we don't spend a lot of time focusing on the correction.

Twelve-Year-Old Girls
By Leslie, 2009
New York

Is Galya perfect? Not by a long shot. Like most normal, American, twelve-year-old girls, she can be lazy, can get mouthy, and sometimes she lies. But the joy that she brings to all those she meets, in her family and her community, far outweighs these minor irritations. She has a positive spirit that is exceptional, especially considering her early history, and her strong spirit certainly helped to save her life.

There is nothing I would rather do than listen to her babble on about nonsense or giggle about something silly. When she laughs, her eyes close completely and her nose turns up so far that I can only say it looks like the nose on the Winnie the Pooh bear I had as a child! Even when she first came to us in 2002, she demanded the affection she had missed in her earlier life, saying such things in her Russian accent as "K'ai slip in you bed?" every single night, or begging me to sit in the back seat of the car with her: "Seet in the back," leaving her Dad to be the chauffer! Now, at twelve, she still wants "cuddle" time.

People often tell my husband and me that we did a wonderful thing. We acknowledge that, but, at the same time, we say that Galya has brought so much joy to us. Somehow we feel that Galya was absolutely meant to be with us and we felt that way on the very first day we were all together. We realize that this will not happen for everyone who adopts. Certainly each adoption has a different degree of adjustment and all have their own problems. Both Tom and I had had a great deal of hardship in our earlier lives. Perhaps it was finally our time to catch a break. I don't mean for anyone to read our story and think that their adoption will be as easy as ours, but love and patience will overcome all but the most serious of challenges.

Biological Families
By Jenny, 2009
Taylor, Arizona

My girls' biological families – birth moms, birth dads, aunts, uncles, cousins – will always and forever be in my heart. They are so special to me and I feel we share something beautiful. I am so thankful that they shared life with me. I have promised my daughters that we can keep in touch with them. I have worked to keep my word, but it has been hard at times. I have called and tried to stay in touch, but have not been able to make contact much with the family of one of my daughters. I've told my daughter that after she graduates from high school we can go back to see her family in her birth country if she wants to. She's eager to do that.

One comment I would make to parents who want to adopt is that there is no way going into adoption that they will be able to predict the emotions that take place. Both of mine were open adoptions, which meant that my children were with their birth moms when I picked them up. I was so excited, with emotions flying high, but when the birth mother handed me my child, the child she so dearly loved (and still does), it was heart-wrenching. I was so ready to take my baby, but it tore me up at the same time because I could easily see how much the whole birth family loved her. My feelings immediately changed in that second – from being excited to being heartbroken. It was such a mix of emotions. When people say, "You're lucky as an adoptive mom not to have experienced the pain of birth," they may be right. But I have experienced the pain of mixed emotions at the moment that a birth mom gives up her baby for adoption.

I thought I was a little better prepared for it the second time around, but it was still very hard. The birth family loved their baby girl; it was evident with their hugs and kisses good-bye. They wanted their daughter to be adopted, and yet it was plain to see on their faces how hard it was to give her to us, her new family.

The love I have for my daughters' birth mothers can never be measured. No matter how many times you adopt, you cannot prepare yourself for that moment or foresee the emotions you will feel.

Fountain of Youth
By Melissa, February 2009
Arizona

It has been so much fun to watch the relationship between my father and my brother Sergei develop. They have a very special bond. When preparing the documents for Sergei's adoption, my dad was so "on top of" each and every little detail, and I could just tell from his commitment to filing the paperwork how excited he was. He was diligent and worked so hard to bring Sergei home as fast as possible. I swear my dad got fifteen years younger when my brother came home. He took up rollerblading and starting playing again like I hadn't seem him do in years! I always knew my dad was happy with his girls, but it has been such a joy to see him have his boy. I love to hear their stories of the annual Boys' Camping Trip with my dad's brothers and all the boy cousins. After the first camping trip, Sergei came home and only wanted to eat Dinty Moore Stew for months. I love that my dad takes Sergei into the garage to build things with wood and tools. As an adult daughter whose parents adopted after I moved out on my own, it has been an absolute joy to see my father so rejuvenated by his relationship with his son!

The Red Thread
By Lindsey, mom and journalist, December 2005
Arizona

For the fifth time this morning, Wen runs into my bedroom calling, "Mama." As soon as he sees me, he breaks into a wild grin and runs away to play trains with his brother Seamus in another part of the house. It happens dozens of times a day, this checking to make sure I am still nearby, that I haven't vanished from his life.

I know he can't possibly remember being abandoned on a doorstep at five days of age, but he's afraid of being abandoned now. He waited three years for a "mama" to come for him. And now that he has her – and a daddy, a sister, and two brothers – he's determined not to lose us.

If only he understood how safe he is. How we could never let him go. How we know in our hearts that he was always meant to be with us, even if he was born on the other side of the world.

When we first began the paperwork to adopt, we intended to bring home a daughter, thinking the sibling rivalry might be more manageable with a girl and boy. We requested a one-year-old – and we never even considered adopting a child with special needs. Our lives are busy, and we weren't sure we would be up to the challenge.

Then I happened to see Wen's picture. Everything was wrong. He was a boy. He was already three years old. And he was born missing a right forearm. Not at all the perfect child we had envisioned. Yet something in my heart told me he was perfect for us. In the photograph, there was a wistful look in his eyes that I recognized. I didn't know why it seemed familiar, but I knew somehow this boy was my son.

When his medical file arrived, we learned the orphanage had given him the name Fu Wei Wen. Fu means "lucky," Wei means "great" and Wen translates as "belonging to someone in the news." How much clearer could it be? We told the adoption agency we no longer wanted a little girl. We wanted Wen.

It was a difficult first meeting. Wen came to us kicking and screaming, and it broke our hearts to see him so afraid. But within hours, he had attached himself to me. The next morning, I was shocked when he called me "Mama" and wouldn't let me out of his sight. That's when I knew for the very first time what it really means to be a mother. It isn't about being pregnant, or giving birth, or nursing, or falling in love with a darling little baby you and your husband created together. It's giving a child, any child, unconditional love…forever.

CHAPTER NINETEEN

How Far We Have Come!

"How far you go in life depends on your being tender with the
young, compassionate with the aged, sympathetic with the striving,
and tolerant of the weak and the strong. Someday in life
you will have been all of these."

~ George Washington Carver

In Russia, Eight Years after My Brother Came Home
By Claire, June 2005
St. Petersburg, Russia

Hello family!

I just got back from Baby Home #14. Igor came and picked me up, since I'm living close to his apartment. He initially told me that we would only stay for about twenty minutes, but when we got to the baby home Valentina had been called unexpectedly to a meeting, so we walked around a bit. Igor showed me the rooms where Paul used to live, and we spoke with a lot of the different women working there. Everyone we spoke to remembered "Seriozha" and they were happy to see the pictures and hear that he is doing well. Some of the questions that different people asked: "Does he speak English with an accent?" "Can he read?" "What does he like to do?" "Does he know that he is Russian?" I told them that Paul is happy and smart and plays the piano and baseball and likes to swim.

Valentina returned after we had been there twenty minutes. She enjoyed hearing Paul's letter (Igor read it aloud in Russian) and was so surprised that Paul wrote it. She also expressed the hope that the whole family would visit in the future. Igor also translated the letter that Mom sent. They both liked hearing all of the news. Igor is going to type out a copy in Russian and bring it to them later. I asked about Paul's "Mama Zoya," and Valentina said that she has retired but comes back often.

I left the toys and candy and your donations with Valentina. She sent some gifts for Paul, two books with beautiful pictures of St. Petersburg, one in English and one in Russian, and a box of nice chocolates. Then Igor and I said goodbye.

Now, here's the best part: As we were walking to the front door, Zoya walked in! Igor told her who I was, and she started crying. She was so, so glad to hear about Paul and to know that he is doing so well. Igor told me later that she had missed Paul so much, and his leaving was hard for her (even though she was also very glad for him) and that Seriozha was her favorite.

It was really a wonderful trip. It was good to see where Paul spent the first three years of his life. Paul, I think it would be very interesting for you to go there and see everyone. I know if you went back for a visit all of those ladies who took care of you would just love it! All of the children there seemed very happy. A lot of them were playing outside and some of them were having lunch when I was there. Valentina really appreciated your letter, and I know that Zoya will read it also.

Lots of Love, Claire

A Mom's Promise
By Kathy, May 2008
Louisiana

Today was a very exciting day that began with one very nervous fifteen-year-old. It was awards day for the middle school. Almira was so nervous about being on stage alone. She is still very shy and does not ever like attention to be on her. You would have thought she was going to have to stand up and give a verbal rendition of her first year of school in the U.S.A.! I assured her that she would be getting an award for Principal's Club (all A's for the year) and she would not be on the stage by herself. She did receive an award for Principal's Club. After that, she received an award for highest GPA in Bible class for the sixth-grade girls. Then she received the "Most Christ-Like" Award for a 6th grade girl. Then the principal kept her up on the stage by herself and presented her the Soaring Eagle Award. So much for Mom's promises that she wouldn't have to be on stage alone!

Principal Stokes explained how she was adopted from Kazakhstan and had been home less than a year. He talked about how she had made so much progress, excelled in the classroom, and adjusted so well to school. He clarified that the Soaring Eagle Award was for a middle school student who goes above and beyond what is expected. I was shaking so much I barely got it on camera! Almira shyly smiled and seemed quite eager to get off the stage and out of the spotlight. After the ceremony she was all smiles and was surrounded by teachers and other students congratulating her. I think she was really surprised and never expected all of the awards and attention. I can't believe how far she has come in just one year. She is truly an exceptional young lady.

Turning Point
By Janna, 2008
California

Exactly three months ago we officially became the parents of this stunning little girl. The first few weeks were tough. There were times I wondered what I had done! But now, a little further down the road, things are going well. We're so blessed! Lili is still Mama's girl, but she is also realizing Daddy's not so bad.

Now that she understands just about everything, we've entered a new phase of behavior. When I tell her to do something, she stands there looking at me and grinning if she doesn't want to do it. I repeat what I've asked her to do and she continues to stand there smiling. After two chances, I start counting to three. She knows if I get to three she's in trouble. Usually by the time I get to two she runs to do whatever it is she's been asked to do, saying "I'm sorry, I'm sorry," as she's running. So, I know it's not a comprehension issue; it's a testing the boundaries issue.

I didn't laugh hysterically when my five-year-old daughter proclaimed, "I not Chinese!" For the record, I don't think she actually knows what that means at this point. She was just being argumentative. She's five; that's her job.

On Halloween when it was time to get dressed in her costume for trick-or-treating, she proclaimed, "I no want to wear Sleeping Beauty dress." I asked, "Would you like to be a chicken?" She loved the chicken costume and walked around clucking between "trick-or-treats."

On a more serious note, we have taken her to see the cardiologist. Everything went well, and our doctor was very pleased with the repair that had been performed in China. Lili will have to have another surgery at some point, but if things go like the cardiologist expects, that won't be necessary until her late teens or early adult years. So far, it has been an amazing journey.

School Progress
By B.J., May 2007
California

School has begun and Aleksandr is pretty on top of writing his name. It has been amazing to see his progress over the last month. He is still in Speech at school but is making tremendous progress. His language improves each day and he is making friends. According to his wonderful teacher, he has his own little 'entourage' and they all look out for one another. He makes us laugh a great deal. But along with this growth and development come greater testing and more talking back. Discipline is becoming a little more commonplace these days but it is all in an attempt to make certain the boys understand their boundaries. Some of that understanding still is a work in progress, but our consistency will pay off.

Zack got his STAR test scores back (A California state standardized test for school goers) and what amazed us was that he scored as well as he did. We reminded ourselves that he had only been here a year when he took that test. It was broken down to writing and language skills, and Math skills. The school district wants kids to score in the 'Proficient' or 'Advanced' range, but is satisfied with 'Basic.' That said, Zack scored at the high end of Basic in language and writing, and a little past the mid-mark for Math, after only being here for a year. Quite an achievement to say the very least! We are very proud of him.

How far they've come in just two short years!

So Much Life
By Tatiana, age 20, June 2009
Arizona

Baby Eva
I feel really lucky to have been adopted. I'm so glad because adoption gave me a new chance at life. I realized this most when I went back to the country of my birth, at age sixteen. But let me start at the beginning.

As a baby in Romania, I was Eva. I was in an orphanage from the time I was born until I was two and a half years old. I, like the other kids that age, was still in a crib, left there most of the day. There wasn't much milk or formula available, I'm told, so we often drank tea – baby bottles filled with tea, and we held the bottles ourselves.

Learning to Give and Receive Affection
You know, those first few years are so important; they are the years when little ones learn to bond emotionally. They need constant touch and handling in order to learn how to bond properly. My mom tells me about when she came to meet me. She picked me up from the crib and I had on soggy, dirty diapers. Of course the caretakers didn't have what they needed to change us more often. Apparently, I didn't want to leave the workers, though, and I pushed my mom away. I didn't want to have much to do with her at all at first and sort of treated her like, "Who are *you*, anyway?" I was hesitant to go with her.

Thinking back on it, I'm sure that I had some attachment problems and difficulty trusting my parents. As a child, you don't realize it, but now I think I was angry in the beginning. I was being passed around among many people and caretakers. I think it took years to resolve those issues. I do have a clear memory – when I was about ten years old – of it becoming easier for me to show affection and share my feelings. I was suddenly more able to hug my mom and tell her I loved her, whereas before that it had been difficult for me. I think I have overcome those challenges now, thanks to my mom. She had to be so patient with us!

My Siblings

I have two other siblings from the town of Miercurea-Ciuc, Romania. Two of us were adopted at the same time, my brother and I. We were from the same orphanage, but we're not related by blood. Then my mom went back for a sister for us two years later. It took that long to get all of the paperwork and arrangements made. My mom worked so hard to bring my sister home because she wanted to get her out of what was a very bad situation: she was neglected, ignored, and barely fed by her birth parents. My sister came to us a few years later, but we were all about the same age.

My mom and dad actually ended up adopting eight children – seven from Eastern Europe and one from Texas. I have two siblings from Romania who are tan-skinned like me, two from Russia, two from Moldova, and one from Texas. I used to feel rather left out, almost shunned, as a kid. I think it's because we were darker skinned and also because we were home schooled. And we were adopted too, so it was just that we were different. Sometimes we just didn't fit in.

I think deep inside I still do have some feelings of confusion. As I grew up, I relied a lot on my family. It was tough for me to separate from them and become a more independent person; at first I didn't want to pull away. I still definitely do not like to be far away from those I love and trust. I want people around me all the time; I'm a people person. I suppose that could be my personality or my years in the orphanage, or both.

Memories

Two early memories stand out for me, and I think I was only three or four years old at the time. I remember how exciting it was when we had finished all of our paper work and my brother and I became U.S. citizens. The second memory was the sealing ceremony that took place in our church. I don't know if I understood the full meaning of the ceremony, but I remember feeling happy. I was also elated about my beautiful, new, fluffy white dress. Those positive feelings were reinforced each time my parents adopted a new child and the new brother or sister was sealed to our family. I enjoyed the attention and affection I received at those special times, but I will honestly say, too, that I didn't necessarily want to share the attention with the new siblings. That probably was because I had missed out on the love and attention I had not gotten during my early years in the orphanage. It's not hard for me to talk about feelings anymore. It's easy now for me to say I was angry in the early years, maybe because I have moved beyond that. Now I don't mind talking about it at all.

A Return to Romania

In 2005, my mom, my Romanian brother and sister and I returned to Romania to visit Tatiana, the woman who had helped my mom and dad adopt us. They've kept in touch with her all these years. (In fact, my parents named me after her when they adopted me.) We went back for about ten days to see the area where we were born, visit with Tatiana, and to take gifts and donations to two different orphanages. My brother's Eagle Project for Boy Scouts was to deliver these items to Romanian orphanages.

The old run-down orphanage where we had lived was gone, so we visited two newer buildings. They were called schools now, instead of orphanages, but the children lived there at least part of the year. Some were kids without homes, so they stayed there; some had disabilities and some were older children. We arrived with duffel bags filled with school supplies, pencil kits, toys, games, balls and dolls. The twenty or so children lined up and received their gifts, and I remember that all of them said thank you to us. We stayed a while and played with them, tossing balls into the air while we all held the edges of a parachute. We all laughed and had fun together. It felt a little sad to leave.

On the Streets

The really heartbreaking part of our trip was seeing so many young people on the streets. Children get turned out from orphanages at age eighteen. Teens and even younger children followed the tourists around. Most of them begged for money and accepted anything that was given to them. Tatiana told us there was no way we could help everyone, but it was hard to send them away without at least a little money.

One experience stood out more than any other. With Tatiana's help, I talked with a young woman, one of many, who made her living on the streets. It was the only way many of them had to survive. We visited with her a while and gave her food. I couldn't help but notice that many of the young women hid behind coats and hoods. They didn't look healthy. Maybe they were ashamed of their lifestyle. They lived on garbage, and many of them were ill. The young woman we visited with told Tatiana to tell me and my siblings how lucky we were to have been adopted. It was then that I really began to understand how fortunate I was to have come home to my family.

Appreciation

Looking back over the years, I see that I have come a long way in my life. I have wondered about my birth mom. I don't even have a picture of her.

My mom tells me that she tried to take a photo of my birth mom when she was in Romania the first time, but my birth mom left before my mom could get her camera. I was angry about that at first, but I'm not anymore. It's not upsetting to me to be adopted or to talk about being adopted. When I was younger, it was even exciting to talk about it, explaining where I came from. Now, I just feel very fortunate. I want to say thank you to my parents for giving me a chance at a real life. Who knows where I would be if you hadn't taken me from the orphanage?

Looking Ahead

It would really be an experience to be able to meet my birth mom. If I did have the chance to meet her, I would be excited to see her – to see what she looks like and to tell her about my life now. It's not likely at all that I'll ever meet her. I also think about how different my life in Romania would have been even if she had been able to raise me.

Now I'm married to a great guy who is a good husband, and we have a baby on the way! At first I didn't think that I was ready to have a baby. I had seen all the work my mom and dad had gone through to adopt us and all the love and devotion my mom had given to me and my brothers and sisters. I considered adoption and thought maybe I could do that some day. Now I look forward to having this baby. It's a beautiful thing. Not all women can have babies, and I will have the opportunity to take care of our baby. She won't go through what I had to. And who knows? Maybe in the future we'll consider adopting. There are so many children who need homes and good parents.

Poem
By Lori, March 2009
Arizona
One year after bringing Lena and Daniel home

> Softness of hair
> Presses my cheek
> Body collapses on my lap
> Laughter connects us all.

A Skeptic Becomes a Believer
By Grace, May 2008
Washington

My grandson was adopted from Ukraine at age seven. To be honest, I was not thrilled that my daughter and her husband were accepting into their lives an older child with challenges; it seemed way too risky to me. Needless to say, they adopted, and my grandson came home to the U.S.A. in the spring of 2005. He did not read or write, was behind other children his age developmentally, and had learning challenges. He was also hyperactive. My daughter and her husband were told that these were all probably the effects of Fetal Alcohol Exposure.

In his first months at home, this child was not very pleasant to be with; he couldn't sit still for even a minute and he demanded attention incessantly. Thank heavens my daughter and her husband were prepared to be patient! With lots of love and compassion, teamwork, and good communication, they have helped this boy immensely. He still has naughty behavior sometimes, just like all children, but he does very well most days in his classroom at school and at home.

Just three short years later, my grandson has calmed down and he interacts well with adults as well as with other kids. In fact, it's now a joy to spend time with him! This precious child is doing well socially, and thanks to his parents' dedication and some special help at school, he has caught up with most of his peers. He has made *incredible* strides and is on the road to doing just fine in all regards. He is, in fact, almost a "different child" than the one the kids brought home three years ago. It seems like a minor miracle to me. I'm amazed, as is the rest of the family, and I'm embarrassed to admit that I was so judgmental of him in his first months here. I have learned a valuable lesson about compassion from my daughter and her husband. The whole family feels honored to have this young man as one of us. He has made us true believers in adoption. And by the way, we have had two more successful adoptions in our extended family since this grandson came home. I'll be the first to admit that love goes a long way in the life of a child.

Misha and Evgeniy's Story Keeps Going
By Sandy, July 2009
Louisiana

Evgeniy (now nine years old) is living with us for the summer on a visa. We love him so much. It is just awesome. We started the adoption process this week, and within six months or so he will be our son. Misha and Evgeniy will be together again as brothers!

Keep on Working
By Susie, October 2008
Florida

Since we have adopted the girls, our lives have changed dramatically for the better. It was such a huge financial strain for us to do it, but we have been rewarded and blessed in so many ways. We didn't much believe in fate, but we do now. Maybe this book will create more adoption awareness and help other children find their forever families. If it helps just one child find a family, it would be so worth all of our hard work and effort.

Why So Many?
By Christy, mom of 12, 2007
Oregon

What motivated me to have so many children? This is the million-dollar question – the question I'm asked most often. My passion was always my love for children. I was the one at every family gathering that was encircled by kids, and I truly loved being surrounded by them. All my spending money was earned from babysitting, and I was in high demand because the kids could sense how much I really enjoyed it. To this day I remain intrigued and bewitched by children's innocence, their honesty, and particularly their enthusiasm. They are so delicate and moldable, both in good and bad ways! I can't imagine any greater opportunity to make a difference than working with the life of a child. Talk about a contribution. If you can make a positive difference in the life of even one single child, you may affect our universe in uncountable ways. There is simply no equipment capable of adding up all the good you might do by investing in another human being, considering all the lifelong impact that person will have on others. So that's why so many: to make the biggest possible difference.

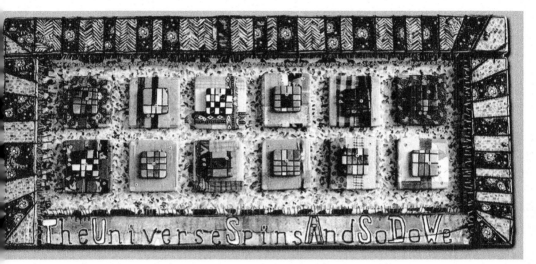

The Universe Spins And So Do We
By Maureen Kelleher   http://www.mkelleherart.com/

APPENDIX A

Parent Readings

"If you want others to be happy, practice compassion.
If you want to be happy, practice compassion."
~ the Dalai Lama

No Cherubs, No Sunshine
By Carol, February 2009
Arizona

The parent side of adoption is that it's lonelier than you think. Other people don't understand some of the things that adoptive families go through. The whole family is adopting the child, not just the mom and dad. Others will sometimes look at you with an expression that says, "What on earth are you doing?" It's evident that they do not agree with the tactics you are using. There are often pieces of information that would help others understand your child and his challenges, but it's not your place to share every bit of your child's private information or history with others. As hard as it is, you have the responsibility of respecting your child's personal information. That's just the way it is. There are usually reasons adoptive families are doing some of the things they do. The hope is that people understand, but if they don't, that's okay too. You know what you have to do to help your child, and it's often not easy.

Once I was at Walmart and the mom in front of me in line was having a really tough time. Her child was acting out uncontrollably. The "old Carol" in me would have had a judgmental thought or might have even rolled her eyes. The "new Carol," the mom who has adopted a child with RAD, simply smiled in an understanding way. As I have found out through adoption, some days the cherubs don't come out and the sun doesn't rise. The book that has helped us more than anything else with our adoption challenges is *When Love Is Not Enough: a Guide to Parenting Children with Reactive Attachment Disorder*, by Nancy Thomas.

"Be kind. Everyone you meet is carrying a heavy burden."
~ Ian MacLaren

RAD Experiences
By "RAD Mother," January 2009
New Mexico

I never thought that my two adopted children would be so different as to temperament and disposition. Not knowing the biological families, their tendencies, emotional make-ups, etc., does have something to do with this; however, I really believe the greater difference between my children was created by the length of time each spent in an orphanage.

Both were placed there at birth. Both were subjected to the lack of manpower (woman power) needed to meet their physical, emotional, and developmental needs. Yet, one child we adopted at a year old, the other when she was almost four. The child we adopted at a year old shows almost no signs now of permanent orphanage damage: she no longer rocks herself, she is no longer underweight, she is developmentally ahead of her age group physically, mentally, and I like to think, emotionally.

The other child is completely different. Now a pre-teen, she still rocks herself – all night long. She still hordes food, lies, often withdraws emotionally when confronted, and indiscriminately shows affection to strangers. When she was six, she was diagnosed with "RAD" – Reactive Attachment Disorder – along with multiple learning disabilities. At the time, we weren't worried about the RAD diagnosis, since we don't particularly believe in labeling people. We were more concerned with the learning disabilities and how to help her get back on track for her age. We wanted her to achieve all that she was capable of achieving in life.

When we first met her in the orphanage, we were impressed that we would finally get a "cuddly child"! All of our other children are so high-maintenance, high energy, and full of life. At the orphanage, this child sat on our lap and wanted to be held. I was in heaven! Soon after the adoption, we realized things were not as they seemed.

We took her back to our hotel room, and a few hours later she turned into a Tasmanian Devil. She literally was bouncing off the walls – screaming, flinging her arms, twirling, babbling, running into things, jumping, etc. My husband and I looked at each other and said, "Oh, my! What have we gotten ourselves into?"

By the next day, after we had lost her in a crowd outside, after she had run from us through the hotel, and again on a street in Russia, I lay with her on the bed holding her arms down in a bear hug type grip so that she wouldn't flail anymore – while I cried. Meanwhile, I prayed: "Dear God. I am old. (Okay. I was not that old, but I had many teenagers who made me *feel* old, and I had been so excited to finally have a "calm child," and here was this strange tiny but mighty tornado of a child!) How am I ever going to handle this little girl? What am I supposed to do with her?"

God is so good! He didn't calm her down in my arms, but he did do something for me. He showed me who she was – who she really was: the person he saw when he looked at her – and he let me see her through his eyes. I am thankful that he did that for me, because there have been so many times I have had to rely on that image of her. In that image, she was glorious! She was beautiful! She was so pure and sweet!

Anyway, the next day we asked our adoption coordinator to find out what was wrong with our daughter – if she needed a special medication or something. Anything. Her answer shocked us. She said, "Well, she is just reacting to being off of the 'calming herbs' they gave her at the orphanage." We read between the lines: hundreds of kids + few workers = drugs to medicate the more active and hyper children into submission. We realized that our daughter was going through some serious withdrawal symptoms.

It took a few weeks for us to understand our daughter's real personality. After getting her to our home (not before losing her in the Seoul airport – she ran away from us and would *not* come when we chased her) and into a routine, she began to thrive in her own small way.

We now understand that RAD plays a larger role in her reactions to this world than we initially gave credit. Researching RAD led us to discouragement at first, as not much hope is given to parents. But we *do* have great hopes for our daughter! She is a survivor. Through trial and error, a few good books, and speaking with other parents of RAD children, we are finding techniques that help our daughter learn better ways to handle life's situations. To make a really long story short, our daughter is an adorable, sweet, energetic, kind-hearted, loving, fun-loving, full-of-life young lady. She is talented. She has so much to offer this world.

A Huge Challenge – and Love to Match It
By "Susan," January 2009
South Carolina

When we first adopted our son, Jay, we knew he would have special needs. My husband and I decided that no matter what the problems would be, we were committed to Jay and would love him unconditionally.

We also assumed from everything that we had researched regarding his behaviors, that he had probably been mistreated in his early years. He had lived his entire life – six years – in orphanages. We believed that with good communication on our part, he would eventually open up to us and share with us what had happened to him, and we would be able to work it out.

We were naïve. For three years we had endured countless tantrums, meltdowns, and much anger. We were always aware, though, that even though he had to face consequences for his behavior, we worked very hard to show him that we loved him no matter what. He was often in trouble at his school and many times there was either a fight or argument on the bus. We made arrangements for him to ride a different bus. After having him tested by the school psychologist, and finding the areas in which we could help him, we signed him up to be in a special needs classroom. There he receives speech therapy, physical therapy, occupational therapy and is surrounded by loving and kind teachers. We had regular interviews with him; we were very open in letting him know that if he wanted to talk about anything, we were there for him and we would listen.

During this third year, however, we found out some shocking news. A neighbor came to us with evidence that our young son had been molesting other children. The more we investigated, the more children we found that he had hurt. My husband and I were stunned to realize that all of this had been going on around us, when we felt that we had been so careful. However, even in our shock, we realized the importance of still letting Jay know that we love him, no matter what. We feel that because he knew that we loved him, he was able to trust us enough to be honest and forthright about what had happened. He was able to be truthful and tell us about what he had done.

We immediately went to every parent of the children and told them what we had learned. We called our church leaders. We spoke with a counselor to see what steps to take. We also went to the police so that they would be aware of what had happened. We visited every family to talk with them; it was incredibly difficult, but of course we had to follow through. We knew that the best way to ensure that their children would get help was to be up front about the situation right away.

We also started Jay in counseling. This counselor has encouraged us wisely every step of the way. She has helped us to understand our son, and yet not to enable him. The counselor, who happens to specialize in working with adoptive families, has helped us understand our son and move ahead to continue to open new doors to healing. Jay has talked with the counselor about his past and the abuse that he endured in the orphanage. Our hope is to break this cycle by providing our son with the ongoing counseling that will help him heal. We have probably made our share of mistakes – this is new territory for us – but we are doing our best to handle this distressing situation in the right way. Throughout all of this challenging time, we have tried to be consistent with Jay, letting him know that despite the negatives that have taken place we do love him, no matter what!

We have had to change our lives, and this has been extremely difficult for us and for our children as well. We are very social people, and yet, we have been willing to cut out a great portion of our social life. We cannot allow Jay to be around children younger than he is, which means families who used to come over often, now cannot come over at all. We have lost connections with some families that used to be friends. A few people have withdrawn from us completely. If we do go out in public, we have to keep Jay by our side at all times, which causes him distress and frustration. It's worth the sacrifice, though, because Jay is worth it.

Our counselor reminds us that Jay will continue testing us and trying to push us away so that he can reject us before we reject him. He will do this until he finally feels that he can trust us to love him unconditionally. He is not there yet, and there is no guarantee that he will ever completely get there, although the counselor does feel hopeful and encouraged that over time Jay will be able to overcome his past hurts. I too feel encouraged. He has actually made some breakthroughs in learning. I have read with Jay daily for the three years he has been with us, and yet learning to read has proved very difficult for him. Just recently, in the last two months or so, he seems to be breaking down some of the barriers; he has begun to learn to read. I think that maybe because of the love we have shown Jay through these extremely difficult times, part of him has begun to heal. It almost reminds me of when Helen Keller discovered the sign language word for *water* and the world began to make sense to her.

This journey has not been an easy one, and yet some positives are coming out of it. Finding out about this situation was the best thing for us.

We have been able to stop our son's hurtful behavior and we have been able to begin the process of helping him heal. It's ironic; we thought that our son would need much physical care and intervention for physical challenges, but more emotional care and growth is what has been needed. Believe it or not, it has also been a journey of great joy. A few weeks ago, I was walking into the house when Jay spontaneously said, "Mom, I love you!" He very seldom says that. Yet line upon line, step by step, and challenge after challenge, we can help him realize that we love him - no matter what.

From Lisa's Journal
By Lisa Finneran
President, ArkAngels for Russian Orphans
Virginia

November 14, 2002 Lina weighs twenty pounds, Igor less than seventeen. Doctor says he's concerned about the discrepancy in their size. Of course, Igor was smaller at birth. But the doctor thinks he should have caught up by now. He thinks there may be some motor skills development problem, which could mean something serious like Cerebral Palsy. I looked up CP in the Internet. It's basically a term used to describe a birth-related brain injury. Could happen *in utero* or during birth. Common in twins, breech birth.

So confused. We expected them to be small, to be delayed. They're in an orphanage. But how much should a baby born at four pounds, twelve ounces weigh at fifteen months? There is four pounds difference between them. Is that really all that much?

And if he is sick, if he does have CP, how much difference does that make? I know we said "healthy infant." But we could do this if we decided to. How to decide? If he does have CP, we might be his only hope. Might be her only hope too, since it's likely the official won't want to split up twins. If we don't adopt them, I would imagine they might never get adopted. Finding a home for twins must be hard enough. Finding a home for twins with problem must be nearly impossible. And I don't even know if we'll get the answers we're looking for. There is an element risk no matter how much information we get. There is an element of risk when you have a biological child.

February 11, 2003 When we emerge on the third floor of the hospital, Anna goes to find the doctor. A woman in a robe wanders by. Her eyes are sunk deep into her head and she looks like she might be a mental patient. But I imagine she's there to have a baby. So sad. Anna comes back and tells us we can't see Elena. They're too busy. The children are getting their massages right now. Come back this afternoon. Anna kept apologizing. But I know it's not her fault. Go with the flow.

Bedtime
By Kristina's Mom, 2008
Texas

Very soon after we arrived home with Kristina, age three, we started a bedtime routine. We had her share a bedroom with her older sister, Elena. We thought that it would be nice for them to have some companionship and not be alone at night. The first night we put Kristina to bed, we read her a story and kissed her goodnight. She seemed to be asleep, so we tip-toed out of the room and gently closed the door. Instantly, she started to scream (not cry). So I ran back in to see what the problem was. She was thrashing around in her bed, with her back arched and screaming so hard that her face was red and sweaty and the veins were sticking out on her neck. I went to work trying to sooth her. I talked, sang about six songs, and stroked her. She would not be consoled. After about an hour of this, she finally fell asleep. I was completely exhausted and totally frustrated. At that time I wondered if I hadn't made the biggest mistake in my life by bringing this child into my home.

After about three nights she started to settle down a lot sooner and easier. But then we soon noticed another problem: Elena was becoming increasingly grouchy, and we noticed her eyes were getting more and more bloodshot every day. I asked Elena what the problem was. She said, "Kristina won't let me sleep. She wakes me up in the middle of the night because she wants a drink of water, or wants to go to the bathroom, or just wants to play. Then when it just starts to get light outside, she wakes me up again and thinks it's time to get up." All of this happened in the space of about four months.

We decided to separate the girls. Each girl had her own room, and Kristina actually seemed to do better at going to bed. Interestingly enough, she doesn't ever bother her mom and dad, but once in a while she will still go and wake her sister. There's that Attachment Disorder again! We didn't know about this (AD) until a little over two years after she was home.

Inconsolable
By Kristina's Mom, 2008
Texas

Three days after bringing three-year-old Kristina home from Russia, she had an accident. She pinched her fingers in the hinge of our folding step-stool in the kitchen. (It was so bad that she actually ended up losing a fingernail.) I immediately ran to help her and to kiss her "owie." Of course she screamed, but the trouble came when I couldn't get her to quiet down at all. I tried to sit down with her on my lap to sooth her, but she just arched her back and pushed against me. The whole time she was screaming the names of all the "mamas" in the orphanage. She didn't want to have anything to do with me; she wanted the "mamas." This hurt me intensely.

My thoughts were something to this effect: "What have I done? I have taken this little girl away from all that she knows. She doesn't understand a word I'm saying and she obviously would rather have someone else console her." Her crying lasted about forty minutes; then she just fell asleep, exhausted, on the couch. I felt so guilty.

I now know that she has Attachment Disorder. It took a little over two years for us to get this diagnosis. Knowing that she has AD has helped us to find answers and to get the help she so desperately needs. She has also been diagnosed with FAS (Fetal Alcohol Syndrome), which also explains a lot. If we had known these diagnoses before we brought her home, it probably wouldn't have stopped us from bringing her home, but it would have saved us all (Kristina, her parents, and her siblings) two years of heartache.

A Difficult Letter to Write
By "Lana," 2003
Delaware

Dear Dave,   2/25/03

I'm having a rough time. I'm embarrassed and ashamed to admit that I'm not handling things well at all. I'm coping…barely…and feel like it is so obvious, but so out of my control. I want so much for this time to be okay, and I had confidence that I would do great through these first months after bringing our boys home. To the contrary, I'm not doing well and seem unable to handle all of the changes and emotions right now. It's very hard to admit it. I know I'm not a failure, but that's the way it feels. I am going through the motions, but I'm not feeling happy. The adjustment is all so much harder than I thought it would be.

I feel fulfillment and contentment – that finally the adoption worked and that the boys are here with us. And when I look at the snow, or celebrate one of our birthdays, or see the kids playing ball, or I get a hug from one of the twins, I feel joy. In the daily routine, though, I feel harried, pressured, and pulled in eight thousand directions, and I feel like I'm completely unable to relax.

I know this feeling will pass – hopefully within days rather than weeks or months, but in the meantime, I'm feeling disappointment in myself. It makes me cry to admit it. I want so much to be the strong, confident person I show to 'the outside world,' but I feel within myself right now that I am not that person. I am competent at getting the basics done to keep our household running, but there is nothing left emotionally right now. I will work on it through prayer and exercise because those are the things that tend to pull me up. Time will help, too.

Thank you for your support and love. Without both, I think I would not be able to meet the demands of our growing family right now. I feel a little better just writing all this down. I love you, and I know this challenge will smooth out. Thank you for your understanding. Love, Lana

(Note: I wrote this letter two months after we got home with our two-year-old twin sons. I hope it helps other parents that are having difficult times to know that they are not alone. The difficulties do pass. Within a few months of writing this note to my husband, our life smoothed out considerably. I think it is worth sharing with other parents, but please don't use our real names. Thanks. Just call me "Lana.")

Tough Times
By Muriel, January 2009
Taylor, Arizona

Many of the babies and some of the children who came to us at our medical foster home weren't expected to live more than a few weeks because of their severe health problems, so we knew that some of them would likely pass away. Many required major surgeries, and some didn't make it through the surgeries. When the first baby died, I got the shock of my life. Whenever a baby died, of course it broke our hearts.

Because of the nature of the health problems and the grave condition that some of the children were in, I had to have a letter on hand from the doctors explaining to social workers, police, emergency workers, and the coroner what type of foster home we ran. The letters explained the extent of each child's problems. Our home was only two minutes from the fire station. One little boy choked on his tongue: Baby Adam. I had to call 9-1-1 to get help. The doctor had to actually sew his tongue down into his mouth so that he wouldn't keep choking on it. One baby died in a worker's arms. We called 9-1-1 immediately and tried to revive the baby, but she didn't make it.

One time a social worker came to inspect our home. I was flabbergasted by her words: "This is really depressing," she said. "How can you rock the babies and care for them knowing they are going to die?" That made me upset. I had never considered my work depressing. I knew my work was important, and I valued each one of those little ones no matter what disabilities they had. We held them and loved them no matter what was wrong with them. I felt like that social worker was in the wrong profession.

One sweet little guy, we called him Baby David, had shunt problems. I took him to the doctor, but the mom wouldn't allow him to get the medical help he needed. She didn't want the baby "repaired." One little girl had Shaken Baby syndrome. She was blind and hard of hearing, but so pretty – and so precious.

Late one night I got a call asking me to take an eight-year-old child with Cerebral Palsy. I told them that I was only licensed to take children up to six years old. They said they would make an exception because they needed me to care for this boy. Honest to goodness, he was skin and bones. He had been starved and neglected; he weighed only eighteen pounds when they brought him to me. Eighteen pounds at eight years old! He also had cigarette burns all over. He was with me six months. He was a different child when he left; he was up to fifty-four pounds.

The most difficult situation of all, though, was when judges allowed the birth families to have the babies back – knowing that they had been abused. Little Stella would come back to us black and blue after time with her birth family. I would check her over and call the hospital. They would take pictures. It broke my heart. The social worker showed the documentation to the judge, but the judge still allowed the family to have visitation rights. One little Thalidomide baby, Baby Rigo, had been abused by his father. After six months with us, the judge let him go back home for visits. He was brought back to us once more after being taken away from his parents again. He kept being sent back to his parents for weekends even though he came back to me with bruises. He would bite like crazy when he came back to us after weekend visits. I think he bit in order to try to defend himself since he had no arms. That was the absolute toughest situation to bear. I just don't know what some of those judges were thinking. As you can see, the tough part of the job for me was not taking care of the babies and their needs, but dealing with the fact that we live in an imperfect world. It's just terrible that any baby or child anywhere is not treated as he or she should be.

> "You must be the change you wish to see in the world."
> ~ Mahatma Gandhi

Help for a Daughter with RAD
By "RAD Mother," March 2009
New Mexico

Our daughter was three pounds at birth, placed in an incubator with a tube down her chest to breathe for her, and was *not* held or even touched often. Orphanage staff told us that they did not have the personnel to handle the children regularly. They took care of their basic needs, meaning they propped bottles in their mouths to feed them and quickly changed their diapers (by putting a new one underneath them when theirs was soiled), all with very little interaction. The infants had to learn "self-preservation and self-comforting techniques." When babies in this situation feel an emotion, their survival instincts take over automatically, and they often withdraw and rock or suck their thumbs to get rid of the uncomfortable feeling brought on by emotion.

What I found through reading and research is that when RAD children ("radishes") feel any intense emotion, whether anger, joy, pain, happiness – it all feels the same to them: uncomfortable – and they don't know what to do with it. They *have* to get rid of the uncomfortable feeling that the emotion produces, and the only way they know how to do this is to force their body to take over and go into the withdrawal mode. Our daughter shows many of the classic signs of RAD. She is not naughty on purpose; she just suffers from an inability to see the outcome of her actions.

With our daughter, anything involving work was a struggle. For instance, she hated homework. It frustrated her and was a huge challenge because of her learning disabilities. She got into a cycle: she cried, whined, and got stuck repeating, "I hate homework. How come I have to do homework?" She then started in with constant chatter and obnoxious noises. After that, she "upped the ante" by rocking the dining room chair. Next she scribbled on her homework. These actions were probably all in an effort (at the unconscious level) to get her automatic withdrawal response to kick in.

Day after day, I patiently erased the paper and told her that we wanted her teacher to be able to read her homework. Sometimes, though, after an hour plus of dealing with these behaviors, my voice was clearly becoming stressed and was *not* happy. She continued to seek the withdrawal action from her body by hitting the table – Bang. Bang. Bang. It became impossible to ignore. At first I reacted with lectures about appreciating what we have, taking care of our belongings, and treating possessions with respect. It didn't work. She was not listening – she was unable to listen. After these episodes, she would finally "withdraw into herself," and I felt terrible not being able to come up with a solution. She did finally do her homework – every time. It took all that build up and all that torture for both of us before her body could take over and give her the relief that she needed. My nerves were fried, and in times like these, after hours of dealing with RAD behaviors, I found myself hating my child, hating myself, and hating my life.

After researching RAD, I realized that my daughter was feeling great anxiety that she *had* to get rid of. She needed to go to her "safe place" inside herself, but she didn't know how to get there. Subconsciously, her body's automatic response would finally take over – finally allowing her to get rid of the anxiety. Once I realized what was happening, it gave me power and inspiration.

My husband and I have found several ways to help our daughter and manage her behavior. I help her find new coping skills to use while her brain stores the new input and stimulation it is receiving. We now break homework into smaller chunks and have her work for fifteen minutes at a time. When I notice her becoming anxious, I help her do a couple of deep cleansing breaths to release her built-up nervousness. I look for motivators that work for her. She loves fruit, so she gets to eat a grape for every homework problem she finishes. It is no longer such a stress for her to do her homework, but rather a kind of game. I also have explained to teachers that homework in large quantities is not conducive to a good family life for us. Our daughter just cannot handle it yet.

I provide natural consequences for inappropriate actions. She thinks they are unfair and she never thinks she is at fault, so repetition and consistency are "key concepts." For instance, when she scratches her sister, she has to wear socks on her hands the rest of the day *and* stand in the corner for an hour. This may seem harsh, but her sister has scars down her arms from her scratches, and I have to help her learn that injuring her sister will result in these consequences. It takes at least thirty minutes for her to get over the, "It's not fair. How come she doesn't have to stand in the corner? I hate standing in the corner," and make the connection that she needs to take responsibility for her actions. After she settles down, we are able to talk about other ways she could have handled the situation: "What could you have done instead of scratching her?" "I could have asked her 'Please.'" It takes a while, but it is helping her find appropriate ways to interact. She hasn't yet quit scratching her sister, but she does not do it very often anymore.

If we make chores into games, she loves it. We have contests, which makes it more pleasant for her to complete daily tasks. To encourage proper behavior before we go into a social situation I say, "Instead of barking like a dog today, you are a pretty princess! How does a princess act?" Then if she retreats to inappropriate behavior, all I have to say is "What is my princess thinking about?" and her poor behavior stops immediately.

"Radishes" often do not show compassion or bond. Despite my daughter's major challenges, she is bonded to us and is very compassionate. When we first got her, we spent months physically holding, rocking, touching, and keeping her close constantly to bond with her. She loves her family. She still can disassociate herself from emotions (which still freaks me out), but I find it happening less and less. With her, family interaction is extremely important in establishing emotional classifications and health, and in strengthening bonds. By being with family, she has bonded with us.

Family interactions provide the greatest possibility to her for over-coming the damage and lack of development she experienced in the institution. Fortunately, my daughter loves spending time with our family, and we do many things as a family to keep our bond tight. Family traditions such as birthday parties, family dinners, holding her while we watch a movie (even though she is ten years old), and singing together while we work have all helped her to establish a more healthy emotional life. Her favorite activity is what we call "Secret Spies." We do service for others without letting them know who did the kind deeds. This is so hard for her because we have to be very quiet about it, which is a huge challenge. She really loves it when we sneak around to neighbors' homes at night leaving goodies on their doorsteps. She always says, "This is the *best* day ever!" And she means it. She loves to look out for others. She has major needs, but she is making steady progress. Yes, it takes a lot of effort to be a mother of a "radish." My daughter is worth the effort.

"We should applaud more frequently those who transform a lost life."
~ Sonia Sotomayor

Transformations
By "Amanda," February 2009
New Jersey

The rage darting from her eyes and seething from her body was enough to destroy anything and everything within her range and enough to challenge even the most seasoned and compassionate parent. Her shouts and screams of "I hate you! Shut up! You are not my Mom!" soon transformed into attempts to bite my arms and kick my stomach. With every ounce of patience and love that I could bring forth in this moment of seemingly unending expression of hate and rage, I validated her by saying that "You are right. I'm not your birth mom. But I *am* your adopted mom, I love you very much, and it's *not* ok to bite or hit me."

When the time-out was over, I watched her slight nine-year-old body shuffle over to and ascend the stairs to retreat to her room. The rest of us who were at home at the time, her younger brother and teenage sister and I, continued with the preparations for dinner.

Her sister (who has been through similar experiences) announced that she would go upstairs to check on our little girl, and when her voice echoed down with a hint of alarm, "Mom, she's not up here," my first thought was that she had found a pretty good hiding place. I know that she can contort herself into some tight closet corners or curl up small under some unassuming blankets; she had eluded me before. When our extensive inside search for my distressed daughter turned up no results, my heart did skip a beat as the statistics for adopted runaways ran through my head.

Her older sister found her wrapped up in her soft yellow blanket lying outside on the blacktop next to our family car. The rage in her soul had been replaced by a sad distant look in her swollen eyes and flaccidity in her limp body. It was a cold evening, and I wanted to scoop her up to hold her and comfort her; instead I followed the advice given by her older sister: "Mom, trust me, she just needs to be alone now." We made sure that she was safe and warm and left her alone to be with her emotions, her older sister checking on her periodically and bringing her warm cocoa. I let go of my dismal helpless feelings of inadequacy, knowing that I must trust the process.

Two hours later she was up in her sister's room working on homework, bringing me a gold chocolate candy and a hug, and saying, "I love you, Mom."

Emotional Times
By Jan, 5/2/08
Minnesota

Dmitry has been home six months, and things are much smoother – in general – than they were in the beginning. He really put me through the paces yesterday, though. I got my feelings hurt and shed lots of tears (a first), but didn't let him see that he "wounded" me. It was a *rough* afternoon and evening. The moral of the story is this: When Dmitry is very tired and Mom is tired, Dad must step in and take over. Thank goodness that this morning our little guy is "lovey and huggy" and sweet as can be. That helps a ton. We're headed to church; the other kids have prepared a duet to sing. I'm counting my blessings.

A Final Word
By Teresa July 2009
Snowflake, Arizona

Adoption, in a way, is as miraculous as birth; everything comes together in space and time in just the right way for a new family to *happen*. Adoption is a "roll of the dice," but after all, isn't that the case with biological parent-hood? Parenting is a challenge, no doubt about it, but I have yet to meet a parent, adoptive or biological, who would go back to life without children. My husband and I have both adoptive and biological kids, and we would never wish for it to be any other way. Life is a challenge, and rela-tionships of all types – not just adoption – require work and dedication. A sense of humor goes a long way, too.

Many adoptive parents I've spoken with have reported having a tough time adapting to changes and new roles. Certainly those feelings are a normal part of the adjustment process. Is it stressful? Yes. It's easier to talk about "going with the flow" than succeeding on a daily basis, especially in the first months of major change. It helps to talk with others who have walked the path of adoption before. Nowadays there is an abundance of information about adoption at our fingertips that was not available ten or even five years ago. The viewpoints here of children and teens add fresh perspectives to the mix of what's already available.

All adoptees will enjoy reading the accounts of others who have had similar experiences. Those who know adopted children and teens will also be interested in reading what young adoptees have to say. My guess is that by reading this book, prospective adoptive parents, family members, teachers, social workers, and others interested in adoption will discover fresh and honest insights about the feelings, challenges, and triumphs of adopted children and teens. I am confident that the accounts written by young adoptees will be valuable to many.

Fortunately, adoption is now more accepted than ever in most countries and is being encouraged by many governments. Whether kids come to their forever families from orphanages or foster care doesn't really matter; all children benefit hugely by having a forever family. Young people have a much greater chance of living a normal and happy life if they have a family to back them up.

Adoption is a win-win situation: it's a positive way to build a family, and it allows children to grow up healthier and to lead a successful life. Almost every single family who adopts will look back ten years after their new children entered the family fold and say, "Everything ended up just the way it was supposed to." The adoption connection is strong and deeply felt.

Some amazing gifts come with adoption. It's an expansion of a family and also an incredible opening up of one's whole world. The vast majority of adoptions are successful. I recommend adoption – just as I would recommend biological parenthood – to everyone who has energy, patience, and *love* to give to a child.

"One word frees us of all the weight and pain of life: that word is *love*."
~ Sophocles

APPENDIX B

Resources and Information of Interest

Adoptive Families
Adoption and parenting guide. *Adoptive Families* magazine and online guide have provided excellent adoption information for over thirty years. http://www.adoptivefamilies.com/

Alexander, Christopher J., Ph.D. "The Inner World of the Adopted Child." *Alexanderphd.com*, 2009. Web. May 2009. <http://alexanderphd.com>.

Antares Foundation
The Antares Foundation is a non-profit corporation which was established in 2004 to help orphans in the North Kazakhstan region of Kazakhstan. Antares Foundation has sponsorship programs, sibling reunions, student-of-the-month program, life skills teaching, and other projects to help children. Antares also coordinates efforts to improve orphanages. http://www.antaresorphans.com E-mail: antares.foundation@yahoo.com

ArkAngels for Russian Adoptions
ArkAngels for Russian Adoptions is a charity founded to raise money for the children left behind in orphanages in Archangelsk, Russia and elsewhere. Money raised through donations and sales is donated to improve the lives of children until they find forever families. http://www.arkangels.org

The Center for Adoption Support and Education (C.A.S.E.)
C.A.S.E. is a non-profit organization which provides support and education to everyone in the adoption community. Its programs benefit children from foster care and adoptive backgrounds, with the goal of helping them grow into successful, productive adults. http://www.adoptionsupport.org

Eldridge, Sherrie. *Twenty Things Adopted Kids Wish Their Adoptive Parents Knew*. New York: Bantam Books. 1999. Print.

Families for Russian and Ukrainian Adoption
FRUA provides information and resources about adoption in Russia, Ukraine, and neighboring countries to families in all stages of adoption. http://www.frua.org

Families with Children from China
FCC provides information and support for who have adopted children from China and for prospective adoptive parents. http://www.fwcc.org

Gowan, Barbara. *Blending In: Crisscrossing the Lines of Race, Religion, Family and Adoption*. iUniverse, Inc. 2008. Print.

Hand In Hand International Adoptions
Hand in Hand is a Hague-approved agency that works with families in all 50 states and with Americans abroad who wish to adopt. Accredited programs in the U.S.A. as well as international programs in the Philippines, China, Haiti, Russia, and Ukraine. Qualified and caring staff in the U.S. and in the foreign countries. Over 35 years of adoption experience. Licensed offices in AZ, IN, CO, MN, and FL. http://www.hihiadopt.org
E-mail: marylee@hihiadopt.org (MaryLee Lane, Founder of Hand in Hand)

A Hand Up
A program dedicated to helping Russian orphans develop a talent so they might later have a chance to support themselves. Sponsored by Golden Cockerel (Russian gifts, books, and dolls). Artists teach children traditional Russian painting techniques; brooches they produce are sold for donations to the program.
E-mail: Walton@goldencockerel.com 1.800.892.5409

Karen's Adoption Links
A comprehensive list of international adoption links and list-serves. http://www.karensadoptionlinks.com/

Kazakhstan Adoptive Families
Site map and links to various resources with information about Kazakh and Russian language, adoption, culture, and travel. http://www.kazakhadoptivefamilies.com

Kelleher, Teresa. *Adopting From China ~ Mandarin*. Arizona: TLC. 2002. Print and Audio CD.
http://WorkNotes.com/AZ/AdoptingFromRussia/Kelleher
E-mail: tk.pacifica@gmail.com

——. *Adopting From Latin America*. Arizona: TLC. 2002. Print and Audio CD.

—. *Adopting From Russia, a Language and Parenting Guide.* Arizona: TLC. 1999. Print and Audio CD.

—. *RUSH Into English, Russian to English for Children.* Arizona: TLC. 2003. Print and Audio CD.

Latin American Parents Association
Volunteer association of adoptive parents (not-for-profit organization) based in New York. LAPA helps prospective adoptive parents and adoptive parents of children from Latin America. LAPA also supplies materials to orphanages. http://www.lapa.com

Little Miracles International Adoption
Little Miracles is a Hague-accredited agency that sponsors several humanitarian projects for orphans in Romania, Kazakhstan, and Russia. http://littlemiracles.org E-mail: info@littlemiracles.org

Maclean, John H. *The Russian Adoption Handbook.* iUniverse, Inc. 2000. Print.

McCreight, Brenda, PhD. "Attachment Disorder and the Adoptive Family." *Life Span Counseling, Brenda McCreight, Ph.D., behavioral challenges/adoption,* 2007. Web. June 2009. <www.theadoptioncounselor.com/free_download.html >

—. *Parenting Your Adopted Older Child.* Oakland, California: New Harbinger Publications, Inc. 2002. Print.

Newman, Janis Cooke. *The Russian Word for Snow: A True Story of Adoption.* New York: St. Martin's Press. 2001. Print.

Nightlight Christian Adoptions
Nightlight is a Hague-accredited adoption agency, licensed by the states of California and South Carolina to provide a variety of adoption-related services, as well as humanitarian work for orphans. http://www.nightlight.org

Riley, Debbie, and Dr. John Meeks. *Beneath the Mask: Understanding Adopted Teens.* Silver Spring, Maryland: C.A.S.E. Publications. 2006. Print.

Thomas, Nancy. *Nancy Thomas Parenting.* 2000–2009. Web. June 2009. <www.attachment.org>.

Thomas, Nancy. *When Love Is Not Enough: A Guide to Parenting Children with Reactive Attachment Disorder.* Colorado: Families by Design. 1997. Print.

Thompson, Dee. *Jack's New Family*. United Writers Press, Inc. 2007. Print.

—. *Adopting Alesia: My Crusade for My Russian Daughter.* Deadwood, Oregon: Wyatt-MacKenzie Publishing. 2009. Print.

What You Should Know before You Adopt a Child. Evergreen, Colorado: The Attachment Center at Evergreen. 1996. Print.